Architecting a Modern Data Warehouse for Large Enterprises

Build Multi-cloud Modern Distributed Data Warehouses with Azure and AWS

Anjani Kumar
Abhishek Mishra
Sanjeev Kumar

Apress®

Architecting a Modern Data Warehouse for Large Enterprises: Build Multi-cloud Modern Distributed Data Warehouses with Azure and AWS

Anjani Kumar
Gurgaon, India

Abhishek Mishra
Thane West, Maharashtra, India

Sanjeev Kumar
Gurgaon, Haryana, India

ISBN-13 (pbk): 979-8-8688-0028-3
https://doi.org/10.1007/979-8-8688-0029-0

ISBN-13 (electronic): 979-8-8688-0029-0

Managing Director, Apress Media LLC: Welmoed Spahr
Acquisitions Editor: Smriti Srivastava
Development Editor: Laura Berendson
Coordinating Editor: Shaul Elson
Copy Editor: April Rondeau

Cover designed by eStudioCalamar

Cover image by Sven Mieke@Unsplash.com

Distributed to the book trade worldwide by Apress Media, LLC, 1 New York Plaza, New York, NY 10004, U.S.A. Phone 1-800-SPRINGER, fax (201) 348-4505, email orders-ny@springer-sbm.com, or visit www.springeronline.com. Apress Media, LLC is a California LLC and the sole member (owner) is Springer Science + Business Media Finance Inc (SSBM Finance Inc). SSBM Finance Inc is a **Delaware** corporation.

For information on translations, please e-mail booktranslations@springernature.com; for reprint, paperback, or audio rights, please e-mail bookpermissions@springernature.com.

Apress titles may be purchased in bulk for academic, corporate, or promotional use. eBook versions and licenses are also available for most titles. For more information, reference our Print and eBook Bulk Sales web page at http://www.apress.com/bulk-sales.

Any source code or other supplementary material referenced by the author in this book is available to readers on GitHub (https://github.com/Apress). For more detailed information, please visit https://www.apress.com/gp/services/source-code.

Paper in this product is recyclable

I dedicate this book to my mother, Prabhawati; my aunt, Sunita; and my wife, Suchi.

— Anjani Kumar

I dedicate this book to my lovely daughter, Aaria.

— Abhishek Mishra

I dedicate this book to my late father, Shri Mahinder Nath.

— Sanjeev Kumar

Table of Contents

About the Authors

Anjani Kumar is the managing director and founder of MultiCloud4u, a rapidly growing startup that helps clients and partners seamlessly implement data-driven solutions for their digital businesses. With a background in computer science, Anjani began his career researching and developing multi-lingual systems that were powered by distributed processing and data synchronization across remote regions of India. He later collaborated with companies such as Mahindra Satyam, Microsoft, RBS, and Sapient to create data warehouses and other data-based systems that could handle high-volume data processing and transformation.

Dr. Abhishek Mishra is a cloud architect at a leading organization and has more than a decade and a half of experience building and architecting software solutions for large and complex enterprises across the globe. He has deep expertise in enabling digital transformations for his customers using the cloud and artificial intelligence.

Sanjeev Kumar heads up a global data and analytics practice at the leading and oldest multinational shoe company with headquarters in Switzerland. He has 19+ years of experience working for organizations in multiple industries modeling modern data solutions. He has consulted with some of the top multinational firms and enabled digital transformations for large enterprises using modern data warehouses in the cloud. He is an expert in multiple fields of modern data management and execution, including data strategy, automation, data governance, architecture, metadata, modeling, business intelligence, data management, and analytics.

About the Technical Reviewer

 **Viachaslau Matsukevich** is an industry expert with over a decade of experience in various roles, including DevOps, cloud, solutions architecture, tech leadership, and infrastructure engineering.

As a cloud solutions architect, Viachaslau has delivered 20+ DevOps projects for a number of Fortune 500 and Global 2000 enterprises. He holds certifications from Microsoft, Google, and the Linux Foundation, including Solutions Architect Expert, Professional Cloud Architect, and Kubernetes Administrator.

Viachaslau authors technology articles about cloud-native technologies and Kubernetes, for platforms such as Red Hat Enable Architect, SD Times, Hackernoon, and Dzone.

In addition to his technical expertise, Viachaslau serves as a technical reviewer for technology books, ensuring the quality and accuracy of the latest publications.

He has also made significant contributions as an industry expert and judge for esteemed awards programs, including SIIA CODiE Awards and Globee Awards (including IT World Awards, Golden Bridge Awards, Disruptor Company Awards, and American Best in Business Awards). Viachaslau has also lent his expertise as a judge in over 20 hackathons.

Viachaslau is also the author of online courses covering a wide array of topics related to cloud, DevOps and Kubernetes tools.

Follow Viachaslau on LinkedIn: `https://www.linkedin.com/in/viachaslau-matsukevich/`

Acknowledgments

We would like to thank Apress for giving us the opportunity to work on this book. Also, thanks to the technical reviewer and the editor and the entire Apress team for supporting us on this journey.

CHAPTER 1

Introduction

In the early days of computing, businesses struggled to keep up with the flood of data. They had few options for storing and analyzing data, hindering their ability to make informed decisions. As technology improved, businesses recognized the value of data and needed a way to make sense of it. This led to the birth of data warehousing, coined by Bill Inmon in the 1980s. Inmon's approach was focused on structured, relational data for reporting and analysis. Early data warehouses were basic but set the stage for more advanced solutions as businesses gained access to more data. Today, new technologies like Big Data and data lakes have emerged to help deal with the increasing volume and complexity of data. The data lakehouse combines the best of data lakes and warehouses for real-time processing of both structured and unstructured data, allowing for advanced analytics and machine learning. While the different chapters of this book cover all aspects of modern data warehousing, this chapter specifically focuses on the transformation of data warehousing techniques from past to present to future, and how it impacts building a modern data warehouse.

In this chapter we will explore the following:

- *History and Evolution of Data Warehouse*
- *Basic Concepts and Features of Data Warehouse*
- *Advantages and Examples of Cloud-based Data Warehouse*
- *Enterprise Scenario for Data Warehouse*

© Anjani Kumar, Abhishek Mishra, and Sanjeev Kumar 2024
A. Kumar et al., *Architecting a Modern Data Warehouse for Large Enterprises*,
https://doi.org/10.1007/979-8-8688-0029-0_1

Objective

This chapter provides an overview of data warehouses and familiarizes the readers with the terminologies and concepts of data warehouses. The chapter further focuses on the transformation of data warehousing techniques from past to present to future, and how it impacts building a modern data warehouse.

After studying this chapter, you should be able to do the following:

- Understand the basics of data warehousing, from the tools, processes, and techniques used in modern-day data warehousing to the different roles and responsibilities of a data warehouse team.

- Set up a synergy between engineering and operational communities, even when they're at different stages of learning and implementation maturity.

- Determine what to adopt and what to ignore, ensuring your team stays up to date with the latest trends in data warehousing.

Whether you're starting a data warehouse team or just looking to expand your knowledge, this guide is the perfect place to start. It will provide you with a background on the topics covered in detail in further chapters, allowing you to better understand the nuances of data warehousing and become an expert in the field.

Origin of Data Processing and Storage in the Computer Era

The history of data processing and storage dates back to the early 20th century when mechanical calculators were used for basic arithmetic operations. However, it wasn't until the mid-20th century that electronic computers were developed, which revolutionized data processing and storage.

The first electronic computer, the ENIAC (Electronic Numerical Integrator and Computer), was built in 1946 by J. Presper Eckert and John Mauchly. It was a massive machine that filled an entire room and used vacuum tubes to perform calculations. ENIAC was primarily used for military purposes, such as computing artillery firing tables.

In the 1950s and '60s, the development of smaller and faster transistors led to the creation of smaller and more efficient computers. The introduction of magnetic tape and magnetic disks in the late 1950s allowed for the storage of large amounts of data, which could be accessed much more quickly than with punched cards or paper tape.

In the 1970s, the development of integrated circuits (ICs) made it possible to create even smaller and more powerful computers. This led to the development of personal computers in the 1980s, which were affordable and accessible to a wide range of users.

Today, data processing and storage are essential to nearly every aspect of modern life, from scientific research to business and commerce to entertainment. The rapid growth of the modern storage solution powered by SSD and flash memory and by internet and cloud computing has made it possible to store and access vast amounts of data from almost anywhere in the world.

In conclusion, the origin of data processing and storage can be traced back to the early 20th century, but it wasn't until the development of electronic computers in the mid-20th century that these processes became truly revolutionary. From massive room-sized machines to powerful personal computers, data processing and storage have come a long way and are now essential to almost every aspect of modern life.

Evolution of Databases and Codd Rules

The evolution of databases began with IBM's development of the first commercially successful database management system (DBMS) in the 1960s. The relational model of databases, introduced by E.F. Codd in the 1970s, organized data into tables consisting of rows and columns, leading to the development of Structured Query Language (SQL). The rise of the internet and e-commerce in the 1990s led to the development of NoSQL databases for handling vast amounts of unstructured data. The Chord protocol, proposed in 2001, is a distributed hash table (DHT) algorithm used for maintaining the consistency and reliability of data across multiple nodes in distributed databases.

Codd's 12 principles for relational databases established a framework for designing and implementing a robust, flexible, and scalable data management system. These principles are relevant in data warehousing today because they provide a standard for evaluating data warehousing systems and ensuring that they can handle large volumes of data, support complex queries, maintain data integrity, and evolve over time to meet changing business needs.

The 12 principles of Codd's rules for relational databases are as follows:

1. **Information Rule**: All data in the database should be represented as values in tables. This means that the database should be structured as a collection of tables, with each table representing a single entity or relationship.

2. **Guaranteed Access Rule**: Each value in the database should be accessible by specifying its table name, primary key value, and column name. This ensures that every piece of data in the database is uniquely identifiable and can be accessed efficiently.

3. **Systematic Treatment of Null Values**: The database should support the use of null values to represent missing or unknown data. These null values should be treated consistently throughout the system, with appropriate support for operations such as null comparisons and null concatenations.

4. **Dynamic Online Catalog Based on the Relational Model**: The database should provide a dynamic online catalog that describes the structure of the database in terms of tables, columns, indexes, and other relevant information. This catalog should be accessible to users and applications and should be based on the relational model.

5. **Comprehensive Data Sublanguage Rule**: The database should support a comprehensive data sublanguage that allows users to define, manipulate, and retrieve data in a variety of ways. This sublanguage should be able to express complex queries, data definitions, and data modifications.

6. **View Updating Rule**: The database should support the updating of views, which are virtual tables that are defined in terms of other tables. This allows users to modify data in a flexible and intuitive way, without having to worry about the underlying structure of the database.

7. **High-Level Insert, Update, and Delete Rule**: The database should support high-level insert, update, and delete operations that allow users to modify multiple rows or tables at once. This simplifies data management and improves performance by reducing the number of database interactions required.

8. **Physical Data Independence**: The database should be able to store and retrieve data without being affected by changes to the physical storage or indexing structure of the database. This allows the database to evolve over time without requiring significant changes to the application layer.

9. **Logical Data Independence**: The database should be able to store and retrieve data without being affected by changes to the logical structure of the database. This means that the database schema can be modified without requiring changes to the application layer.

10. **Integrity Independence**: The database should be able to enforce integrity constraints such as primary keys, foreign keys, and other business rules without being affected by changes to the application layer. This ensures that data is consistent and accurate at all times.

11. **Distribution Independence**: The database should be able to distribute data across multiple locations without being affected by changes to the application layer. This allows the database to scale horizontally and geographically without requiring changes to the application layer.

12. **Non-Subversion Rule**: The database should not be susceptible to subversion by unauthorized users or applications. This means that the database should enforce access controls, encryption, and other security measures to protect against unauthorized access or modification of data.

Traditional tabular systems based on Codd rules were relevant, but with the rise of the internet and e-commerce, there was a huge increase in the volume and variety of data being generated. To handle this data, new NoSQL databases were developed, which are more flexible and scalable, especially for unstructured data. In building a universally accepted data warehouse, it's important to consider the strengths and weaknesses of both traditional and NoSQL databases and follow best practices, such as data quality, data modeling, data governance, and security measures. In the upcoming section of this chapter, we will explore this transition in a step-by-step manner while giving special attention to the areas that remain relevant for creating a strong and widely accepted modern data warehouse.

Transitioning to the World of Data Warehouses

In the 1970s, the dominant form of database used in business was the hierarchical database, which organized data in a tree-like structure, with parent and child nodes. However, as businesses began to collect more data and as the need for complex querying and reporting increased, it became clear that the hierarchical database was not sufficient.

This led to the development of the network database, which allowed for more complex relationships between data, but it was still limited in its ability to handle large volumes of data and complex querying. As a result, the relational database model was developed, which organized data into tables consisting of rows and columns, allowing for more efficient storage and easier retrieval of information.

However, the relational model was not without its limitations. As businesses continued to collect more data, the need for a centralized repository to store and manage data became increasingly important. This led to the development of the data warehouse, which is a large, centralized repository of data that is optimized for reporting and analysis.

The data warehouse is designed to handle large volumes of data from multiple sources and to provide a single source of truth for reporting and analytics. Data warehouses use specialized technologies, such as extract, transform, load (ETL) processes, to extract data from multiple sources, transform it into a common format, and load it into the data warehouse.

Data warehouses also use specialized tools for querying and reporting, such as online analytical processing (OLAP), which allows users to analyze data across multiple dimensions, and data mining, which uses statistical and machine learning techniques to identify patterns and relationships in the data.

The world transitioned to data warehousing from databases in the 1970s as businesses realized the limitations of the hierarchical and network database models when handling large volumes of data and complex querying. The development of the data warehouse provided a centralized repository for storing and managing data, as well as specialized tools for reporting and analysis. Today, data warehouses are a critical component of modern businesses, enabling them to make data-driven decisions and stay competitive in a rapidly changing market.

During this pivotal transition in the world of data management, numerous scientists and experts made significant contributions to the field. Notable among them are Bill Inmon, revered as the originator of the data warehouse concept, which focuses on a single source of truth for reporting and analysis; Ralph Kimball, a renowned data warehousing expert who introduced dimensional modeling, which emphasizes optimized data modeling for reporting, star schemas, and fact tables; and Dan Linstedt, who invented the data vault modeling approach, which combines elements of Inmon and Kimball's methodologies and is tailored for handling substantial data volumes and historical reporting. In addition, Claudia Imhoff, a business intelligence and data warehousing expert, founded the Boulder BI Brain Trust, offering thought leadership; Barry Devlin pioneered the business data warehouse concept, which highlights business metadata's importance and aligns data warehousing with business objectives; and, lastly, Jim Gray, a computer scientist and database researcher, who contributed significantly by introducing the data cube, a multidimensional database structure for enhanced analysis and reporting. In conclusion, these luminaries represent just a fraction of the visionary minds that shaped modern data warehousing, empowering businesses to harness data for informed decision-making in a dynamic market landscape.

Data Warehouse Concepts

In today's world, businesses collect more data than ever before. This data can come from a variety of sources, such as customer transactions, social media, and Internet of Things (IoT) devices. However, collecting data is only the first step; to truly unlock the value of this data, businesses must be able to analyze and report on it. This is where the data warehouse comes in. The following are aspects of the data warehouse:

- A data warehouse is a large, centralized repository of data that is optimized for reporting and analysis. The data warehouse is designed to handle large volumes of data from multiple sources, and to provide a single source of truth for reporting and analytics. It is a critical component of modern business intelligence, enabling businesses to make data-driven decisions and stay competitive in a rapidly changing market.

- Data warehouses use specialized technologies, such as extract, transform, load (ETL) processes, to extract data from multiple sources, transform it into a common format, and load it into the data warehouse. This allows businesses to bring together data from disparate sources and create a single, unified view of the data.

- Data warehouses also use specialized tools for querying and reporting, such as online analytical processing (OLAP), which allows users to analyze data across multiple dimensions, and data mining, which uses statistical and machine learning techniques to identify patterns and relationships in the data.

- One of the key features of the data warehouse is its ability to handle historical data. Traditional transactional databases are optimized for handling current data, but they are not well suited to handling large volumes of historical data. Data warehouses, however, are optimized for handling large volumes of historical data, which is critical for trend analysis and forecasting.

- In addition, data warehouses are designed to be easy to use for business users. They use specialized reporting tools that allow users to create custom reports and dashboards, and to drill down into the data to gain deeper insights. This makes it easy for business users to access and analyze the data they need to make informed decisions.

There are several common concepts in data warehouses that are essential to understanding their architecture. Here are some of the most important concepts:

- **Data Sources**: A data warehouse collects data from a variety of sources, such as transactional databases, external data sources, and flat files. Data is extracted from these sources and transformed into a standardized format before being loaded into the data warehouse.

- **ETL (Extract, Transform, Load)**: This is the process used to collect data from various sources and prepare it for analysis in the data warehouse. During this process, data is extracted from the source systems, transformed into a common format, and loaded into the data warehouse.

- **Data Marts**: A data mart is a subset of a data warehouse that is designed to meet the needs of a particular department or group within an organization. Data marts are typically organized around specific business processes or functions, such as sales or marketing.

- **Data Modeling**: In the field of data warehousing, there are two main approaches to modeling data: tabular modeling and dimensional modeling. Tabular modeling is a relational approach to data modeling, which means it organizes data into tables with rows and columns. Dimensional modeling involves organizing data around dimensions (such as time, product, or location) and measures (such as sales revenue or customer count) and using a star or snowflake schema to represent the data.

- **OLAP (Online Analytical Processing)**: OLAP is a set of tools and techniques used to analyze data in a data warehouse. OLAP tools allow users to slice and dice data along different dimensions and to drill down into the data to gain deeper insights.

- **Data Mining**: Data mining is the process of analyzing large datasets to identify patterns, trends, and relationships in the data. This technique uses statistical and machine learning algorithms to discover insights and make predictions based on the data.

- **Metadata**: Metadata is data about the data in a data warehouse. It provides information about the source, structure, and meaning of the data in the warehouse, and is essential for ensuring that the data is accurate and meaningful.

Data Sources (Data Format and Common Sources)

In a data warehouse, *data source* refers to any system or application that provides data to the data warehouse. A data source can be any type of system or application that generates data, such as a transactional system, a customer relationship management (CRM) application, or an enterprise resource planning (ERP) system.

The data from these sources is extracted and transformed before it is loaded into the data warehouse. This process involves cleaning, standardizing, and consolidating the data to ensure that it is accurate, consistent, and reliable. Once the data has been transformed, it is then loaded into the data warehouse for storage and analysis.

In some cases, data sources may be connected to the data warehouse using extract, transform, and load (ETL) processes, while in other cases, they may be connected using other data integration methods, such as data replication, data federation, or data virtualization.

Note   Data sources are a critical component of a data warehouse, as they provide the data that is needed to support business intelligence and analytics. By consolidating data from multiple sources into a single location, a data warehouse enables organizations to gain insights into their business operations and make more-informed decisions.

There are various types and formats of data sources that can be used in a data warehouse. Here are some examples:

- **Relational databases**: A common data source for a data warehouse is a relational database, such as Oracle, Microsoft SQL Server, or MySQL. These databases store data in tables with defined schemas and can be queried using SQL.

- **Flat files**: Data can also be sourced from flat files, such as CSV files, Parquet, Excel, or any other formatted text files. These files typically have a delimited format with columns and rows.

- **Cloud storage services**: Cloud storage services, such as Amazon S3 or Azure Data Lake Storage, can also be used as a data source for a data warehouse. These services can store data in a structured or unstructured format and can be accessed through APIs.

- **NoSQL databases**: NoSQL databases, such as MongoDB or Cassandra, can be used as data sources for data warehouses. These databases are designed to handle large volumes of unstructured data and can be queried using NoSQL query languages.

- **Real-time data sources**: Real-time data sources, such as message queues or event streams, can be used to stream data into a data warehouse in real-time. This type of data source is often used for applications that require up-to-date data.

- **APIs**: APIs can also be used as a data source, providing access to data from third-party applications or web services.

Format of the data coming from multiple sources can also vary depending on the type of data. For example, data can be structured or unstructured, semi-structured, such as JSON or XML. The data format needs to be considered when designing the data warehouse schema and the ETL processes. It is important to ensure that the data is properly transformed and loaded into the data warehouse in a format that is usable for analysis.

Data can flow to the data warehouse through different systems, some of the most used of which include the following:

- **Transactional databases**: Transactional databases are typically the primary source of data for a data warehouse. These databases capture and store business data generated by various systems, such as sales, finance, and operations.

- **ERP systems**: Enterprise resource planning (ERP) systems are used by many organizations to manage their business processes. ERP systems can provide a wealth of data that can be used in a data warehouse, including information on customer orders, inventory, and financial transactions.

- **CRM systems**: Customer relationship management (CRM) systems provide data on customer interactions that can be used to support business analytics and decision-making.

- **Legacy systems**: Legacy systems are often used to store important historical data that needs to be incorporated into the data warehouse. This data may be stored in a variety of formats, including flat files or proprietary databases.

- **Cloud-based systems**: Cloud-based systems, such as software-as-a-service (SaaS) applications, are becoming increasingly popular as data sources for data warehouses. These systems can provide access to a variety of data, including customer behavior, website traffic, and sales data.

- **Social media**: Social media platforms are another source of data that can be used in a data warehouse. This data can be used to gain insights into customer behavior, sentiment analysis, and brand reputation.

*One effective approach for documenting data-related artifacts, such as data sources and data flows, is using **data dictionaries** and **data catalogs**. These tools can capture relevant information about data elements, including their structure and meaning, as well as provide more comprehensive details about data sources, flows, lineage, and ownership. By leveraging these tools, implementation teams and data operations teams can gain a better understanding of this information, leading to improved data quality, consistency, and collaboration across various teams and departments within an organization.*

Note   When categorizing data into structured or unstructured sources, you'll find that older systems like transactional, ERP, CRM, and legacy tend to have well-organized and -classified data compared to that sourced from cloud-based systems or social media. It's not entirely accurate to say that all data from cloud platforms and website analytics activities are unstructured, but analyzing such data requires additional computing power to derive significant insights. With the adoption of cloud computing, organizations are increasingly storing unstructured data.

ETL (Extract, Transform, Load)

ETL stands for extract, transform, load. It is a process used to move data from one or more source systems, transform the data to fit business needs, and load the data into a target system, such as a data warehouse.

The ETL process is an essential component of a data warehouse, as it enables organizations to consolidate and integrate data from multiple sources into a single, unified view of their business operations. Here is a brief overview of the ETL process:

- **Extract**: The first step in the ETL process is to extract the data from the source systems. This can be done using various methods, such as APIs, file transfers, or direct database connections.

- **Transform**: Once the data has been extracted, it needs to be transformed to fit the needs of the data warehouse. This may involve cleaning the data, consolidating duplicate records, converting data types, or applying business rules and calculations.

- **Load**: After the data has been transformed, it is loaded into the target system, such as a data warehouse. This can be done using various methods, such as bulk inserts, incremental updates, or real-time streaming.

The ETL process can be complex and time-consuming, particularly for large datasets or complex data models. However, modern ETL tools and technologies, such as cloud-based data integration platforms, have made the process more efficient and scalable.

A well-designed ETL process is critical to the success of a data warehouse, as it ensures that the data is accurate, consistent, and reliable. By providing a unified view of business data, a data warehouse enables organizations to gain insights into their operations, identify trends and patterns, and make more informed decisions.

There are many ETL (extract, transform, load) software tools available, both commercial and open source. Here are some examples:

- **Informatica PowerCenter**: Informatica PowerCenter is a popular ETL tool that offers a wide range of data integration and transformation features, including data profiling, data quality, and metadata management.

- **Microsoft SQL Server Integration Services (SSIS)**: SSIS is a powerful ETL tool that is part of the Microsoft SQL Server suite. It provides a wide range of data integration and transformation features, including data cleansing, data aggregation, and data enrichment.

- **Talend Open Studio**: Talend Open Studio is an open source ETL tool that offers a broad range of data integration and transformation features, including support for Big Data platforms like Hadoop and Spark.

- **IBM InfoSphere DataStage**: IBM InfoSphere DataStage is a comprehensive ETL tool that offers advanced data integration and transformation features, including support for real-time data processing and complex data structures.

- **Oracle Data Integrator (ODI)**: ODI is a powerful ETL tool that offers a broad range of data integration and transformation features, including support for Big Data and cloud platforms.

- **Apache NiFi**: Apache NiFi is an open-source data integration and transformation tool that provides a flexible, web-based interface for designing and executing data workflows. It supports a wide range of data sources and destinations and can be used for real-time data processing and streaming.

- **Azure Data Factory**: Azure Data Factory is a cloud-based data integration service offered by Microsoft Azure. It allows you to create, schedule, and manage data integration pipelines. It provides 90+ built-in connectors for seamless data integration from various sources, including on-premises data stores. Azure Data Factory enables easy design, deployment, and monitoring of data integration pipelines through an intuitive graphical interface or code. This helps you manage your data more efficiently, reduce operational costs, and accelerate business insights.

- **AWS Glue**: AWS Glue is a serverless ETL service by Amazon Web Services that automates time-consuming ETL tasks for preparing data for analytics, machine learning, and application development. It enables you to create data transformation workflows that can extract, transform, and load data from various sources into data lakes, warehouses, and other stores. You can use pre-built transformations or custom code with Python or Scala for ETL. AWS Glue is based on Apache Spark, allowing for fast and scalable data processing, and integrates with other AWS services like Amazon S3, Amazon Redshift, and Amazon RDS. This service simplifies the ETL process and frees up time for analyzing data to make informed business decisions.

These are just a few examples of the many ETL tools available for data integration and transformation. The choice of ETL tool depends on the specific needs and requirements of the organization, as well as the available resources and budget.

ETL and ELT

ETL (extract, transform, load) and ELT (extract, load, transform) are both data integration techniques that are used to transfer data from source systems to target systems. The main difference between ETL and ELT lies in the order of the data processing steps:

- In ETL, data is first extracted from source systems, then transformed into the desired format, and finally loaded into the target system. This means that the transformation step takes place outside of the target system and can involve complex data manipulation and cleansing.

- In ELT, data is first extracted from source systems and loaded into the target system, and then transformed within the target system. This means that the transformation step takes place within the target system, using its processing power and capabilities to transform the data.

- The choice between ETL and ELT depends on several factors, including the complexity and size of the data being processed, the capabilities of the target system, and the processing and storage costs. ETL is more suitable for complex data transformation, while ELT is more suitable for large data volumes and systems with advanced processing capabilities.

Data Mart

A data mart is a subset of a larger data warehouse and is designed to serve the needs of a particular business unit or department. Data marts are used to provide targeted, specific information to end users, allowing them to make better, data-driven decisions.

A data mart is typically designed to store data that is relevant to a specific business area or function, such as sales, marketing, or finance. Data marts can be created using data from the larger data warehouse, or they can be created as standalone systems that are populated with data from various sources.

Data Mart Architecture

The architecture of a data mart can vary depending on the specific needs of the business unit or department it serves. However, some common elements are typically found in a data mart architecture:

- **Data sources**: The data sources for a data mart can come from various systems and applications, such as transactional systems, operational databases, or other data warehouses.

- **ETL process**: The ETL process is used to extract data from the source systems, transform it to meet the needs of the data mart, and load it into the data mart.

- **Data mart database**: The data mart database is the repository that stores the data for the specific business unit or department. It is typically designed to be optimized for the types of queries and analyses that are performed by the end users. (In modern day, in some cases this may be a temporarily transformed datastore refreshed periodically with no history.)

- **Business intelligence tools**: Business intelligence (BI) tools are used to analyze the data in the data mart and provide reports, dashboards, and other visualizations to end users.

Advantages of Data Marts

Data marts are a crucial component of modern data management and analytics strategies, offering several advantages that organizations can leverage to drive informed decision-making and enhance their competitive edge. These streamlined subsets of data warehouses are designed to cater to specific business units or departments, providing a focused and efficient approach to data access and analysis. Some of the key advantages of a data mart, with examples, are as follows:

- **Targeted data**: Data marts provide a subset of the larger data warehouse that is specifically designed to meet the needs of a particular business unit or department. This makes it easier for end users to find the data they need and make well-informed decisions.

- **Improved performance**: Data marts are designed to be optimized for the types of queries and analyses that are performed by the end users. This can improve query performance and reduce the time it takes to access and analyze data.

- **Reduced complexity**: By focusing on a specific business area or function, data marts can simplify the data architecture and make it easier to manage and maintain.

Examples of Data Marts

An organization comprises various departments, including Sales, Marketing, Finance, etc., each with distinct analytics needs and specific information consumption requirements. Therefore, to effectively address these diverse needs, different datamarts are essential.

- **Sales data mart**: A sales data mart might be used to provide information on customer orders, product sales, and revenue by region or by salesperson.

- **Marketing data mart**: A marketing data mart might be used to provide information on customer demographics, campaign performance, and customer acquisition costs.

- **Finance data mart**: A finance data mart might be used to provide information on budgeting, forecasting, and financial reporting.

In conclusion, data marts are an essential component of a data warehouse, providing targeted, specific information to end users and enabling them to make better, data-driven decisions. By designing data marts to meet the specific needs of individual business units or departments, organizations can improve performance, reduce complexity, and achieve their business objectives more effectively.

Data Modeling

In the field of data warehousing, there are two main approaches to modeling data: **tabular modeling** and **dimensional modeling**. Both approaches have their strengths and weaknesses, and choosing the right one for your specific needs is crucial to building an effective data warehouse.

Tabular Modeling

Tabular modeling is a relational approach to data modeling, which means it organizes data into tables with rows and columns. This approach is well suited to handling large volumes of transactional data and is often used in OLTP (online transaction processing) systems. In a tabular model, data is organized into a normalized schema, where each fact is stored in a separate table, and the relationships between the tables are established through primary and foreign keys.

The advantages of tabular modeling include its simplicity, ease of use, and flexibility. Because data is organized into a normalized schema, it is easier to add or modify data fields, and it supports complex queries and reporting. However, tabular models can become more complex to query and maintain as the number of tables and relationships increases, and it can be slower to process queries on large datasets.

Dimensional Modeling

Dimensional modeling is a more specialized approach that is optimized for OLAP (online analytical processing) systems. Dimensional models organize data into a star or snowflake schema, with a fact table at the center and several dimension tables surrounding it.

The fact table contains the measures (i.e., numerical data) that are being analyzed, while the dimension tables provide the context (i.e., descriptive data) for the measures.

Also, dimensional modeling is optimized for query performance, making it well suited for OLAP and especially reporting systems. Because data is organized into a star or snowflake schema, it is easier to perform aggregations and analyses, and it is faster to query large datasets. Dimensional models are also easier to understand and maintain, making them more accessible to business users. However, dimensional models can be less flexible and more complex to set up, and they may not perform as well with transactional data.

In conclusion, both tabular and dimensional modeling have their places in data warehousing, and the choice between them depends on the specific needs of your organization. Tabular modeling is more suited to handling large volumes of transactional data, while dimensional modeling is optimized for OLAP systems and faster query performance.

In modern warehousing with data and delta lakes, tabular models structured in facts and dimensions are still effective. There are multiple tools available to balance between extreme normalization and extreme classification. While tabular models provide a simpler structure and facilitate querying of data, dimensional models make it more ready for analytics and reporting needs.

Understanding Dimensional Modeling in Brief

In data warehousing, dimensions, facts, and measures are essential concepts that are used to organize and analyze data. A dimension is a category of data that provides context for a fact, while a fact is a value that describes a specific event or activity. Measures are numerical values that quantify facts.

Dimensions

A dimension is a grouping or category of data that provides context for a fact. Dimensions can be thought of as the "who, what, when, where, and why" of a dataset.

For example, a sales dataset might include dimensions such as date, product, customer, and location. Each of these dimensions provides additional information about the sales data and helps to contextualize it.

Dimensions can be further classified into the following types:

- **Degenerate Dimension**: A degenerate dimension is a dimension that is not stored in a separate dimension table but is included in the fact table.

- **Conformed Dimension**: A conformed dimension is a dimension that is used in multiple fact tables in the same data warehouse. It is designed to ensure the consistency and accuracy of data across the different fact tables. For example, let's consider a retail company that sells products through multiple channels, such as brick and mortar stores, online stores, and mobile apps. The company has a data warehouse that stores data about sales, inventory, and customer behavior.

  In this scenario, the "customer" dimension is a good example of a conformed dimension. The customer dimension contains attributes such as customer name, address, age, gender, and purchase history. This dimension is used in multiple fact tables, such as sales fact table, customer behavior fact table, and inventory fact table.

  By using a conformed dimension for customer data, the data warehouse ensures that all the information related to customers is consistent and accurate across all the fact tables. It also simplifies the data model and reduces the risk of data inconsistencies and errors.

  Another advantage of using conformed dimensions is that they can be reused across multiple data marts or data domains. This means that the same customer dimension can be used for sales analysis, customer behavior analysis, and inventory management analysis without duplicating the data or creating a separate dimension for each fact table.

- **Junk Dimension**: A junk dimension is a collection of flags and indicators that are not related to any specific dimension. These flags and indicators are grouped together into a single dimension table to simplify the data model and improve query performance.

Junk dimensions are used when you have many low-cardinality flags that are not related to any specific dimension, and it's not worthwhile to create a separate dimension for each flag.

The name *junk* comes from the fact that the dimension contains seemingly unrelated attributes that don't fit neatly into any other dimension. Examples of attributes that can be included in a junk dimension are as follows:

- **Boolean indicators**: "yes" or "no" flags that describe the presence or absence of a particular condition

- **Flags**: "on" or "off" indicators that specify the status of a particular process or workflow

- **Codes**: short codes that describe the result of a particular event or transaction

- **Dates**: dates or timestamps that indicate when a particular event occurred

By consolidating these attributes into a single dimension table, you can simplify the data model and improve query performance. The junk dimension table acts as a bridge table between the fact table and the other dimensions in the data model.

For example, let's consider an e-commerce website that sells products online. The website has a fact table that records the sales transactions and several dimensions, such as product, customer, and time. The fact table contains several low-cardinality flags, such as "shipped," "cancelled," "returned," and "gift-wrapped," which are not related to any specific dimension. Instead of creating a separate dimension table for each flag, these flags can be consolidated into a junk dimension table. The junk dimension table will have a record for each unique combination of these flags, and the fact table will reference the junk dimension table using a foreign key.

Junk dimensions can be an effective way to simplify a data model and reduce the number of dimension tables required in a data warehouse. However, care should be taken to ensure that the attributes in the junk dimension are truly unrelated and do not belong in any other dimension. Otherwise, the use of a junk dimension can lead to data-quality issues and analysis errors.

- **Role-Playing Dimension**: A role-playing dimension is a dimension that is used in different ways in the same fact table. For example, a **date dimension** can be used to analyze sales by order date, ship date, or delivery date. Role-playing dimensions are useful when the same dimension table is used in different contexts with different meanings. By reusing the same dimension table, the data model can be simplified, and the data can be more easily analyzed and understood. However, it's important to ensure that the meaning of each use of the dimension table is clearly defined to avoid confusion and errors in data analysis.

- **Slowly Changing Dimension (SCD)**: A slowly changing dimension is a dimension that changes slowly over time. SCDs are classified into six types:

  - **Type 1 SCD**: In a Type 1 SCD, the old values are simply overwritten with new values when a change occurs. This approach is suitable for dimensions where historical information is not required.

    Suppose you have a price master table that contains information about products such as name, price, and details. If the price of a product changes, you might simply update the price in the price master table without keeping track of the historical price.

  - **Type 2 SCD**: In a Type 2 SCD, a new row is added to the dimension table when a change occurs, and the old row is marked as inactive. This approach is suitable for dimensions where historical information is required.

    Continuing with the price master table example, if you want to keep track of the historical price of each product, you might create a new row for each price change. For example, you might add a new row with a new product version number and a new price whenever the price changes. This way, you can keep track of the historical prices of each product.

- **Type 3 SCD**: In a Type 3 SCD, a limited amount of historical information is maintained by adding columns to the dimension table to store previous values. This approach is suitable for dimensions where only a limited amount of historical information is required.

  Suppose you have an employee table that contains information about employees such as name, address, and salary. If an employee gets a promotion, you might add a new column to the table to store the new job title. You would only store the most recent job title, and not keep track of historical job titles.

- **Type 4 SCD**: Create a separate table to store historical data. This type of SCD is useful when historical data needs to be stored separately for performance reasons.

  Suppose you have a customer table that contains information about customers such as name, address, and phone number. If you want to keep track of historical addresses, you might create a new table to store the historical addresses. The new table would contain the customer ID, the old address, and the date the address was changed.

- **Type 5 SCD**: Combine SCD Types 1 and 2 by adding an additional column to track the current and historical values. This type of SCD can be useful when there are a large number of historical changes, but only the current value is needed for most queries.

  Continuing with the customer table example, if you want to keep track of the current and historical phone numbers for each customer, you might create a new column in the customer table to store the current phone number, and then create a new row in a separate phone number table for each phone number change. The phone number table would contain the customer ID, the phone number, the start date, and the end date.

- **Type 6 SCD**: Combine SCD Types 2 and 3 by adding an additional column to track the current and previous values. This type of SCD is useful when historical data is important, but only the current and previous values are needed for most queries.

    Suppose you have a product table that contains information about products such as name, price, and description. If the price of a product changes, you might create a new row for the new product version and store the new price in that row. You might also add a new column to the product table to store the previous price. This way, you can easily access the current and previous prices of each product.

- **Time Dimension**: A time dimension is a special type of dimension that is used to track time-related data. It provides a way to group and filter data based on time periods such as hours, days, weeks, months, and years.

- **Hierarchical Dimension**: A hierarchical dimension is a dimension that has a parent–child relationship between its attributes. For example, a product dimension can have a hierarchy that includes product category, sub-category, and product.

- **Virtual Dimension**: A virtual dimension is a dimension that is created on the fly during query execution. It is not stored in the data warehouse and is only used for a specific analysis or report.

Facts

A fact is a value that describes a specific event or activity. Facts are typically numeric and can be aggregated to provide insight into a dataset. For example, a sales dataset might include facts such as the total sales revenue, the number of units sold, or the average sales price.

Facts are associated with dimensions through the fact table, which contains the measurements (**Measures**) for each event or activity. The fact table typically contains foreign keys to link the fact table to the dimension tables.

Facts are the numerical data that we want to analyze. They are the values that we measure and aggregate in order to gain insights into our data. In a sales data warehouse, the facts could include sales revenue, quantity sold, and profit.

Each fact has a corresponding measure that defines the unit of measurement for the fact. For example, revenue could be measured in dollars, while quantity sold could be measured in units.

The fact table contains the numerical values, and it is linked to the dimension tables through foreign key relationships. The fact table is typically wide and has fewer rows than the dimension table.

Best practices for designing facts include the following:

- **Choose appropriate measures**: It is important to choose measures that are meaningful and appropriate for the business.

- **Normalize the data**: Normalizing the data in the fact table can help to reduce redundancy and improve performance.

- **Use additive measures**: Additive measures can be aggregated across all dimensions, while non-additive measures are specific to a single dimension.

Measures

Measures are the values that we use to aggregate and analyze the facts. Measures are the result of applying mathematical functions to the numerical data in the fact table.

For example, measures could include average sales, total sales, and maximum sales. Measures can be simple or complex, and they can be derived from one or more facts. Measures can be pre-calculated and stored in the fact table, or they can be calculated on the fly when the user queries the data warehouse.

Best practices for designing measures include the following:

- **Choose appropriate functions**: It is important to choose functions that are appropriate for the business and the data being analyzed.

- **Use consistent units of measurement**: Measures should use consistent units of measurement to avoid confusion.

- **Avoid calculations in the query**: Pre-calculate measures that are frequently used to improve performance.

The dimensional modeling technique provides a powerful method for designing data warehouses. The key concepts of dimensions, facts, and measures are essential to the design of a successful data warehouse. By following best practices for designing dimensions, facts, and measures, you can create a data warehouse that is easy to use, efficient, and provides meaningful insights into your data.

Schematics Facts and Dimension Structuring

A key aspect of a data warehouse is its schema, which defines the structure of the data in the warehouse; it's the way to structure the facts and dimension tables or objects.

There are several different types of schemas that can be used in a data warehouse, as follows:

- **Star Schema**: In this schema, the fact table is surrounded by dimension tables, which contain the attributes of the fact data. This schema is easy to understand and query, making it a popular choice for data warehouses.

- **Snowflake Schema**: This schema is like the star schema, but it normalizes the dimension tables, which reduces redundancy in the data. However, this makes the schema more complex and harder to query.

- **Fact Constellation Schema**: This schema is a combination of the star and snowflake schemas, and is used to model complex, heterogeneous data.

Cubes and Reporting

In the realm of data warehouses and data analytics, the concept of cubes and reporting holds significant value as it enables data to be transformed into meaningful insights for intended users. Without proper representation, data remains inconsequential and fails to provide any actionable insights.

The idea of cubes refers to the multidimensional structure of data that allows for complex data analysis, where data is organized into multiple dimensions and measures. This structure enables users to slice and dice the data from different angles, providing a better understanding of the underlying patterns and relationships within the data.

Reporting, meanwhile, is the process of presenting data in a structured and organized manner, using charts, tables, and other visual aids to provide insights that are easy to comprehend. By presenting data in a visually appealing manner, reporting makes it easier for users to understand the underlying trends and make informed decisions based on the insights obtained from the data.

OLAP

OLAP, or online analytical processing, is a critical component of data warehousing that facilitates complex and interactive data analysis. It is a technology used for organizing and structuring data in a way that enables users to perform multidimensional analysis efficiently. OLAP systems are designed to support complex queries and reporting requirements, making them invaluable for decision-makers and analysts in business intelligence and data analytics. In the next section we will try to understand OLAP better.

Online Analytical Processing, Cubes, Reporting, and Data Mining

In today's data-driven world, organizations are constantly dealing with large volumes of data. This data can come from a variety of sources, including customer interactions, sales transactions, social media, and more. Analyzing this data can provide valuable insights that can help organizations make informed decisions and stay ahead of the competition. One way to analyze data is through OLAP (online analytical processing) and the use of cubes.

OLAP and Cubes

OLAP is a multidimensional data-analysis technique used to support business intelligence (BI) applications. It enables users to analyze large volumes of data from different angles and perspectives.

The main idea behind OLAP is to create a multidimensional data model that allows users to perform complex queries and analysis with ease. OLAP, in the background, can use data stored in either tabular or dimensional models structured in different schema types; e.g., star or snowflake.

Cubes are the foundation of OLAP. They are multidimensional structures that organize data into hierarchies, dimensions, and measures. A cube can have multiple dimensions, each representing a different aspect of the data. For example, a sales cube might have dimensions such as time, product, region, and customer.

Cubes provide a fast and efficient way to analyze data. They can aggregate data across multiple dimensions, allowing users to drill down and explore data at different levels of granularity. This makes it easier to identify trends, patterns, and anomalies in the data.

Categorization of OLAP

OLAP can be categorized into different types based on its architecture and the way it processes data. Here are some of the different types of OLAP and their examples and query techniques:

- **ROLAP (Relational OLAP)**: This type of OLAP works directly with relational databases and SQL queries. The data is stored in a relational database, and queries are executed against the database to generate reports. ROLAP is useful for handling large volumes of data and complex queries.

  - **Example:** Microsoft SQL Server Analysis Services

  - **Query Technique:** SQL queries

- **MOLAP (Multidimensional OLAP)**: This type of OLAP stores data in a multidimensional cube structure, which allows for faster processing of data and complex calculations. MOLAP cubes can be pre-aggregated, which improves query performance.

  - **Example**: IBM Cognos TM1

  - **Query Technique**: MDX (multidimensional expressions)

- **HOLAP (Hybrid OLAP)**: This type of OLAP combines the features of both ROLAP and MOLAP. It stores the data in a relational database and uses a multidimensional cube structure for querying.

  - **Example**: Oracle Essbase

  - **Query Technique**: SQL and MDX

- **DOLAP (Desktop OLAP)**: This type of OLAP is designed for small-scale data analysis and runs on a desktop computer. It can be used to perform ad-hoc queries and analysis.

  - **Example**: Microsoft Excel

  - **Query Technique**: Point-and-click interface or formula-based calculations.

- **WOLAP (Web-based OLAP)**: This type of OLAP runs on a web browser and allows users to access data remotely. It is useful for collaborative data analysis and reporting.

  - **Example**: MicroStrategy Web

  - **Query Technique**: Point-and-click interface or SQL-like queries.

Querying Technique

While there are multiple programmable ways to query data from an OLAP cube, such as SQL and other programming languages, MDX has been one of the most prominent options to query cube data.

For almost two decades, MDX has been used as a primary powerful way to query and analyze multidimensional data, allowing users to gain insights from complex datasets that would be difficult to analyze using traditional relational database queries; however, with the evolution of data lake and delta lakes the preferences have changed.

MDX (Multidimensional Expressions) is a query language used to retrieve data from multidimensional databases that store data in a cube format, typically used in OLAP (online analytical processing) systems. It was invented by Microsoft and was first introduced in 1997 as part of their SQL Server Analysis Services product. Since then, it has become a widely adopted standard in the OLAP industry, and is supported by many vendors, including IBM, Oracle, and SAP.

MDX works by providing a flexible syntax for querying multidimensional data, allowing users to extract information from different dimensions and levels of a cube. MDX queries can retrieve data from a single cell or from multiple cells within a cube and can perform calculations and aggregations on the data.

Some of the key features of MDX include the following:

- **Hierarchies**: MDX supports hierarchies, which allow users to navigate through data in a structured way. Hierarchies are arranged in a tree-like structure, where each level represents a different attribute of the data.

- **Measures**: Measures are the numeric data stored in a cube, and MDX provides a way to perform calculations on them. Measures can be aggregated over different dimensions and levels to provide different perspectives on the data.

- **Cross-join**: MDX supports cross-join operations, which allow users to combine different sets of data into a single result set. This is useful for comparing data across different dimensions.

- **Filters**: MDX allows users to apply filters to their queries to restrict the data returned to specific subsets.

A basic MDX query example:

```
SELECT {[Measures].[Sales]} ON COLUMNS,
{[Month].[Year].MEMBERS} ON ROWS
FROM [SalesCube]
WHERE [Product].[Category].[Electronics]
```

This MDX query retrieves the total sales for each year in the [Time] dimension, for the [Product] category "Electronics," from the [SalesCube] multidimensional database.

The query is composed of several parts:

- **SELECT**: specifies which data to retrieve—in this case, the [Measures].[Sales] data on the columns axis.

- **ON COLUMNS:** specifies that the [Measures].[Sales] data should be displayed on the columns axis.

- **{[Month].[Year].MEMBERS}**: specifies that the [Time].[Year] hierarchy should be used on the rows axis, and that all the members of the hierarchy should be included in the query.

- **ON ROWS**: specifies that the [Month].[Year] hierarchy should be displayed on the rows axis.

- **FROM [SalesCube]**: specifies the name of the multidimensional database (in this case, [SalesCube]) that the data is being retrieved from.

- **WHERE [Product].[Category].[Electronics]**: specifies a filter that restricts the results to the [Product].[Category].[Electronics] category.

This query will return a table with the total sales for each year in the [Time] dimension, for the [Product] category "Electronics."

Reporting Techniques

There are several reporting techniques that can be used to present OLAP data. These include the following:

- **Tabular Reports**: This is the simplest form of reporting, displaying data in a table format.

- **Pivot Tables**: A pivot table allows users to rearrange data in a cube to create a custom view of the data. Users can drag and drop dimensions and measures to create different perspectives.

- **Charts and Graphs**: Charts and graphs are a visual way to represent data. They can be used to highlight trends, patterns, and anomalies in the data.

- **Dashboards**: Dashboards provide an at-a-glance view of key performance indicators (KPIs). They can be customized to show data from multiple sources and provide real-time updates.

There are several reporting tools available for OLAP data, including the following:

- **Microsoft Excel**: Excel has built-in support for OLAP data through its PivotTable and PivotChart features. It allows users to easily create reports and visualize OLAP data.

- **Tableau**: Tableau is a popular data visualization tool that supports OLAP data sources. It provides a wide range of visualization options and allows users to create interactive reports.

- **Power BI**: Power BI is a business intelligence tool that allows users to connect to OLAP data sources and create interactive reports and dashboards.

- **SAP BusinessObjects**: SAP BusinessObjects is a suite of business intelligence tools that includes a reporting tool that supports OLAP data sources.

- **IBM Cognos Analytics**: Cognos Analytics is an enterprise reporting tool that supports OLAP data sources. It provides a range of visualization and reporting options and supports complex data modeling.

- **Oracle BI**: Oracle BI is a suite of business intelligence tools that includes a reporting tool that supports OLAP data sources.

- **Power BI**: Power BI supports establishing relationships between data stored in different data sources, including OLAP cubes. When connecting to an OLAP cube, Power BI uses the Analysis Services connector to retrieve data and metadata from the cube.

Data Mining

Data mining is the process of extracting useful insights from large volumes of data. It involves using statistical and machine learning algorithms to identify patterns and relationships in the data. Data mining can be used to do the following:

- **Predict future trends**: By analyzing historical data, data mining can help predict future trends and behaviors.

- **Identify anomalies**: Data mining can help identify anomalies in the data that may indicate fraud, errors, or other issues.

- **Segment customers**: By analyzing customer data, data mining can help identify different customer segments and their behaviors.

- **Optimize processes**: Data mining can be used to identify inefficiencies in processes and suggest improvements.

Here are some examples of how data mining can be used in conjunction with OLAP:

- **Market-basket analysis**: This technique is used to identify relationships between products that are frequently purchased together. OLAP can be used to analyze sales data by product, time, location, and other dimensions, while data mining can be used to extract patterns in the data that identify which products are often purchased together.

- **Fraud detection**: OLAP can be used to analyze financial transactions by account, date, location, and other dimensions, while data mining can be used to detect patterns of fraudulent activity that may be difficult to detect through traditional analysis.

- **Customer segmentation**: OLAP can be used to analyze customer data by demographics, purchase history, and other dimensions, while data mining can be used to identify clusters of customers with similar characteristics and behaviors.

- **Churn analysis**: OLAP can be used to analyze customer retention by product, location, and other dimensions, while data mining can be used to identify patterns in customer behavior that indicate a likelihood of churn.

There are several data mining and OLAP tools available in the market. These tools provide users with a wide range of options for data mining and OLAP and can be used to analyze large and complex datasets. They are often used in industries such as finance, health care, and retail, where large amounts of data need to be analyzed to gain insights into customer behavior, fraud detection, and other areas. Here are some of the most popular ones:

- **Microsoft SQL Server Analysis Services**: Microsoft SQL Server Analysis Services is an OLAP and data mining tool that is widely used in the industry. It provides multidimensional analysis and data mining capabilities, as well as support for data visualization tools such as Power BI.

- **IBM Cognos Analytics**: IBM Cognos Analytics is a business intelligence tool that includes OLAP and data mining capabilities. It provides users with a range of visualization and reporting options, as well as support for data discovery and predictive analytics.

- **Oracle BI**: Oracle BI is a business intelligence tool that includes OLAP and data mining features. It provides users with a range of analytical and reporting options, as well as support for data discovery and predictive analytics.

- **SAS Analytics**: SAS Analytics is a data analytics platform that provides users with a range of tools for data mining, OLAP, and predictive analytics. It includes features such as data exploration, model building, and automated modeling.

- **Tableau**: Tableau is a data visualization tool that provides users with a range of data exploration and visualization options, as well as support for OLAP and data mining. It includes features such as drag-and-drop data visualization and dashboard creation.

- **RapidMiner**: RapidMiner is a data science platform that provides users with a range of data mining and predictive analytics capabilities. It includes features such as data integration, visualization, and automated modeling.

OLAP, cubes, reporting techniques, and data mining are powerful tools that can help organizations analyze large volumes of data and extract valuable insights. By using these tools, organizations can make informed decisions and stay ahead of the competition. Whether you are a small business or a large enterprise, these techniques can help you better understand your data and improve your overall performance.

Metadata

Metadata is information about data. It describes the structure, contents, and context of data. In a data warehouse, metadata is particularly important because it helps users understand the data structure, context, and meaning of the data and ensures that the data is being used effectively and efficiently.

As it's a critical component of any data warehousing system and relevant in the past, future, and current stages of the data warehouse, investing in a robust metadata management system can make better use of an organization's data and derive greater insights from it.

There are several types of metadata that are commonly used in data warehousing, as follows:

- **Technical metadata**: This type of metadata describes the physical structure of the data, including tables, columns, indexes, and relationships between tables.

- **Business metadata**: This type of metadata describes the meaning and context of the data. It includes information about the source of the data, the business rules that apply to the data, and how the data should be used.

- **Operational metadata**: This type of metadata describes how the data is being used in real-time. It includes information about who is accessing the data, how often it is being accessed, and what queries are being run.

- **Usage metadata**: This type of metadata describes how users are interacting with the data. It includes information about which reports are being run, which queries are being executed, and which data is being exported.

Metadata is typically stored in a metadata repository, which is a centralized database that contains information about the data warehouse. This repository can be used to manage metadata across different tools and applications, and to ensure that all users are working with consistent and accurate information.

With the large amount of data that data warehouses store, managing metadata can be a challenging task. This is where metadata management tools come in. These tools help automate metadata management, making it easier to maintain accurate and up-to-date metadata.

Let's consider the need for metadata management with a use case of a large retail organization with a complex data warehousing environment.

The company has several databases, data marts, and data warehouses, each with different data structures and business rules. It is challenging for users to find the data they need, and there is a high risk of data inconsistencies and errors. The company decided to implement a metadata management tool to streamline metadata management.

Example: The company decides to use the Informatica Metadata Manager. They start by configuring the tool to connect to their databases, data marts, and data warehouses. *The tool automatically discovers and documents metadata from these sources,* providing a comprehensive view of the organization's data assets. Users can now search for data assets across different systems, view the relationships between assets, and see the history of changes to assets.

The company also uses the tool to *create a business glossary, which provides a common language for describing data.* They define terms such as *customer, product,* and *sales* and link these terms to the relevant data assets. This makes it easier for users to understand the context and meaning of the data they're working with.

As a result of implementing the metadata management tool, the company can improve the accuracy and consistency of its data, reduce the risk of errors, and make it easier for users to find and understand the data they need.

Following are some of the most popular metadata management software solutions for data engineering:

- **IBM Infosphere Information Server**: IBM Infosphere Information Server is a comprehensive metadata management solution that provides data lineage, impact analysis, and governance capabilities.

- **Collibra**: Collibra is a cloud-based metadata management platform that provides a data governance framework. The platform includes features such as data discovery, business glossary, and data lineage.

- **Alation**: Alation is a cloud-based metadata management solution that provides a collaborative data catalog. It includes features such as data discovery, data cataloging, and data lineage.

- **Talend Metadata Manager**: Talend Metadata Manager is a metadata management solution that provides data lineage, data mapping, and impact analysis capabilities. It can be used with the Talend Data Integration platform.

- **Informatica Metadata Manager**: Informatica Metadata Manager is a metadata management solution that provides a centralized view of metadata across the organization. It includes features such as data discovery, data lineage, and impact analysis.

Note   In response to the changing data landscape, metadata management software is becoming more advanced and incorporating new features. This applies to different types of data storage such as traditional data warehouses, data lakes, delta lakes, and data mesh. Organizations are using these software tools more effectively to optimize their data management.

The following modern tools with specific usage scopes are also frequently used in addition to the well-known and evolved tools:

- **Microsoft Purview**: Microsoft Purview is a cloud-based metadata management solution that allows users to discover, classify, and manage data assets across the organization. It includes features such as data discovery, data cataloging, and data lineage.

- **Apache Atlas**: Apache Atlas is an open-source metadata management solution that provides data governance capabilities for Hadoop and other Big Data platforms. It includes features such as data discovery, data classification, and data lineage.

- **Cloudera Navigator**: Cloudera Navigator is a metadata management solution that provides data discovery, data lineage, and data governance capabilities for Hadoop and other Big Data platforms.

- **SAP Metadata Management**: SAP Metadata Management is a metadata management solution that provides a centralized repository for metadata across the organization. It includes features such as data discovery, data lineage, and impact analysis.

- **MANTA**: MANTA is a metadata management solution that provides automated data lineage and impact analysis for databases, data warehouses, and Big Data platforms.

- **AWS Glue**: AWS Glue is a fully managed extract, transform, and load (ETL) service that can be used to manage metadata for data stored in Amazon S3. It includes features such as data cataloging, data lineage, and data discovery.

- **Databricks Delta**: Databricks Delta is a unified data management system that can be used to manage metadata for data stored in Databricks. Delta provides features such as schema enforcement, data versioning, and data lineage.

- **Databricks Unity Catalog**: Databricks Unity Catalog is a metadata management solution that is built into the Databricks Unified Analytics Platform. It provides a unified metadata catalog for all data sources within the Databricks workspace, including data stored in Databricks Delta Lake, Apache Spark, and external data sources such as AWS S3 and Azure Data Lake Storage.

Data Storage Techniques and Options

Once you have a basic understanding of the various components of a data warehouse, it is crucial to familiarize yourself with the available storage options and techniques used to store data at different stages of data processing and consumption. There are several factors to consider when choosing a storage technique or option, including the amount of data, the frequency of data updates, and the query performance requirements.

Popular storage techniques and options for data warehouses include the following:

- **Relational databases**: These are the most common storage systems for data warehouses. They are efficient at handling large volumes of structured data and can support complex queries. Examples include MySQL, Oracle, and Microsoft SQL Server.

- **Columnar databases**: These databases store data in columns rather than rows, which can improve query performance for large datasets. Examples include Amazon Redshift, Google Big Query, Apache Cassandra, SAP HANA, and Vertica.

- **In-memory databases**: These databases store data in memory, which can dramatically improve query performance, but at a higher cost. Examples include SAP HANA, Oracle TimesTen, VoltDB, Microsoft SQL Server In-Memory OLTP, and MemSQL.

- **NoSQL databases**: These databases are designed to handle unstructured or semi-structured data, which can be useful for data warehouses that need to incorporate a variety of data types. Examples include MongoDB, Cassandra, and Neo4j.

- **Cloud-based storage**: Cloud-based data warehouses can be a cost-effective and scalable option, as they allow organizations to store and process large volumes of data without investing in expensive hardware.

  - **Data lakes**: These are large repositories of raw, unstructured data that can be used for a variety of purposes, including data exploration, machine learning, and analytics. Examples include Amazon S3, Google Cloud Storage, and Azure Data Lake Storage. In most cases the underlying technology is object storage, which is optimized for storing unstructured data such as images, videos, and audio files. Examples include Amazon S3 and Google Cloud Storage.

Overall, the choice of schema and storage options in a data warehouse will depend on the specific needs and goals of the organization.

Evolution of Big Data Technologies and Data Lakes

The evolution of Big Data technologies and data lakes has been a game-changer in the realm of data management and analytics. Initially, organizations primarily relied on traditional relational databases to handle their data. However, as data volumes surged exponentially, these systems proved inadequate. This led to the emergence of Big Data technologies, characterized by distributed computing frameworks like Hadoop and Spark, which could handle massive datasets by dividing them across clusters of machines. The concept of data lakes also emerged during this evolution. In the next section we will examine this evolution in detail.

Transition to the Modern Data Warehouse

Earlier in this chapter, we discussed the evolution of data warehousing, starting with OLTP-based systems, which were sufficient for most enterprise needs. However, with the growth of the internet, e-commerce, social media, and IoT, data collection, processing, and consumption faced many challenges.

The transition from a traditional data warehouse to a modern data warehouse has been driven by the need for faster and more efficient processing of large amounts of data.

There are several key factors that have led to this transition, as follows:

- **Increased volume and variety of data**: With the rise of Big Data, organizations are dealing with larger and more complex datasets than ever before. This has led to the need for new technologies and techniques that can handle this data at scale.

- **Real-time processing**: Modern data warehouses need to support real-time data processing and analytics, which requires faster processing times and more efficient data storage and retrieval.

- **Cloud computing**: The availability of cloud computing services has made it easier and more cost-effective for organizations to store and process large amounts of data. Cloud-based data warehouses offer greater scalability, flexibility, and accessibility than traditional on-premises solutions.

- **Self-service analytics**: Modern data warehouses support self-service analytics, which allows business users to access and analyze data without relying on IT teams. This requires a more flexible and user-friendly data warehouse architecture.

Another major challenge with the older system involved the hardware and scalability. As the amount of data and the complexity of queries continued to grow, the data warehouse engineers and designers started facing multiple challenges, including the following:

- **Limited processing power**: Older data warehouse systems often had limited processing power, which made it difficult to handle large volumes of data and complex queries. Today, many data warehouses use parallel processing to distribute queries across multiple servers, which can significantly improve performance.

- **Limited storage capacity**: Older data warehouse systems also had limited storage capacity, which meant that organizations had to prioritize which data to store and which to discard. Today, cloud-based data warehouses offer virtually unlimited storage capacity, allowing organizations to store and analyze large volumes of data without having to worry about running out of storage space.

- **Slow query performance**: Query performance can be slow in older data warehouse systems due to the large amount of data that needs to be scanned. Today, many data warehouses use columnar storage, which allows for faster query performance by only scanning the columns that are needed for a specific query.

- **Difficulty in integrating different data sources**: Older data warehouses often required extensive data modeling and ETL (extract, transform, and load) processes to integrate data from different sources. Today, modern data warehouses use tools and technologies such as data virtualization and data pipelines to streamline the integration of data from different sources.

- **Inability to handle real-time data**: Older data warehouses were typically designed to handle batch processing of data, which meant that real-time data was not readily available. Today, many data warehouses use streaming data processing technologies to handle real-time data and enable real-time analytics.

All these issues led to the evolution of new database systems, collectively called Big Data systems. These widely used NoSQL and distributed databases in multiple ways, leading to the development of multiple systems. A few were built on a master–slave model, while others were built on completely distributed peer-to-peer technology.

One of the biggest challenges initially faced by distributed databases was maintaining the consistency and reliability of the data across multiple nodes. To address this issue, the Chord protocol was proposed in 2001 by Ion **Stoica et al.** This distributed hash table (DHT) algorithm enabled efficient and consistent lookup of data across a large network of nodes. The Chord protocol relies on a consistent hashing function and a set of rules for routing and maintaining replicas of data across nodes. It has since become one of the most widely used DHT algorithms for distributed databases, implemented in numerous systems and applications.

Although there are currently no widely used Big Data systems directly built on the Chord protocol, multiple techniques used to manage synchronization and partitions between different nodes holding or processing data are inspired in some way by the Chord protocol.

Note   Today, the modern data warehouse is powered by Big Data systems that rely on the myriad options of distributed computing frameworks and storage technologies, such as Apache Hadoop, Apache Spark, Apache Cassandra, and Amazon S3, which are designed to handle the unique challenges of processing and storing large volumes of data across clusters of machines.

The progress achieved in the data warehouse industry has not been sudden, but rather has undergone a significant transformation over the last few decades. Modern data warehousing solutions have made considerable enhancements in terms of hardware and scalability, exceeding the capabilities of previous versions.

We will delve into some of the major hardware and scalability advancements in modern data warehouses, and discuss real-life instances of how the following upgrades have empowered organizations to manage vast volumes of data effortlessly:

- **Cloud-Based Data Warehouses**: One of the biggest hardware improvements in modern data warehouses has been the adoption of cloud-based data warehousing solutions. These solutions offer virtually unlimited storage capacity and the ability to scale up or down as needed. Organizations can leverage cloud-based data warehouses to handle large amounts of data without having to invest in expensive hardware or infrastructure. For example, Airbnb uses Amazon Redshift, a cloud-based data warehouse, to store and analyze over 10 petabytes of data, allowing them to make data-driven decisions that improve the user experience for their customers.

- **Distributed Processing**: Another key hardware improvement in modern data warehouses is the use of distributed processing. This technique involves distributing queries across multiple servers, allowing organizations to handle large volumes of data and complex queries with ease. Apache Hadoop, an open-source distributed processing framework, is commonly used in modern data warehouses. For example, Yahoo uses Hadoop to process over 100 petabytes of data each day, providing insights that drive their search, mail, and news products.

- **Columnar Storage**: Another important hardware improvement in modern data warehouses is the use of columnar storage. Unlike traditional row-based storage, columnar storage stores data in columns, which makes it easier and faster to retrieve specific data. This approach is especially effective for data warehousing, where queries often involve aggregating data from large datasets. For example, Adobe uses columnar storage in their cloud-based data warehouse, Adobe Experience Platform, to store and analyze large amounts of customer data. This allows them to gain insights that help them improve their products and services.

- **Real-Time Analytics**: Modern data warehouses also enable real-time analytics, allowing organizations to make decisions based on the most up-to-date data available. Real-time analytics requires hardware that can handle a high volume of data with low latency. For example, financial services company Capital One uses Apache Kafka, a distributed streaming platform, to handle real-time data from their mobile and web applications. This allows them to analyze customer data in real-time and make decisions that improve their products and services.

These technologies provide critical features such as fault tolerance, scalability, and high performance for processing and analyzing Big Data. These solutions offer significant hardware and scalability improvements over their predecessors and allow organizations to handle massive amounts of data with ease, enabling them to gain insights that drive better business decisions. From cloud-based data warehouses to distributed processing, columnar storage, and real-time analytics, modern data warehousing solutions provide organizations with the tools they need to succeed in today's data-driven world.

Big Data systems, which are the foundation of modern data warehousing, have enhanced flexibility, scalability, and cost-effectiveness. They have enabled the handling of vast quantities of unstructured and semi-structured data, processing of data in parallel, and provision of real-time analytics. The significance of Big Data technologies in data warehousing is growing and will continue to be critical in the future. With businesses generating massive amounts of data, these technologies will become increasingly indispensable for managing and analyzing data.

Here are some ways in which Big Data technologies are being used in data warehousing:

- **Data Ingestion**: Big Data technologies are used to collect data from various sources, including social media, mobile devices, and IoT devices. This data is then transformed into a structured format and loaded into a data warehouse.

- **Data Storage**: Hadoop Distributed File System (HDFS) is used to store large amounts of unstructured data, while NoSQL databases are used to store semi-structured data.

- **Data Processing**: Big Data technologies, such as Hadoop and Spark, are used to process large datasets in parallel. These technologies can also handle complex processing tasks, such as natural language processing, machine learning, and predictive analytics.

- **Data Analytics**: Business intelligence tools, such as Tableau and Power BI, are used to analyze data stored in the data warehouse. These tools can connect to data sources, including Hadoop and NoSQL databases, and create visualizations and reports based on the data.

- **Data Governance**: Big Data technologies are used to enforce data governance policies, including data security, data quality, and data lineage.

In recent years, we've seen a major shift in the way companies handle Big Data. Rather than relying on traditional data warehousing methods, more and more organizations are turning to data lakes. A data lake is a centralized repository that allows businesses to store, manage, and analyze large amounts of structured and unstructured data in real-time. This approach provides organizations with the flexibility and scalability needed to handle the ever-increasing volume, velocity, and variety of data.

Traditional Big Data Technologies

Before the emergence of data lakes, companies used traditional Big Data technologies like data warehouses, which were designed to store structured data. Data warehouses were initially created to support business intelligence and reporting applications, and cleansed, transformed, and then stored data for analysis. This approach worked well for many years, but as the amount and types of data continued to grow, data warehousing became expensive and complex.

Data warehousing required complex ETL (extract, transform, and load) processes to extract data from multiple sources, transform it into a structured format, and then load it into a centralized repository. This process was time-consuming, costly, and required specialized skills to implement and maintain.

The Emergence of Data Lakes

With the advent of data lakes, companies can store structured and unstructured data in a centralized repository without the need for ETL processes. Data lakes use a flat architecture, which means data is stored in its original format, without the need for transformation. This approach allows businesses to store vast amounts of data from multiple sources, with a variety of data types, such as social media posts, customer reviews, machine logs, and more.

Data lakes are designed to be scalable, flexible, and cost-effective. They allow organizations to store data in its native format, which can be processed and analyzed by different applications and tools. This flexibility provides businesses with the agility they need to respond to changing market conditions, make data-driven decisions in real-time, and discover new insights from their data.

The Benefits of Data Lakes

One of the most significant benefits of data lakes is their ability to perform real-time analytics on vast amounts of data.

Traditional data warehousing technologies were limited by their inability to process unstructured data as well as the need for complex ETL processes. With data lakes, businesses can analyze data in real-time, without the need for preprocessing, making it easier to gain insights and make data-driven decisions.

Another advantage of data lakes is their cost-effectiveness. Unlike traditional data warehousing methods, which required expensive hardware and software licenses, data lakes can be deployed on cloud platforms such as Amazon Web Services, Google Cloud, or Microsoft Azure, providing businesses with a scalable, cost-effective solution for storing and analyzing data.

Data lakes have become a popular choice for storing large amounts of data, including unstructured data. However, as with any technology, there are issues that need to be considered when working with data lakes and unstructured data. Some of the common issues that arise with data lakes and unstructured data are as follows:

- **Lack of Structure**: Unstructured data can be difficult to work with because it lacks the structure that is typically found in structured data. This can make it challenging to query, analyze, and visualize the data. To address this issue, businesses must use tools and technologies that can process and analyze unstructured data.

- **Data Quality**: Unstructured data can be messy, incomplete, or inconsistent, which can lead to issues with data quality. This is especially true when data is coming from multiple sources. To address this issue, businesses need to have strong data governance policies and processes in place to ensure that data is accurate and consistent.

- **Data Security**: Unstructured data can be more difficult to secure than structured data. This is because unstructured data can be stored in a variety of formats, making it more difficult to manage and control access to the data. Businesses must implement strong security measures to protect unstructured data, such as access controls and encryption.

- **Data Swamps**: Data swamps, also known as data dumps or data wastelands, are situations where large amounts of data are accumulated and stored in a disorganized, unstructured manner without any clear purpose or plan for analysis. This can lead to significant challenges for companies, including security risks, data inconsistencies, and difficulties in processing and analyzing the data.

In other words, a data swamp is a data repository that is poorly managed and lacks the necessary structure and governance to make the data useful. Data swamps can occur when businesses attempt to store all their data in a single repository without proper management, which can lead to a disorganized and unmanageable mess.

One example of a well-known real-life data swamp caused significant trouble for a major credit reporting agency in the United States in 2017. The agency suffered a data breach that exposed the personal information of more than 140 million customers, including their names, Social Security numbers, birth dates, and addresses.

An investigation into the breach found that the agency had failed to implement basic security measures to protect the sensitive data it collected and stored. The agency had stored the data in a large, unsecured database that lacked basic protections such as encryption and multi-factor authentication. The data was also poorly organized and maintained, making it easy for hackers to access and steal the information.

This highlights the dangers of data swamps and the importance of implementing proper data management and security practices. To avoid data swamps, companies should focus on implementing clear data management policies, including data governance, data quality, and data security measures. This can involve implementing data classification systems, defining data ownership and access policies, and regularly reviewing and maintaining the data to ensure it remains relevant and accurate.

In addition, companies should consider investing in data management and analytics platforms, such as data lakes or data warehouses, that can help organize and process large amounts of data in a structured manner. These platforms can provide the scalability and flexibility needed to store and analyze large volumes of data, while also providing the necessary security and governance features to protect sensitive information.

To avoid data swamps, businesses must implement proper data governance policies and processes. This includes defining data quality standards, establishing data lineage, and monitoring data usage to ensure that data is being used effectively.

Implementing governance, structure, and improved data identification and validity in a data lake makes it a strong contender to replace traditional data warehouses. However, since data warehouses are primarily used to store processed and structured data for end users, replacing them can be challenging. Therefore, many organizations have optimized their data lakes to bridge the gap left by traditional data warehouses.

Data Lakes as Data Warehouses

Although data lakes and data warehouses are often viewed as distinct concepts, they do share some similar functionalities, and it is possible to leverage a data lake as a data warehouse. Here's how:

- Data warehouses are specifically designed to store structured data and facilitate business intelligence and reporting applications. To accomplish this, structured data must be cleansed, transformed, and then stored for analysis. Data lakes, however, are designed to store large quantities of structured and unstructured data in its raw form, without any transformations. This makes data lakes much more adaptable and scalable than data warehouses.

- Data lakes can store both structured and unstructured data, making it possible to utilize them as a data warehouse. By transforming the raw data stored in the data lake into structured data, it is feasible to create a data warehouse that can be used for traditional business intelligence and reporting purposes.

- To transform data stored in a data lake into a structured format, tools such as Apache Hive, Data Bricks, etc., can be used. Apache Hive can query data stored in a data lake and transform it into a structured format. This transformed data can then be loaded into a data warehouse like Amazon Redshift, Azure Synapse, or Google BigQuery, which can be utilized for traditional business intelligence and reporting purposes.

Leveraging a data lake as a data warehouse provides numerous benefits, such as enhanced flexibility in the types of data that can be stored and analyzed.

Data lakes can store both structured and unstructured data, making it easier to manage complex and diverse datasets. Additionally, this approach provides scalability, as data lakes can handle vast amounts of data without the need for complex ETL processes.

Data Lake House and Data Mesh

A data lakehouse combines the flexibility of data lakes with structured data warehousing features, allowing organizations to efficiently manage diverse datasets. Meanwhile, a data mesh is a decentralized data management approach that treats data as products owned by domain teams, promoting collaboration, reusability, and scalability while addressing the challenges of growing data complexity. In the next section we will review each of these concepts and applications in detail.

Transformation and Optimization between New vs. Old (Evolution to Data Lake House)

In the world of data management and analytics, the terms *data warehouse* and *data lake* have been used to describe two different approaches to storing and analyzing data. However, in recent years, a new concept has emerged that combines the best of both worlds: the data lake house.

The evolution of data management has taken a significant leap from traditional data warehousing to data lakes and now to data lake houses. To understand the evolution of data management, let's first take a look at the concepts of data warehousing and data lakes.

A data warehouse is a centralized repository that stores structured data from various sources, such as databases, applications, and data feeds. Data warehouses are typically designed to support business intelligence and analytics applications, providing a single source of truth for the organization. Data warehouses are often expensive to build and maintain, and the structured nature of the data makes it challenging to store and analyze unstructured data, such as social media feeds, videos, and images.

Data lakes, however, are designed to store raw, unstructured data in a centralized repository. Data lakes can store data from a variety of sources, including social media feeds, IoT devices, and other unstructured data sources. Data lakes are more cost-effective than data warehouses and can provide greater flexibility in analyzing data. However, data lakes lack structure, making it difficult to organize and process data for analytics purposes.

The data lake house is a new concept that combines the best of both data warehouses and data lakes. It is designed to provide a centralized repository that stores both structured and unstructured data. This repository is highly scalable and can accommodate large volumes of data from various sources.

The data lake house provides a unified and integrated view of all data, making it easier to manage and analyze the data. This approach eliminates the need for multiple data repositories and simplifies data management, ensuring data consistency and accuracy. The data lake house can also handle both batch and real-time data, making it ideal for streaming and IoT data.

Data lake houses provide businesses with the flexibility and agility to manage and analyze data in real-time, enabling them to make informed decisions based on the latest information. The ability to combine structured and unstructured data in a single repository makes it easier to extract insights from the data, improving business performance.

In conclusion, the evolution of data management has led to the development of the data lake house, which combines the best of both data warehouses and data lakes. The data lake house provides a centralized, integrated, and scalable repository for both structured and unstructured data, making it easier to manage and analyze data in real-time. This approach is ideal for businesses that need to handle large volumes of data from various sources and require fast and accurate analytics to support decision-making. The data lake house is an exciting new development in data management and analytics, providing businesses with the flexibility and agility they need to stay competitive in today's data-driven world.

A Wider Evolving Concept Called Data Mesh

The data mesh is a paradigm shift in data management that focuses on data as a product. It seeks to decentralize data ownership and management, making data more accessible, understandable, and manageable by small, self-organizing teams.

The data mesh approach recognizes that data is no longer a centralized resource that can be managed and controlled by a few experts. Instead, data is a distributed resource that is generated by various teams and departments within an organization. To effectively manage and use this data, a new approach is needed that emphasizes distributed ownership and governance.

The data mesh approach emphasizes the following principles:

- **Data as a product**: Data is treated as a product that is designed, developed, and managed by small, self-organizing teams that are responsible for delivering business value.

- **Domain-driven design**: Data products are organized by domain, with each domain having its own data product manager responsible for managing the data products within that domain.

- **Federated data governance**: Data governance is distributed and owned by the domain data product managers, with central governance providing a framework and guidelines.

- **Self-serve data infrastructure**: Data infrastructure is designed to be self-serve, with each domain team having access to the tools and infrastructure needed to develop and manage their data products.

- **Data operations**: Data operations are designed to be automated, with tools and processes in place to ensure that data products are available, reliable, and scalable.

Note   The data mesh approach is designed to address the challenges of data management in the modern era. It emphasizes distributed ownership and governance, making it easier to manage and use data products. This approach is particularly well-suited to organizations that have a large and complex data landscape, with data generated by various teams and departments.

In conclusion, the evolution of data management has seen a shift from traditional data warehousing to data lakes and now to data lake houses. However, as the volume and complexity of data continue to grow, the data mesh is emerging as the next evolution in data management. The data mesh approach emphasizes distributed ownership and governance, making it easier to manage and use data products. This approach is well suited to organizations that have a large and complex data landscape, with data generated by various teams and departments. As the data mesh continues to evolve, it is likely to become the new standard in data management and analytics.

Building an Effective Data Engineering Team

A data warehouse project typically involves a team of people with diverse skills and expertise. Here are some of the key roles and responsibilities in a data warehouse project:

- **Project Manager**: The project manager is responsible for overseeing the entire data warehouse project, ensuring that it is completed on time, within budget, and to the required quality standards. They coordinate the efforts of the team and communicate with stakeholders about project progress and issues.

- **Data Architect**: The data architect is responsible for designing the overall architecture of the data warehouse, including the data model, ETL process, and data integration strategy. They ensure that the data warehouse is scalable, efficient, and able to meet the needs of the business.

- **ETL Developer**: The ETL developer is responsible for designing and building the ETL process that extracts data from source systems, transforms it into a standard format, and loads it into the data warehouse. They ensure that the ETL process is efficient, reliable, and scalable.

- **Database Administrator**: The database administrator is responsible for ensuring the performance, security, and availability of the data warehouse. They optimize the database for performance, monitor it for errors, and ensure that backups are performed regularly.

- **Business Analyst**: The business analyst works with stakeholders to understand the business requirements for the data warehouse. They identify the key metrics and KPIs that the business needs to track and analyze and ensure that the data warehouse is designed to meet those needs.

- **Data Analyst**: The data analysts are responsible for managing and analyzing data in a data warehouse. They perform tasks such as data cleansing and transformation, data exploration and analysis, report generation, data quality management, and data governance.

They ensure that the data is clean, accurate, and meaningful, and provide business users with the insights they need to make data-driven decisions.

They use SQL, data visualization, and statistical analysis to explore the data and identify trends, patterns, and relationships.

- **Quality Assurance (QA) Analyst**: The QA analyst is responsible for testing the data warehouse to ensure that it meets the requirements of the business. They perform functional and performance testing, identify defects and issues, and work with the development team to ensure that they are resolved.

These are just some of the key roles and responsibilities in a data warehouse project. The size and scope of the project will determine the exact roles needed, and some individuals may wear multiple hats, depending on their skills and experience.

An Enterprise Scenario for Data Warehousing

An enterprise scenario for data warehousing is characterized by the need to integrate data from multiple sources across different departments and business units. In large organizations, data is often siloed, meaning it is stored in separate systems or databases that are not easily accessible to other parts of the organization. This can make it difficult to get a complete picture of the business and make informed decisions. A data warehouse in an enterprise scenario can help solve this problem by providing a central repository for all of the organization's data.

One of the key requirements of an enterprise data warehouse is scalability. As the amount of data and the number of users accessing the data warehouse grow, the system must be able to handle the increased load. This may require a distributed architecture, where data is spread across multiple servers or even data centers. It may also require specialized hardware and software designed for high-performance data processing.

Another critical aspect of an enterprise data warehouse is security. Data is often one of an organization's most valuable assets, and protecting it is essential. An enterprise data warehouse must be designed with security in mind, including features such as user authentication and authorization, data encryption, and audit trails to track access to the system.

In an enterprise data warehouse scenario, data quality is also crucial. The data must be accurate, complete, and consistent to ensure that the insights derived from it are reliable. To achieve this, the data warehouse must include data quality checks and validation processes to ensure that data is correctly entered and updated.

Finally, an enterprise data warehouse must be able to support a variety of analytical applications and tools. This includes both business intelligence and data science tools that allow users to visualize and analyze data, extract insights, and make informed decisions. An enterprise data warehouse must be designed to support different types of queries and analytical workloads, such as ad hoc reporting, OLAP analysis, and predictive modeling.

In this chapter, we have explained multiple options like data lake, data lake house and data mesh that can be used to create an enterprise data warehouse, the topic here just describes the need to cater to different aspects when building an enterprise data warehouse.

Summary

In conclusion, this chapter has provided a comprehensive overview of the evolution of data warehousing and data storage concepts, from the traditional data warehouse to the modern data warehouse, data lake, data lake house, and data mesh. As we continue through subsequent chapters, we will delve deeper into these concepts and explore how to build a modern data warehouse that incorporates proper security, governance, and design to accommodate both structured and unstructured data. With this foundation, we can stay up to date with the latest data engineering practices and make informed decisions to optimize our data management and analytics processes.

CHAPTER 2

Modern Data Warehouses

In the last decade, numerous technology updates have happened in the area of data warehousing. In addition, customer expectations increase with each passing year.

The first question that comes to mind is, What is a modern data warehouse? What characteristics make it modern? What makes it future-ready? What are the expectations for a data warehouse in modern times from the perspective of distributed process, storage, streaming, processing data in the cloud, or in general?

In this chapter, you will get answers to these questions. You will understand the need for modern data warehousing in modern times, which will help you grasp the next set of chapters with ease.

In this chapter, we will explore the following:

Introduction and Characteristics of Modern Data Warehouse (MDW)

- Challenges faced by data warehouses

- Modern data warehouse (MDW) technical features

Big Data

- Introduction to NoSQL databases

- Types of NoSQL databases, like key–value, document, column

Enterprise Scenario for Modern Cloud-based Data Warehouse

- Case study

- Enterprise scenario for modern cloud-based data warehouse

Advantages of Modern Data Warehouse over Traditional Data Warehouse

- Advantages of modern data warehouse over traditional data warehouse

© Anjani Kumar, Abhishek Mishra, and Sanjeev Kumar 2024
A. Kumar et al., *Architecting a Modern Data Warehouse for Large Enterprises*,
https://doi.org/10.1007/979-8-8688-0029-0_2

Objectives

This chapter describes the technical challenges faced by modern times and the reasons why a modern data warehouse is required to meet these technical requirements. The chapter further discusses the features of modern databases and the classification of modern databases.

After studying this chapter you should be able to do the following:

- Provide an overview of challenges faced by modern data warehouses and the features of modern data warehouses.

- Show understanding of big data and the types of NoSQL databases.

- Identify scenarios and requirements while setting your and stakeholders' expectations while building long-term solutions.

Introduction to Characteristics of Modern Data Warehouse

In the modern era, we have to handle the following requirement challenges raised by business, along with the four V's.

Data Velocity

"If an organization is a car, they need real-time data to navigate both external and internal bumps and reach their goals timely and safely."

—Anonymous

Organizations across all industries want to capture data frequently, fast to faster. As the event happens, management wants to know the event happened, and its intensity and repercussions. As the trends go, reporting data requirements has moved from quarterly to monthly, monthly to weekly, weekly to daily, daily to hourly, to every couple of seconds. It is important to mention that there is no industry left untouched by high-speed reporting of business data. Health care, automobiles, media, environmental, and real-time campaign data are only a few of the many I could mention.

Real-time data relates to the high velocity/speed of data. As the name suggests, data is captured in real time, processed in real time, and reported in real time. This processing can be done near the place where data are getting generated to save microseconds. The storage of data is generally done for a short stint, but you can always hook up a parallel stream to store the data for long-term analysis.

In real-time data, less latency is expected in write operations, but ideally is seen in both read and write operations. This reduces latency in the overall data pipeline, from ingestion to output, in the full data-flow cycle. *Latency* is defined as the time between when a request for data is sent and when a response is provided back to the requester. As time goes by, with the speed of the internet increasing, the speed at which data moves has increased.

Except for internet speed, computation is the most significant contributor to latency. With the advent of cloud computing, processing speed has increased by leaps and bounds. For example, social media on mobile can share location data, video, and images with other users with ease and speed.

Many industries exhibit this high-velocity usage, such as social networking conversations; GPS feeds; voice-to-text feeds; IOT (Internet of Things) feeds from devices from home like bulb, fan, door, etc.; water supply consumption; robotic manufacturing; face-recognition; cyber security threat assessment , and more.

Data Variety

Variety is defined as the ability to ingest from and integrate with a variety of formats of data, both structured and unstructured.

Operational systems like Enterprise Resource Planning (ERP), and Customer Relationship Management (CRM) systems generate numeric and text data in a .csv or Excel-like format, in the form of rows and columns; these are structured data and are categorized as conventional sources. However, images, video, audio, and a variety of other formats of data are unstructured data and are categorized as unconventional data. Unstructured data can be found in a variety of places, including radio frequency identification (RFID), data from industrial or home devices, image and video feeds from social networking sites, payment transaction data, global positioning system (GPS) data, call center voice feeds, email, SMS, and so on.

Data variety happens in many ways: Having a variety of files, with variance in file formats both structured and unstructured; variety in different formats of data files; or the file format is the same but column numbers or sequences vary. We must have the ability to handle the unpredictability of file structures.

The basic premise of the traditional data warehouse was to narrow variety and structured content. Enabled by new AI and analytics solutions, the modern data warehouse (MDW) has significantly expanded our horizons by enabling a wide variety of data formats and sources; for example, images and videos from social media, emails, blogs, SMS data, GPS data, and so forth.

There are 500+ varieties of format with varying sizes; for example, BMP, CALS, DDZ, GIF, JPEG, HTML, SKB, VOL (video), and more. Each format is compatible with other formats, or not, but can be analyzed in different ways; for example, by tagging audio or video files, or forensic voice comparison with reference data. Actual data can be computed using metadata. Network distances can be calculated using graphic data. Emotions can be analyzed in text, emoticons, tweets, social media messages, text, etc. These are a few examples, but not all can be accessed and processed in same way.

Complexity or variety is changing in the rapidly shifting landscape of DW technologies. The data is processed, transformed, compiled, and ingested from a variety of sources using Extract Transform Load (ETL)/Extract Load Transform (ELT).

Figure 2-1 demonstrates the variety of data that flow through the ingestion pipeline, which include data from multimedia, xml, email systems, traditional RDBMS (Relation Data Base Management Systems), data streaming, legacy data, cloud platform, internet, and mobile applications.

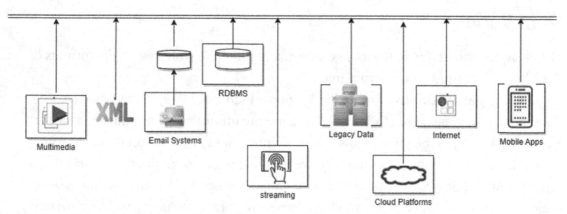

Figure 2-1. *Variety of data sources*

Volume

As the volume of data is increasing, we need to plan for the storage and processing of terabytes or petabytes of data in real time. This is a characteristic of Big Data. However, in modern times cheap storage and processing is possible, and there are multiple vendors and solutions available in the market with the capability of catering to scalability, distributed storage, and high processing querying requirements. Organizations will turn to cloud computing. Organizations will turn to cloud computing to process and cloud storage to store data for real-time reporting. Data scientists can dig deep and analyze data to find patterns and create predictive models to see future directions and prescriptive models. The amount of data that needs to be stored for prescriptive analytics is big. With the advent of cloud solutions, this volume of data can be handled with modern solutions.

Data Value

Data value is the ability to transform data into information and then into insights, and to create value from data when and wherever and in whichever format required. This means, that safe and secure support for business intelligence reports, automation and artificial intelligence (AI) capabilities is essential in modern times.

At a minimal level, data value is the ability to create reports and dashboards. At the second upper level, it is an ability to automate manual activities. At the third level, it is the ability to integrate with code and create predictive models, use statistical methods, and enable machines to improve with experience and learn to make integrated decisions. Having the ability to offer multi-language support and create queries—e.g., SQL, Python, R, etc.—is a value addition for business.

Fault Tolerance

Fault tolerance is the ability of a system to continue operating properly in the event of the failure of one or more of its components. A fault-tolerant design enables a system to continue its intended operation when some part of the system fails. Fault tolerance is an important consideration for any system that must be highly available. By incorporating fault tolerance into the design of a system, it is possible to reduce the risk of system downtime and ensure that the system can continue to operate even in the event of failures.

Managing, processing, and storing large-scale data requires high availability, reliability, reduced costs, and improved security in data warehouses. One of the performance points is handling the faults that occur during computation; e.g., handling disk failures. If a unit of work fails in hardware, then the system must automatically restart the same task on an alternate node and not restart the entire query from the beginning. This is a critical value addition and differentiating factor in systems handling real-time databases; e.g., payments, orders booking, etc.

Scalability

Because not only the volume of data is captured. Sometimes the data flowing into an organization's system is high volume for a few hours, but then drops in volume for several hours. An MDW should be easily scalable, or at least with little effort, and should be able to scale horizontally or vertically on the fly.

Interoperability

An MDW should be able to connect with the legacy and on-premises data warehouse and any new DW coming onto the market. In organizations where multiple cloud environments are available, they should be able to connect with each other.

Reliability

Data must be processed and executed accurately and completely such that the expected output is achieved as intended, every time, always.

Note   Out of the four V's—volume, variety, velocity, and veracity—there is one that is inherent in the others—veracity. It means data should be accurate, error-free, reliable, consistent, bias-free, and complete, along with having multilingual capability. We are not counting this important factor because it is applicable in traditional data warehouses as well. It applies in all technologies and practices in all business cases.

Modern Data Warehouse Features: Distributed Processing, Storage, Streaming, and Processing Data in the Cloud

With the advent of 5G connectivity, edge computing is building a case for the platform that hyperscale cloud providers offer as part of their distributed cloud solutions.

There are multiple use cases for modern data warehouses in analytics, cloud-native applications, and edge computing to increase the capabilities in operations management, security and compliance, data analysis, resilience, enterprise integration, developer services, edge-computing immersive experience, and data/event reporting, among others.

There are multiple features of the modern data warehouse that make it modern. With the advent of processing, memory capabilities are enhanced in many technologies. There are a couple of features that were not available before that are available now. All these features may or may not be available in one single database solution. An ultimate solution could be a hybrid of two or more databases.

Distributed Processing

Distributed processing is a revolutionary development in computing models in analytics, scientific tasks, and more computation-heavy applications, as processing loads of direct and dependent jobs as processing tasks is getting bigger in size and more complex, and it would be expensive in terms of resources spent on a single processor to handle them alone. In distributed processing, computation tasks are distributed to multiple processors for efficient processing. Distributed computing offers advantages over traditional processing in terms of real-time scalability, reliability, flexibility, and speed in processing. These products are generally found in SaaS (Software as a Service) platform vendors that offer expanded functionality and cost effectiveness.

Flexibility and Speed in Implementation

It is easier to add computing power in a few minutes by adding a few servers in a cloud or/and computing capacity from a single window, than to take weeks and months going through the purchasing cycle and implementation of on-premises hardware.

Flexibility and Speed in Processing

Distributed processing reduces the risk of failure arising out of lack of enough computing power for jobs to run or waiting for dependent jobs to complete. The more data there is to process, the more time is saved in processing with this strategy.

Flexibility and Better Control on Costs

All vendors propose the flexibility to choose distributed processing when required and switch it off when required to save computer resources. CPU and memory are important factors in cost saving for cloud-based distributed computing. One caveat is that without governance and policy controls, this functionality can be misused by individuals, and instead they can get a massive bill. Flexibility means offering a broad range of virtual machine (VM) sizes, non-virtualized servers, VM on a single tenant's hosts, and multiple hypervisor choices.

Storage

Storage technology has evolved rapidly, as Gordon Moore predicted. You can say the performance capability of chips is roughly doubling every 18 months, and this amount of time is decreasing every year. The size of devices with the same storage are getting smaller compared to previous years. From a data-warehousing perspective, storage is used as a placeholder before processing, while processing, and after processing data according to business rules.

Note   Gordon Moore was one of the pioneers of integrated circuits who gave a prediction which is known as Moore's Law.

Storage as a Service

The storage capacity growth trend seen from cloud vendors is moving positively toward consumption-based offerings. Given the need to reduce time and costs, and to increase the ease of IT storage administration, support and maintenance will be moving toward storage as a service (STaaS) and artificial intelligence for IT operations (AIOps).

Storage Solutions

Storage infrastructure vendors provide solid-state arrays (SSAs), hybrid arrays, and software-defined storage (SDS) solutions that are deployed to support primary storage workloads. Storage in terms of modern data warehousing has some criteria.

Advances in cloud-native technologies; managed STaaS offerings; advanced AIOps features; consumption-based, SLA-metric-driven sourcing; and vendor-based asset financing and management programs set the stage for the next phase of the enterprise storage industry.

In-memory Storage

In-memory systems are data warehouse management systems (DBMS) where data is stored within computer memory itself instead of on a physical hard drive. This approach creates faster access and gets high I/O performance of system resources. This is critical for real-time applications like transaction processing and other applications that need to read and write data quickly. Three important factors of performance are memory, processing, and I/O. The physical design of most systems tries to speed up processing by reducing memory/storage access.

One of the approaches to doing so is by duplicating the data within or near a system where processing is performed; e.g., one version is placed in a database for operational OLTP (online transaction processing) systems, and another version in data warehouses for OLAP systems. This is because OLTP is I/O heavy, while OLAP is computationally heavy and requires different optimization routines. In-memory database applications can get you the best of both worlds in a single system. However, make sure that sensitive data is encrypted before storage and that there is regular back-up of data.

An in-memory-based approach can be implemented for column-based storage as well as for relational databases; e.g., Oracle's *TimesTen* for in-memory relational DB, *SAP HANA* for a column-based data warehouse, and *Starcounter* for OLTP solutions.

Streaming and Processing

Most organizations are processing data in the cloud in some capacity and increasing investments in new cloud-based initiatives. As cloud use cases spur the streaming and processing of data to increase application portability, automation, maintenance, security, and standardization, the effectiveness of cloud models is helping organizations anticipate and respond to changes (such as during the pandemic) to increase the adoption of cloud services.

As cloud services are essential in digital transformation across industries, regions, and boundaries, use cases such as smart cities, connected vehicles in automobiles, virtual healthcare, and more push for new data-streaming processing-speed requirements. Using cloud computing increases the ability to assess risks proactively, helps the organization's strategic planning, and supports mainstream operations. Cloud has a huge impact on business applications, business operating models, and IT architectures. The influence of cloud on IT operating models extends through IT operations management, security, networking, and business functions; e.g., clouds are becoming more prominent in technology purchasing. Serverless applications help organizations spend less time on infrastructure and more time on business functionality. Composable applications have the ability to provide pre-packaged functional capabilities to support businesses' quest to be agile, dynamic, and adaptive.

Here are some of the examples of specialized services that provide solutions for high with fast streaming and fast processing:

(QCaaS) Quantum computing as a service provides access to quantum computing (QC) systems and associated services, enabling them to explore enterprise-relevant use cases and devise quantum algorithms for a highly specialized set of problems; e.g., optimization, simulation, search, linear systems, and security-related use cases.

SaaS operations (SaaSOps) are the operational aspects of business end users who use SaaS applications in the cloud, and those who deploy their own software in the cloud and want to operate the software like a SaaS provider. It also includes other functionalities, such as ITOps, PlatformOps, SecOps, AIOps, MLOps, and site reliability engineering (SRE) capabilities. SaaSOps remains a fragmented model. Many SaaSOps aspects are performed separately. However, currently, there is no consolidated approach from SaaS providers to address data warehouse observability.

SaaS (software as a service)-centric APIs are cloud application services whose primary interface method is programmatic, accessed via request- or event-based APIs. The intent of SaaS-centric APIs is to contribute a set of Application Programming Interface (API) building blocks for further development of custom application functionalities, as well as experience and related processes. SaaS-centric APIs allow packaged business functionality, such as banking, commerce, or mapping services, to be used as building blocks in larger applications. This empowers organizations to create application experiences that are more advanced than relying on starting from scratch. This translates to business empowerment and faster, safer, and more efficient innovation.

Cloud high-performance computing services (HPC) offer modernized supercomputing environments for data processing that lead to digital innovation with integrated cloud services, automation, elasticity, and AI-based management. Cloud High performance Computing (HPC) market providers offer platforms that support scalable access to specialized HPC architectures, enabling enterprises to address diverse and complex use cases, including traditional computational engineering applications and advanced AI.

Edge computing uses distributed computing, in which data storage and processing are placed in the location of data creation and use, respectively. Edge computing locates data and workloads and optimizes for factors like latency, bandwidth, autonomy, and regulatory/security considerations. Edge-computing locations are found near places where physical sensors and digital systems converge to the cloud or a centralized on-premises data center. Edge computing improves efficiency and cost control by keeping computation processing close to the edge, where the data is generated or acted upon, for better automation and quality control, offering more business opportunities and growth with better customer experience and real-time business interactions.

Artificial intelligence (AI) services are used to automate tasks, improve efficiency, and make better decisions. AI services can be used in a variety of industries, including health care, finance, retail, and manufacturing. This provides a single or a collection of components and services on the cloud; e.g., AI modeling tools, APIs for pre-built services, and associated middleware that enables the designing, building, training, deployment, and consumption of machine learning (ML) models running on the cloud. These services include vision, language, and automated ML services to create new models and customize pre-built models. The adoption of these services is rapidly accelerating among developers and citizen data scientists for use with language, vision, and ML applications to automate and accelerate the achievement of business objectives.

Some of the capabilities of AI services are *natural language processing (NLP)* of human language, which can be used for machine translation, text analytics, and chatbots. *Computer vision* enables computers to see and understand the world around them and can be used in use cases for image recognition, object detection, and facial recognition. Machine (M/C) learning enables computers to learn from data without being programmed by a human element and can be used in use cases such as fraud detection, predictive analytics, and customer segmentation. Robotics deals with the design, construction, operation, and application of robots and can be used in use cases such as manufacturing, health care, and logistics.

Autonomous Administration Capabilities

Database administrators ensure that databases run efficiently and securely. They are responsible for maintaining databases. They monitor and update anti-malware software. Modern platforms for data warehouses should have autonomous administrative capabilities with minimum but be flexible enough to be interjected at any point of time.

Self-repair is an important ability of a system that can regularly check, detect, and repair or heal damage or malfunctions within its day-to-day operations without human intervention; e.g., automatic updates of major and minor database versions. This will increase reliability, reduce maintenance costs, and increase security and uptime.

High availability means having working database clusters without disruption. Having easily deployable and highly available databases offered via a managed service is a significant benefit for all kinds of workloads and applications. A highly available database is typically a cluster of three nodes, which is composed of a primary database node and two replicas. While undergoing maintenance or in case of node failure, there is another node available to make sure your application does not experience downtime. In case of a database on a virtual machine, the service will replace the non-working/problem nodes with working nodes, use monitoring tools to see the real-time state of the VM, and use that feedback to check the state of faulty nodes. A DHCP (dynamic host configuration protocol) server can be configured and reclaim new network addresses. Organizations can set up the node monitor to conditionally re-spawn/restart. Irrespective of the reason for the shutdown, a notification email is recommended for administrative activities. The expectation for modern data warehouses is that downtime should be less than three microseconds.

The self-securing capability includes multiple things. First, it includes patching of the operating system and security patching while running, without or with only minimal disruption. Second, having encryption always on encrypts selected columns in the DB that can be queried. Third, databases have the ability to regularly monitor for bugs and cyber-attacks and other levels of security, which can be proactively found, if not fully resolved. In case of disruption, the database should be able to remediate from the last version of the database as soon as possible.

Self-driving

A self-driving database requires three high-level steps. The first step is to enable monitoring of the administrative activities of the database. The second step is to collect data and monitor past events. Third is to create predictive models; e.g., a forecasting framework predicts the query arrival rates using time-series models combined with behavior modeling, which constructs machine learning models that predict the run-time behavior of database management systems. And, in the last, what action needs to be taken to enable autonomous database management systems that proactively plan for optimization actions? It automatically applies the actions and provides explanations of its decisions. Some examples of algorithms are Monte Carlo tree search and receding horizon control.

A self-driving DBMS enables automatic system management, Sys-DevOps, and removes any impediments. First, workload forecasting predicts the query, workload patterns, storage, and processing requirements using machine learning, time-series learning model, behavior modeling and AI.

Self-tuning and Configuration

Modern data warehouses utilize machine learning and deep learning algorithms to analyze current workloads to forecast future workloads. At the same time, they control and fine-tune the number of CPUs required and customize temporary storage and query performance. Modern data warehouses have the ability to use hybrid storage to reduce the latency of OLAP/OLTP workloads.

Self-automatic backup is included as part of the business continuity and disaster recovery service, and this includes restoration to a point in time within a preconfigured retention period. The options for full backup of data and logs can be set by the customer to their desired frequency, recovery point, and time objective. It offers self-automatic multi-regional support for backup and self-recovery from a failover point.

Self-partitioning divides a big portion into smaller partitions. This is generally done to improve the performance and security by querying a small set of data parallelly. For example, with multiple parallel processing, partitioning advisors work closely with an MPP (multiple parallel processing) engine to partition with three objectives: combining the best of directed and stochastic search algorithms; balancing and exploiting the best solutions and exploring the search space; and maintaining a pool of potential solutions that consider alternative algorithms.

Self-scaling via horizontal and vertical scaling offers easy database node resizing so you can scale your database resources up or down as needed. Even horizontal scaling helps by adding capacity via additional servers, portioning the servers, and loading them. However, vertical scaling adds capacity to a server by increasing memory, processors, and so forth, making the same server bigger and better. The use cases are different for horizontal and vertical scaling. However the best-case scenario is having the capability of hybrid scaling where, depending on the use case, one or both capacities can be chosen.

Hybrid: As we know, OLTP and OLAP systems work with different objectives in mind. One is writing optimized, which OLAP is a read-optimized engine. A major development would be to transform DBMS to support both OLAP and OLTP workloads at the same time. The modern DW is able to adjust its configuration to accommodate both types of workloads at run time, depending on technical or business requirements.

Multi-tenancy and Security

Single-tenant architectures are provider managed and have a dedicated infrastructure and software instance, but the tenant retains full control over the software and infrastructure customization. Most single-tenant delivery models provide a high degree of user control, engagement, security, reliability, and backup capability. A single-tenant environment is an isolated one, so tenants are more flexible than in a shared infrastructure model. However, multi-tenant architecture is suitable for organizations that need to get up and running fast and are interested in reducing costs and maintenance overhead. However, companies should be aware of the limitations of the software in terms of performance, security, and customization.

Multi-tenant architecture shares resources between multiple tenants and can improve performance of the overall system. However, modern multi-tenant systems use advanced mapping and resource distribution mechanisms to make efficient use of resources and thus improve performance and reduce maintenance costs. Because resources are shared, the advantages are lower costs per user and efficient utilization of resources. Most vendors offer improved performance with strict service level agreements (SLAs) at an additional cost. It is easy to set up and has lower maintenance costs, from a customer perspective. This is used for processing or operations whether on-premises, off-premises, or hybrid.

Because of limited isolation between tenants in multi-tenant, and less than single tenant, and thus with more access points, attackers can more easily identify and exploit vulnerabilities in one tenant's environment and use them to attack other tenants.

The second type of threat to database servers is a software security threat via old versions of server patches, SQL injection, authentication gaps, and lack of backups, which create vulnerabilities.

The third issue is related to data; e.g., data sanitization, during data in motion, and regulatory compliance. This issue can be resolved through policies and procedures or through policies related to governance through people component out of PPT (People, Technology, and Process) framework.

The increasing risk of security breaches of sensitive data requires proactive data management. Anti-ransomware and cybersecurity solutions are needed to implement the NIST framework, and advanced detection methods that reduce the threat exposure window should be used. Storage systems need to be adapted to include requirements of the National Institute of Standards and Technology (NIST), and the Cyber Security Framework (CSF) can be seen as a security checklist for storage infrastructure demands.

Performance

Performance is about ensuring all the system resources are used optimally in the process of meeting the application's requirements. Last but not least, the cost of database performance is often measured in terms of how quickly data are fetched from and returned to their respective applications.

Multiple layers that might impact DW performance are:

Physical layer, like disks, RAM, OS, Server processes

Data schema layer, like tables, container, data types, volumes, and location

Network layer performance, like network speed, etc.

Application layer on-premises, off-premises, or hybrid, size of application

Modern data warehouses have the same definition of performance as traditional warehouses. There are three factors of DW performance:

1. ***Workload*** of the data warehouse is the combination of number and complexity of online transactions, regular batches, ad-hoc jobs, and configuration of server settings, like frequency of logs, back-ups, etc. Workloads can be predicted with confidence after analyzing historical data. The workload can be planned and optimized depending on the patterns. However, DBAs (database administrators) don't have historical data in the case of a new server setup. Workload has a major influence on performance.

2. ***Throughput*** is the measure of the DW's ability to carry out the amount of processing involved with the workload, size of server, and type of job. This can impact overall throughput, including I/O, CPU speed, size of RAM, parallel processing capabilities of server, and efficiency of operating system.

3. ***Contention for system resources.*** This is the condition in which two or more components of the workload are competing to use the same resources. Common examples are multiple users writing/updating a single row, resulting in long waits. As the contention increases throughput decreases for a traditional

71

DW. A modern DW handles this by choosing scalable cluster architectures to distribute workload and avoid contention. Databases use automatic sharding and replication to improve availability and performance while reducing contention.

There are ways to improve performance by providing indexes. Network speed, increasing number of buffers and buffer size, partitioning, range, and list, database tuning, hashing, and joining eliminate system-wide and application-specific bottlenecks.

There are multiple dimensions of performance: storage, I/O, and processing.

Storage Efficiency

Advancement in storage management includes integrating with data and analytics tools, AI operations, and AI operation platforms.

It also includes ultra-low latency for power-efficient, high-density edge data center infrastructure for storage.

The use of consumption-based and pay-for-use subscription licenses can replace (capital expenditure) CAPEX spending by (operation expenditure) OPEX, instead spending on hybrid cloud and edge infrastructure with cloud-native benefits.

Cloud vendor offerings reflect that the storage capacity growth trend is positively moving toward consumption-based offerings. We need to reduce time spent and increase ease of IT storage administration, support and maintenance. This points toward using storage as a service (STaaS) and artificial intelligence for IT operations (AIOps). More than 40 percent of on-premises IT storage administration, support, and maintenance will be replaced by storage as a service (STaaS) and artificial intelligence for IT operations (AIOps), which is an increase from less than 10 percent in 2022. The external enterprise storage arrays deployed to support primary storage workloads will adopt nonvolatile memory express over fabric (NVMe-oF), compared with fewer than 10 percent in 2022.

Data compression is an important technique and factor affecting performance and must be considered in a modern data warehouse. Lossless compression is used for financial or health-care data that is sensitive in nature. This data needs to be preserved without loss of its original form; lossless compression uses efficient encoded schemes to represent data.

Lossy compression is the opposite of lossless compression. This is for non-sensitive data that has no need to be preserved in its original form. The data removed is small.

Type of data, compression ratio, frequency, total time required, I/O effort to compress/uncompress, and compression algorithm itself are important factors in considering which type of compression should be used. For example, in I/O-intensive applications like image or text processing, compression provides a 35 percent to 60 percent gain in performance. In some use cases, compression shifts the computation load of data processing from I/O to CPU, but in some cases CPU compute–intensive application performance gains from data compression are negligible. Hadoop clusters are shared resources, hence a diminishing I/O load for one app can increase the bandwidth of other apps as they use the same bandwidth of I/O.

In some use cases, data compression is undesirable and even reduces performance; e.g., custom binary input files. In other cases, such as sequence files and derivative files, compression is always preferable. Compression is also preferable for intermediate files used for the shuffling and sorting of data.

In storage administration, along with its risks and associated costs, maintenance and support can be replaced by AI operations and STaaS (storage as a service) management capabilities. However, storage SME needs to be reskilled for software and AI/ML development initiatives.

In life-cycle management with centralized cloud-native control and data services capabilities, replace quality metrics with metric-based SLA sourcing. Both in-line compression and deduplication can be turned on and off at an individual logical unit number (LUN) level.

Scalable Storage

Multi-node shared storage architecture has the ability to store multiple file formats. It scales from tens of terabytes to multi-petabyte configurations and includes a comprehensive set of data services, such as replication and snapshots.

Reliability, Availability, and Serviceability (RAS):

Reliability, availability, and serviceability (RAS) are important factors in performance. *Reliability* means the ability of the DW system to consistently provide accurate and timely data. *Availability* means the ability of the DW system to be up and running always and when needed. *Serviceability* is the ease with which the system can be maintained and repaired when issues arise.

RAS is essential in providing data integrity in storage systems, implementing memory controllers—including memory mirroring, enhanced error checking and correction code (ECC) scrubbing, and memory sparing—which can be highly efficient.

Implementing multiple bit errors—and with the ability to locate and correct these errors—memory scrubbers have the ability to schedule or continually read and write to memory locations, looking for failures. The engine detects, logs, and attempts to correct errors in advance. It writes an error log that allows system management to measure the time-based deterioration of dual in-line memory modules (DIMM). DIMM sparing can be used as a fail-over mechanism. Reliability can be enhanced in PCI (Payment card industry) by error detection and signal integrity.

Multiple Parallel Processing (MPP)

Having a partitioning advisor working closely with an MPP (multiple parallel processing) engine for partitioning has two objectives. Combining techniques like distributed processing, clustering, and partitioning can greatly enhance performance and efficiency. This means that multiple queries or operations can be run in parallel on the databases in the same query, if they are not dependent on the same sequence path.

Flexibility and Speed in Implementation

As part of automated development, the Data warehouse Automation (DWA) tool generates the necessary system components without manual coding. The modern data warehouse automated development service includes automated development of code, data definitions, shell scripts, documentation, testing scripts, lineage, ETL/ELT logic, scheduling, and configuration scripts. The modern data warehouse automated maintenance service includes automated operating system patches, major and minor database version upgrades, and backups.

Real-time Processing

Advanced AIOps capabilities can favorably reduce IT administrative activities and reduce hardware admin and support costs.

Managed STaaS offerings include advanced AIOps features; consumption-based SLA metrics driving sourcing; and vendor-based asset financing and management programs.

Container-based services require a scalable persistent-data storage tier for effective usage.

Big Data

Traditional data warehouses like SQL, MySQL, PostgreSQL, and Maria DB are relational databases (RDBMS) that organize data as a series of two-dimensional tables, like rows and columns, which is easy to understand. RDBMS are ACID (atomic, consistent, isolated, and durable) compliant.

Before setting expectations for NoSQL databases, which are another name for Big Data, let's quickly recap the CAP and BASE theorems.

CAP Theorem

According to the CAP theorem (Figure 2-2), any distributed system can satisfy only two out of three properties:

> *Consistency*: This means that everyone who reads the database should read consistent information. This means that for every read instance, the database fetches the last write consistently.

> *Availability*: This means that the database should be always available for reading and writing. This is possible if the database has confirmation from the node about its availability. Read and write will be able to succeed when active nodes can confirm that they are live and available within reasonable response time

> *Partition tolerance*: This means that the database system will keep functioning without interruption in the event of data loss or system failure.

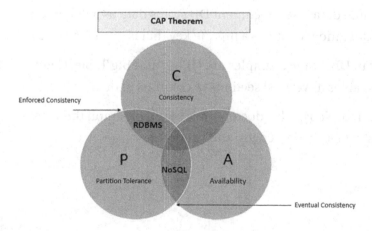

Figure 2-2. *CAP Theorem*

Note   The partition tolerance property is a must for NoSQL databases.

Relational databases focus on the cross-section of partition tolerance and consistency. However, NoSQL is not only SQL databases. NoSQL databases focus on the cross-section between partition tolerance and availability.

The NoSQL databases work on the BASE principle, where **BASE** stands for the following:

- **B**asic **A**vailability: The database should be available most of the time.

- **S**oft State: Temporary inconsistencies are allowed.

- **E**ventual Consistency: The system will come to a consistent state after a certain period.

What Are NoSQL Databases?

Open source or not, NoSQL databases are non-relational, distributed databases that enable organizations to analyze huge volumes of data with the benefit of high availability, zero fault tolerance, and high scalability. These databases are compliant with the BASE principle, which is the opposite of the ACID property.

There are the following four types of NoSQL databases:

1. Key–Value DB: DynamoDB, Riak

2. Document DB: MongoDB, CouchDB. This is an extension of the key–value database. Document DB stores data as a document. Each document contains a unique key that is used for retrieval.

3. Column DB: Some examples are HBase and Big Table. Column DB stores tables as vertical sections of columns of data.

4. Graph DB: Neo4j. This document is based on graph theory and stores data as nodes, edges, and properties.

Key–Value Pair Stores

The word *key–value* is made up of *key* and *value*. Two pieces of data are associated with each other, and the key is a unique identifier that points them to each other. The value in a key–value pair is either the data being identified or a pointer to that data. The values can be of any scalar data type, like complex structures or integers, blob, list, JSON, etc., and can be stored as an array, string, JSON, etc. The performance of this type of store is excellent and can be used to store data for a plethora of use cases.

The concept of the key–value pair has existed since time immemorial. Any index directory is a good example, or telephone directory, dictionary, and so on. In the previous example, the key is the unique identifier of a person, business name, or phone number, and the respective values are the person's name, business name, and phone number. Some common use cases for key–value databases are storing personal data, such as addresses, telephone numbers, etc.; product recommendations; caching and servicing; session management of multiplayer online games, and more. The question can be asked that since the same thing can be implemented in RDBMS as views, why would we use a key–value store. Key–value stores and other NoSQL methods have the advantages of speed, easy implementation, less need of programming skills, better pricing, and ease of integrating with features of web applications.

Figure 2-3 explains that a key–value store is basically a hash table. You link each data value with a unique key, and the key–value store uses this key to store the data by using a hashing function. The even distribution of hashed keys across data storage is a factor in the selection of hashing functions.

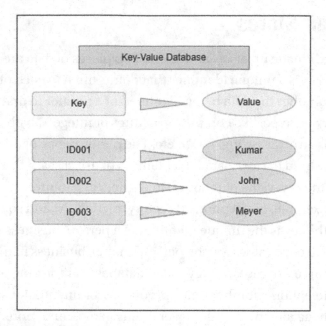

Figure 2-3. *Key–value pair database*

Key–value pairs consist of two elements: *partition key* and *unique identifier*.

The *unique identifier* is an identifier of a row that is unique for each row in the same partition. Items/values in the same partition are stored in row key order. If a new row is added to a table, it is ensured that the row is unique and that there is a unique identifier in terms of keys.

The *partition key* uniquely identifies the partition contained in the row. The stored values are not identified by the storage system software by itself. Hence, Table schema information must be provided and interpreted by the application. In other words, the key–value store retrieves the stored values by using the key as a reference point of lookup.

When an application retrieves a single row, the partition key enables Azure to go to the correct partition, and a unique identifier lets Azure identify the row in that partition being sought. In a range query, the application searches for a set of rows in a partition, specifying the start and end points of the set as row keys. This type of query is also very efficient and quick, if you have designed your keys according to the queries performed by the application.

Most key–value databases are intended for semi-structured databases and mostly support simple queries for retrieving data and insert/delete instances—only for writing instances. To modify a value (either partially or completely), an instance must overwrite the existing data for the entire value.

A key–value DB operation can be very fast for reading and writing. The DB is optimized for lookups and best used in use cases intended for the same. Key–value databases are very flexible, scalable, extendable, and distributable across multiple nodes on separate machines. This ability is a valuable, desirable, and strong feature of modern data warehouses. As time goes on, we are generating more and more data that is semi-structured in nature. Key–value DBs do not allow null values as keys or values. Irrespective it is not much, but as the number of nodes increases, storage capacity also increases.

In-memory caching is used in key–value databases to minimize read and write processing time; e.g., web applications can store user session details or customer product preferences by tracking users and storing data in key–value storage. As an example of another use case, real-time recommendations and advertising are often powered by key–value stores because the stores can quickly access and present new recommendations or ads as a web visitor moves throughout a site.

Some of the famous popular key–value DBs in the market are Riak, Redis, Project Voldemort, and Azure Storage Tables.

Document Databases

A document DB is a type of NoSQL DB and is very much an extension of a key–value DB. A document database has all the points of key–value DBs except that a document DB stores a document, which is a collection of fields. Fields can store a simple value or complex elements, such as lists or parent child hierarchy. Document DBs come in a variety of forms, such as JSON, BSON, XML, YML, and .txt.

A second difference is that the fields in the document enable an application to query and filter data by the values in those fields. A document DB does not require that all documents have the same structure. The structure of encoded data is semi-structured and can allow for complicated queries. This freeform approach provides a great deal of flexibility. Applications can store different data in documents as business requirements change. The data in a document can be stored in multiple forms, such as lists, collections, and so forth, and are retrieved by unique keys, such as a customer number or an order number.

Documents do not need to have the same structure as the way they are stored in RDBMS. Data applications can handle multiple structures of data in document DBs as business requirements change. There are multiple factors that are critical to decide when opting for a document database. Document DB can be easily partitioned and is distributable across multiple nodes, so it is highly scalable and high-performing. Because of the lack of rigid format structure, these DBs can store semi-structured and unstructured data and handle the changing schema from a data-modeling perspective.

Such databases can be helpful in scenarios where users need to work with binary data and perform low-level operations, like putting encryption algorithms on these binary bits within data. Document DBs have myriad business use cases for personalization engines, content management, games, IOT applications, and more. One of example of a document database is MongoDB.

MongoDB stores data as JSON/BSON documents to provide more flexibility for scaling and querying data as an application evolves. *Mongo* means "humungous," which means it is built for large volumes of data. MongoDB provides flexibility in terms of being schemaless when updating linked applications. This means we can start creating documents without needing to first establish a fixed structure. It provides features like GridFS, sharding, indexing, JavaScript interface to MongoDB, and rich query language. There are features for search flexibility, like graph search, geo-search, map-reduce queries, and text search.

However, before simply choosing MongoDB, we need to look at both its strengths and its weaknesses before deciding which platform to use or which approach to use; e.g., while setting up concurrent locations, updating a consistent field in several locations can cause lags in performance compared to a relational database as there will be a delay in data write operations. Also, like in other NoSQL languages, there can be a steeper learning curve for developers who are familiar with other databases because queries are written with a JSON syntax, instead of SQL.

Columnar DBs

Column DB is another type of NoSQL database where data are stored in a row and column table structure, like in a relational database, but are grouped in separate columns instead of rows. It means that, unlike traditional databases, the absence of predefined keys or column names provides schema-free flexibility when it comes to adding columns in real-time.

Figure 2-4 tries to demonstrate how all unique key values of three columns are stored and linked by unique keys.

Traditional- Row Oriented

Unique ID	FirstNm	SecondNm	GPA
ID001	Sanjeev	Kumar	4.0
ID002	Abhishek	Mishra	3.9
ID003	Anjani	Kumar	3.8

Wide Column oriented

Unique ID	FirstNm
ID001	Sanjeev
ID002	Abhishek
ID003	Anjani

Unique ID	SecondNm
ID001	Kumar
ID002	Mishra
ID003	Kumar

Unique ID	GPA
ID001	4.0
ID002	3.9
ID003	3.8

Figure 2-4. *Document database*

A column DB is one in which you can store a large amount of data within a column instead of a row. First, putting columnar data together allows compression algorithms to reduce the volume of disk storage required. Second, the main point of a column DB is its ability to store large amounts of data within a single column. Third, it improves read efficiency because there is no need for a row identifier, and this does allow for more rapid analysis of those column values.

However, when similar values are together in a columnar structure, it is not so good in terms of compression, and hence not so good performance-wise. Because one single insert could result in many rewrites as the data is shuffled to ensure similar values are adjacent to each other, if the data has frequent inserts and updates, this efficiency will eventually be lost.

So, the preceding criteria should be considered when deciding between column DB and traditional DB. While querying in CQL (Cassandra Query Language), column DBs allow for rapidly finding the location of fields and returning data. Data may need to be shuffled around to allow a new data row item to be inserted. In this case, traditional transactionally oriented databases will probably perform better in an RDBMS. Column DBs will best fit for business cases where speed of access to non-volatile data is important; for example, in (DSS) decision support system databases using a semantic layer to create visualization tools or create applications where speed of data access is the main differentiator. For example, you only need to review external data from commercial vendors to see business analytics.

Some examples of Column DBs are Apache Cassandra, HBase, and Cosmos DB. For Cassandra; instead of declaring a primary server; data is distributed in a cluster of nodes, each of which can process client requests. This provides an "always available" architecture that is extremely appealing for enterprise applications where having no downtime is critical. To write very large amounts of data efficiently, the trade-off option between read and write speed options are provided based on BASE principal. Even though there are several levels of trade-off between data consistency and availability for developers, when performing a write operation, replicas of a new record are stored across multiple cluster nodes and are created in parallel. Only a subset of those nodes needs to complete a replica update for the write operation to be considered successful, which means that the write operation can finish in less time.

Graph Databases

Graph DBs use flexible representation to manage data. Data is stored using a graph structure. Graph DBs consist of two elements: (1) nodes (entities) and (2) edges (relations).

We typically look for global patterns and structures though graph DBs. Global pattern finding is done through visualization of interconnectedness of different points, represented through network graphs. It helps in dissemination of existing interconnected systems and different components or groups. It uses graph algorithms to model the existing system and create predictive algorithms.

Figure 2-5 explains one simple example of tracking the flow of money through multiple banks and countries. For example, a banned organization sends money to Person A, present in the United Kingdom, who sends it to another person, in the United States, who is a family member (e.g., brother) of a politically influential person.

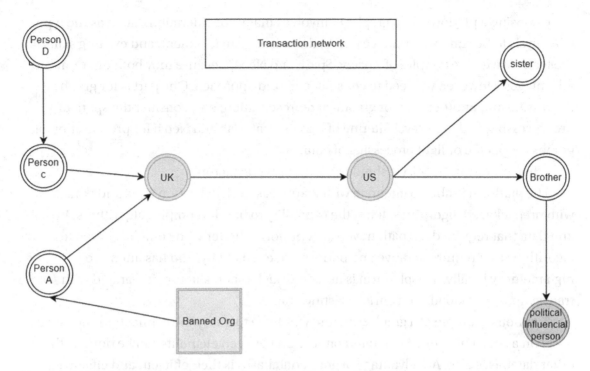

Figure 2-5. *Anti-money laundering through a graph DB*

For example, analysis of international and local payments for all network diagrams between sender of payments and receiver of payments is helpful for tracking money laundering and/or illegal activities. This analysis creates new opportunities for further data analysis and conclusions.

Graph databases are data processing–intensive databases. It requires both scale up and scale out abilities. For efficiency, their design focuses on powerful, multi-core, large memory machines; efficient data structures and multi-threading; and efficient algorithms. A valuable capability is their ability to handle different algorithms; e.g., weighted, unweighted, directed, undirected, cyclic, acyclic, sparse, dense, monopartite, bipartite, and k-partite, etc.

There are multiple types of processing done by graph databases. It could be based on nodes, relationships between nodes, processing these nodes within a subgraph independent of other subgraphs, while communicating to other subgraphs, etc. Graph databases focus on faster read and write using small queries. Graph DBs focus on high current scalability and operational robustness.

Choosing a platform for a graph DB involves many considerations, such as the type of analysis to be run, performance needs, the existing environment, and existing skills in the team. We gave examples of Apache Spark and Neo4j because they both offer unique advantages. However, we need to consider a hybrid approach. One part is for graph processing and another part for graphical representation; e.g., consider the spark of preprocessing and high-level filtering of massive datasets and Neo4j for presentation of graphs or specific or light processing of data.

When choosing Neo4j, we should consider several factors.

The platform is able to integrate with graph-based visualization tools and comes with prepackaged algorithms. It has the capability to handle complex algorithms and data that require deep path traversal. It performs better with complex, iterative algorithms that require iterative and performance sensitivity, and has intensive high memory locally. The platform is designed such that results are integrated with transactional workloads and enrich existing graphs.

A famous example of a graph structure would be to query the connections between users on a social network. Such interconnection between elements can be done with other databases also. An advantage of graph databases is their efficient and effective querying for highly interconnected data; e.g., famous automobile manufacturer Jaguar Land Rover uses graph analytics to give the business an interconnected view of supply chain and demand end to end, enabling it to form efficient answers to complex business questions. Graphs provide the means for understanding relations between sales, inventory, logistics, and supply chain, but, most important, it continues to learn.

Case Study: Enterprise Scenario for Modern Cloud-based Data Warehouse

The U.S. State Government school, having more than 1,000 schools, is a massive data consumption organization, from studying how disconnected students feel after two years of COVID isolation and its effect on individual grade-level performance in comparison to statewide trends, to the effect of a change in curriculum on student achievement in certain tasks as related to overall employee performance, to school establishment/abolishment of Community isolation at the time of COVID. It has undertaken exciting multi-year trend analysis to view "wholeness" trends seen in student and teacher performance, as well as comparative analysis of our numbers in respect to other statewide local education authorities and large urban cities across the country.

The problem statement that was coming from leadership was: There were multiple data marts available in organizations for students, teachers, academics, finance, human resources, etc., but from the department's view/perspective, the data warehouse/BI (Business Intelligence) essentially consists of SharePoint folders holding old spreadsheets and reports from which they often re-key/modify data. Analytics tools like power BI and Tableau were used, but in limited ways and selectively. However, the choice by default for analytical reporting tools is Excel. An organization relies on putting our static reports that have presumptions about the Business understand or definition of data, and these presumptions may have changed with time; e.g., a student's home situation could be different this year than it was last year.

After further analysis, it was clear that the problem was multidimensional and deeper rooted than initially assessed.

The IT systems and departments were working in silo environments, not collaborating or coordinating with each other frequently. One of the issues was related to governance. There was not a stewardship or ownership framework nor a data-governance framework that could work with the governance council and governance steering committee. Another issue was related to team efficiency and skills that needed to be upgraded to match the solution proposed. Last but not least, another issue was related to systems' not talking to each other, which was related to the interoperability of systems. This led to an increase in the cost of rework resulting from misunderstanding of requirements, which led to delays and an indirect increase in costs.

After discussions with users and stakeholders, the following storage and processing requirements were listed and finalized:

- Ability of the data warehouse platform to enable machine learning (ML) that can support all formats and frequencies.

- Ability to store data in multiple cloud environments, such as S3 from Amazon or Blob storage from Azure, to reduce storage costs.

- Ability to support data versioning so that one can find out what, how, and when data has changed over time and which are the current and historical versions of data.

- Enables direct data access so that users can query the data directly from raw data.

- Enable users to have insights and build transformation logics and improve/clean the quality of the data.

- Ability for self-service analytics for data analysts across all departments.

- Ability to connect directly to other cloud or non-cloud platforms and connect directly to BI tools, like Tableau, Power BI, and so on.

- Platform should be able to reduce data redundancy's happening in the presence of the multiple tools and platforms used for cleaning data warehouses for processing.

- Enable a single enterprise-level combined cloud data platform for the whole organization within the existing architectural framework.

The new solution should be enabled by a new system design that implements similar data management features to those in a data warehouse, directly on the kind of low-cost storage used for data lakes. Merging them into a single system means that analysis, data science, and machine learning teams can move faster because they are able to use data without needing to go to and fro for access to multiple systems.

Given these requirements, it is an easy and common but wrong approach to use multiple specialized systems or data warehouses for different departments for analysis. Having a multitude of systems introduces more complexity for governance and, importantly, introduces redundancy, data quality issues, and delays as analysts/users need to move or copy data between different systems.

After analyzing multiple analytics platforms, the solution that ticked all the boxes for a requirement traceability matrix along with a long list of analytical business use cases was the Databricks Unified Analytics Platform for Lakehouse.

Note   Requirement traceability Matrix (RTM) is Document which helps to map initial requirements to final artifacts and output of development. RTM is required. It's used to prove that requirements have been fulfilled. This document is created at the time of requirement gathering and used in testing and scoping.

This enterprise-level modern data warehouse is expected to allow the organization to optimize machine learning algorithm requirements at scale, streamline workflows of inter- or intra-departmental teams, and reduce complexity. Simplified infrastructure management reduces OPEX costs through the automation of cluster management, auto-scaling, auto-backup, and on-the-spot instance management. It increases collaboration within the team through collaborative workspaces, integration with CI/CD, DevOps, and interactive notebooks. This effectively reduces silos within departments and prevents duplicated work efforts.

Advantages of Modern Data Warehouse over Traditional Data Warehouse

Traditional data warehouses are not only relational or dimensional types but also hierarchical and object oriented. Network databases have their own advantages, disadvantages, and purposes from use case to use case. The traditional data warehouse analytics is structured, centralized, and controlled. Analytics is curated, summarized, contained, and predicted, and data movement is batch oriented.

There are modern use case requirements that require a data warehouse to handle the four Vs of data: high data velocity, ingestion of a variety of data, provide veracity, and handle variability of data. Expectations from modern data warehouses are changing and increasing over time. Data movement is done in real time, and there is more automation, performance, and integration with modern applications.

The following characteristics of modern data warehouses distinguish them from the traditional ones:

> *Smart*: A modern DW uses AI/ML to learn, alert, adjust, make recommendations, and administer and use the environment efficiently and effectively. The data architecture for modern data warehouses is not just automated, but also uses (ML) machine learning and (AI) artificial Intelligence to build the tables, views, schemas, objects, and flexible data and architecture models that enable data to flow. It uses AI/ML to identify data types and common keys in tables, identify relations, map tables, join tables as part of data integration, and provide extensions to identify and fix data-quality errors. It provides recommendations related to data and analytics as part of business intelligence, and more. Recent trends and advances have been to automate the processing of unstructured data, like audio, video, images, and so on. Traditional DWs were not designed, optimized, and purposed for these types of data, only for the metadata of these files.

Security: A modern data warehouse is a security fortress; it is able to provide access to authorized users while securing it from hackers and intruders and complying with all the state, national, and international privacy regulations across industries, including the Health Insurance and Portability and Accountability Act (HIPAA) and General Data Protection Regulation (GDPR). Security is provided at multiple levels, such as physical, server, application, network, folder/schema, table, and row. Security is even provided at the data level by using encryption, masking data at rest or in motion, masking personally identifiable information, providing fraud protection services, tracking usage of metadata in catalog, tracking lineage, and tracking changes using an audit trail.

Flexibility: A modern data warehouse needs to be flexible enough to support a variety of complex business requirements from all departments; e.g., from a technology point of view, flexible storage requirements; flexible processing requirements like loading/ extract transformation; loading operation with data refresh rates and scheduling rates (e.g., batch, near real-time, real-time); concurrent query operations; flexible deployment in on-premises, private, public, and hybrid clouds; and integration within and among multiple clouds. Another technical requirement regards flexibility with data processing engines from a variety of other data warehouses, both relational and NoSQL. A modern data warehouse has the ability to be the architecture and handle multiple business use cases' requirements. Currently, all the features of the specified flexibility are not present in a single data warehouse. Trends clearly indicate we are moving in the direction of having one solution for all. The expectation for the modern data warehouse is high performance, flexibility, and ability to handle diverse data applications, including real-time monitoring, traditional SQL analytics, and AI/ML.

Automation: The ability to handle multiple dimensions of automation, like self-observation, learning engine, self-repair, data quality, integration, and advantages is self-explanatory. Modern DW motivation is the reduction of the amount of work required to build, operate, and maintain a DW. The modern data warehouse has automated architecture in which data flows continuously, so designers must automate everything from ingestion to reports or dashboards in a visualization layer using schedulers, machine learning, and metadata injection. This process first profiles the data and then tags it while data is ingested from external sources, and then maps it to existing tables and attributes designed by data architects. This process is able to compare and detect changes in source and target schemas, objects, and applications. Once anomalies are detected, alerts are triggered to notify the stakeholders, and the issue is reported in operational dashboards. These automated data operations of monitoring, predicting failures, and avoiding them adds operational value by reducing the cycle time of accessing ready-to-use data.

Interoperable: First, this capability enables users to connect to and ingest data from various types of storage platforms, both on-premises and cloud, remote and local. Second, this is able to operate with MDM (master data management) tools, ETL (extract, transform, and loading), data modeling, data lineage, DevOps, governance, and metadata tools. For example, IBM data stage and Informatica have parallel connectors to modern data warehouses, enabling high-speed data transfer with custom data transformation algorithms executed on data nodes. It is integrable with analytical, ML, an statistical analysis packages.

Interconnectivity: An organization that does not have one but rather a collection of analytical servers, data warehouses, data lakes, data marts, and so on needs to have these be integrated together logically, with metadata and data virtualization (federation), so that it appears as a single logical system for integration by providing interfaces between multiple servers with multiple data integration methods. First, we combine the logic data warehouse with an abstraction layer on top and then automate manual tasks in the LDW and other systems. This provides features that allow the system to provide prescriptive advice to the users about what data elements to use, which datasets/tables to join, and, additionally, provides a significant degree of ability to self-administer the platform.

Resilient: If a modern data warehouse architecture is resilient it means it has the capability of being highly available, able to recover from disaster scenarios quickly, and able to provide a backup and restore DB from the point of failure. This is very important for highly critical data applications ranging from payment applications in the banking security industry or IOT-based application in automotive industries. All cloud vendors use hundreds of server farms and are designed with built-in redundancy and fail-over backup recovery with high service level agreements by setting up mirror images in geographically distributed data centers across regions, countries, and other parts of the world.

Elastic: With the varying processing demands across time and a range of requirements, modern data warehouses require scalable architecture that adapts to such variations on demand. A positive trend is that all companies providing cloud services platforms (public, private) provide on-demand and auto and on-demand elastic scalability at low prices. Elastic architectures help administrators by their not having to spend time to calibrate capacity, increase or throttle usage if necessary, avoid risk of overspending on hardware, and decrease time to market. Elasticity has many factors to consider that vary, from type and criticality of application to environment of deployment, such as development, QA, test environment setup, and setting up analytic sandboxes.

Self-service: In the traditional setup, the IT department built everything in a data warehouse. However, modern DW architecture enables splitting the responsibility between IT and business by allocation as per ownership and stewardship frameworks. The IT department does the heavy lifting by ingesting data from core operations and standardizing architecture building blocks like tables, schemas, data dictionary, and business dictionary, and then providing access to these tables, views, and schemas to data scientists, data explorers, data analysts, and business data consumers of various departments. From there, business units are provided ownership of data. They can generate reports if they have the skills, desire, and needs. Business units are made effective by focusing on the strength of the analytical skills of their analysts so that they can focus on core skills, and IT data engineers focus on data warehouse engineering skills by focusing on data preparation. Similarly, data scientists are provided access to raw data in the landing area or in a purpose-built sandbox where they can mix raw corporate data with external data to create predictive or AI models. This capability along with providing data catalogs and governance is important for encouraging innovation capabilities across the enterprise for digital transformation.

Adaptable: In a modern enterprise data warehouse architecture system, data flows smoothly from source systems to business end users. The purpose of the modern data warehouse architecture is to manage data flow by creating a series of multi-directional, dependent, and interconnected data pipelines that serve various changing business needs. These pipelines are built using data views, snapshots, and deltas, including reference and master data. These architecture building blocks are continuously reused, repurposed, and replenished to ensure the steady flow of high-quality and relevant data to the business.

Low Latency: Speed and cost of implementation are interrelated and are important factors for shifting to a modern data warehouse architecture. Data ops is used for debug fixing, DevOps for migration, activities like customizable template library for writing/creating/exporting metadata. Having automatic code/ETL scripts/programs/jobs running schedule generation using a metadata repository reduces a lot of development time and effort, and reduces risk of mistakes. The ability to self-observe the data warehouse combined with easy access controls to restrict or open traffic to the database nodes and easy database node resizing so you can scale your database resources up or down as needed reduces database admin/maintenance time. Another dimension is low latent processing; e.g., data grids of in-memory databases provide a distributed reliability, scalability and consistency that is shareable across multiple distributed applications. These applications perform concurrent transactional and/or analytical operations in the low-latency data grid, thus drastically reducing the use of traditional high-latency storage. Some of the advantages are data grid consistency, availability, and durability via replication, partitioning, and persistent storage.

Simplicity: In principle, simple architecture is the best architecture. Given the complexity involved and diversity of the technical and business requirements of modern data warehouses, it is important to simplify these requirements and spend some time on design and approach; e.g., look at the big picture, long term, and create a multi-year road map. Take into consideration internal and external factors, such as size of enterprise, vision, organization culture, business environment, and trends. Plan ahead, and if required minimize data movement and data redundancy, and create standardization across enterprises. Sometimes traditional BI tools are sufficient at the time for small organizations, but not as they grow. At the end of the day, it boils down to cost and benefit analysis. Map all benefits you want to come out of BI tools with their technical and non-technical capabilities.

Summary

In this chapter, we learned the basics of modern data warehouses. We explored some characteristics of modern data warehouses, like fault tolerance, scalability, interoperability, and reliability, including the 4 Vs.

We discussed the associated features of distributed processing, big data storage, streaming, and processing data on cloud along with autonomous administration capabilities, multitenancy, and security.

Then we discussed the concepts with which NoSQL databases are concerned. We discussed how modern DWs are different from traditional DWs.

Next, we discussed Big Data and the CAP and BASE theorems. Then we discussed types of NoSQL data warehouses, like key–value DBs, document DBs, column DBs, and graph DBs.

We also discussed actual business use cases of an enterprise scenario and a customized solution of a modern cloud-based data warehouse was provided. Next, we discussed advantages of modern data warehouses over traditional data warehouses. Every warehouse has its strengths and weaknesses. A modern data warehouse's capabilities can make it unique and modern; e.g., smart, secure, flexible, automated, interoperable, interconnectivity, resilient, elastic, self-servicing, adaptable, low-latency, and yet simple and customer-centric.

It is thought that all customers want a panacea solution for all use cases so that they can replace traditional DWs with modern DWs. However, we have not reached that point yet. As of now, the choice of data warehouse solution depends on specific business requirements. The overall solution could be a hybrid of traditional and NoSQL/Big Data solutions; e.g., combining multiple NoSQL solutions like columnar, document DB, or key–value along with dimensional or relational databases.

In the next chapters, we will discuss modern concepts like data lakes, lakehouse, delta lake, data mesh, and data orchestration in detail.

CHAPTER 3

Data Lake, Lake House, and Delta Lake

Relational databases keep structured data that are easy to retrieve and consume. You can define data dependencies and relationships with ease and can quickly perform operations on the data, along with any associated relationships, using the Structured Query Language (SQL). However, when the volume of the data grows, then new challenges occur when it comes to extracting meaningful information from the data that can generate enhanced insights.

This development led to the evolution of the data warehouse, where you can ingest tons of relational data using the extract, load, and transform (ETL) process. You can then access it by using business intelligence (BI) tools to gather deeper insights from the data. However, modern data comprises a lot of unstructured data, like images, videos, text, and documents, that are generated from a wide variety of data sources. This led to the evolution of the data lake, where tons of unstructured non-relational data can be stored along with structured relational data. However, when the data in the data lake evolved and the amount of data storage needed increased, it became challenging to manage, mine, and seek the unstructured data in the data lake. This led to the evolution of the lake house, and Databricks came up with the delta lake, which serves as an important component of the Databricks lake house implementation.

In the previous chapter, we explored the concept of a modern data warehouse in detail. In this chapter, we will discuss the concept of data lakes, lake houses, and delta lakes and learn how to design and implement cloud-based solutions in these areas.

© Anjani Kumar, Abhishek Mishra, and Sanjeev Kumar 2024
A. Kumar et al., *Architecting a Modern Data Warehouse for Large Enterprises*,
https://doi.org/10.1007/979-8-8688-0029-0_3

Structure

In this chapter, we will explore the following areas:

- Data Lake, Lake House, and Delta Lake Essentials
- Data Lake, Storage, and Data Processing Engine Synergies and Dependencies
- Implement Lake House in Azure
- Implement Lake House in AWS

Objectives

After studying this chapter, you should be able to

- understand the fundamentals of data lakes, lake houses, and delta lakes; and
- design and implement cloud-based solutions for data lakes, delta lakes, and lake houses.

Data Lake, Lake House, and Delta Lake Concepts

Let us start with understanding the concept of the data warehouse. Using the extract, transform, load (ETL) process, structured relational data gets ingested into the data warehouse. It keeps tons of structured data that can be easily queried using Structured Query Language (SQL). Business intelligence tools connect to the data warehouse and extract meaningful insights from the stored data. The main goal of a data warehouse is to store data that can be consumed later to derive essential insights using business intelligence tools. The data warehouse is highly performant, and the business intelligence tools can run it with ease and speed. Data can be ingested by adhering to the database atomicity, consistency, isolation, and durability (ACID) properties. Figure 3-1 depicts a data warehouse.

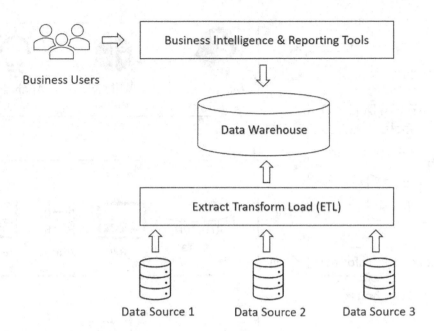

Figure 3-1. *Data warehouse architecture*

The data warehouse has been a perfect choice to serve as a data mart for structured data that can be consumed later to gather meaningful insights. However, as the data world evolved, unstructured non-relational data started to get generated at a very fast pace. Enterprises ended up generating tons of unstructured data that needed to be stored and managed along with the structured data. This led to the evolution of data lakes, which can store both structured and unstructured data. Enterprises ingested raw data like text files, videos, and images into the data lake. While consuming the data, enterprises processed it and used it for complex use cases like machine learning and artificial intelligence, along with gathering insights. The data warehouse helps you with getting business intelligence insights, and the data lake can be used for complex use cases involving machine learning, data analytics, and artificial intelligence. Figure 3-2 depicts a data lake. The data from various sources get ingested into the data lake. The data is further processed and used for machine learning, artificial intelligence, and business analytics purposes. The data can also be consumed by the data warehouse, where business users can run business intelligence tools to get business insights from the data.

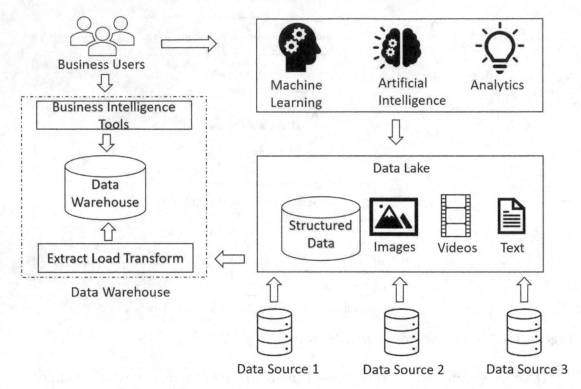

Figure 3-2. *Data lake architecture*

As the storage space needed for the data in the data lake increased, new complexities came up, like extracting data in a performant way, managing and governing the data, bringing in granular security to the data, and enforcing ACID (atomicity, consistency, isolation, and durability) based transactions. Enterprises were generating tons of data and consuming just a small portion of it. A lot of data stored in the data lake could not be consumed to generate any insights. Accessing the data from the data lake got slower as the amount being stored grew.

The data lake house is the solution to these problems. It is based on a modern data platform and stores a very large volume of structured and unstructured data, and also offers faster data retrieval. The data lake house is a fusion of a data lake and a data warehouse and brings in the best capabilities from each. The storage layer and the compute layer that processes the data stored in the storage layer are isolated and can scale independently. The following are the advantages of using a data lake house:

- Can store huge volumes of structured and unstructured data

- Can transact with data using ACID (atomicity, consistency, isolation, and durability) principles

- Low-cost storage with faster retrieval options

- Reliable, scalable, and durable data solution

- Metadata, indexing, versioning and caching features that make data querying highly performant and fast

- Can use Structured Query Language (SQL) to retrieve data

- Can build business intelligence–, machine learning–, and artificial intelligence–based solutions using a data lake house

- Can support open data storage formats like plain text, XML, JSON, parquet, and many more

- Can support streaming of real-time data

- Can enforce schema and governance and make the data stored usable

In the case of a data lake house, data from different sources gets ingested into the lake house in the raw format. On top of the lake house, there is an additional layer that keeps the curated data that can be accessed using Structured Query Language (SQL) or technologies like Spark SQL. Figure 3-3 depicts data lake house architecture.

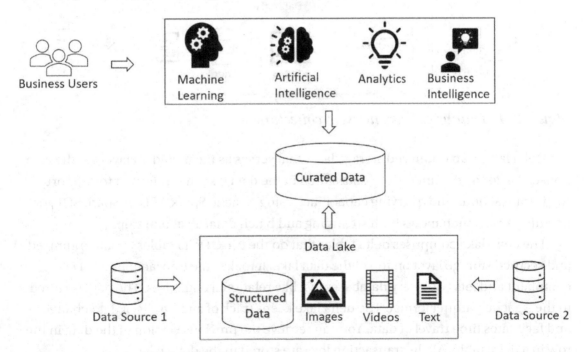

Figure 3-3. *Lake house architecture*

Figure 3-4 depicts the Databricks lake house architecture. Raw data is ingested into the underlying data lake. On top of that, there is a metadata and governance layer. Data is stored in an open file format, like parquet files, in the data lake. The metadata layer brings in capabilities like querying data using SQL, facilitating ACID transactions, indexing, data versioning, and many such features. There is also a Unity Catalog layer that brings in data governance, sharing, and auditing capabilities to the data stored in the lake house.

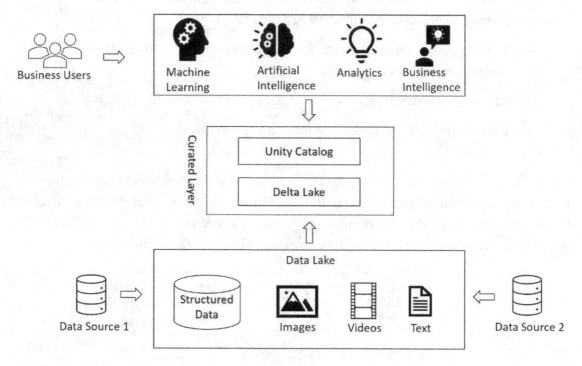

Figure 3-4. *Databricks lake house architecture*

Delta lake is an optimized storage layer that serves as the metadata layer for the lake house. It extends the underlying data stored in the data lake in raw format to support ACID transactions and querying capabilities using Apache Spark APIs or Spark SQL, or anything similar. It handles both streaming and batch data, all at one stop.

The delta lake comprises delta tables that do the trick. Delta tables are an optimized and secured storage layer on top of the data lake. It makes the transactions ACID compliant and lets you query databases just like relational databases. The data is stored in the Apache parquet format. The delta lake keeps track of audit trails of data changes and facilitates time travel of data. You can retrieve the previous version of the data in the row in a delta table. All the transaction logs are stored in the delta lake.

The Unity Catalog facilitates a one-stop data governance and compliance mechanism for the data stored in the delta log. You can define the security standards and governance once and use them everywhere across the delta lake. It supports tracing the data lineage and can help you trace data asset creation and usage across all languages and personas. It facilitates the auditing of the data stored in the delta lake. It supports data discovery by tagging and documenting the data.

You can follow the medallion architecture to store data in bronze, silver, and gold tables. Ingested raw data is stored in the bronze table. Filtered and cleaned data is stored in the silver table, and the processed data for business consumption is stored in the gold table. You can achieve this medallion architecture using the delta lake in the lake house data platform for Databricks. Figure 3-5 depicts the medallion architecture for the lake house.

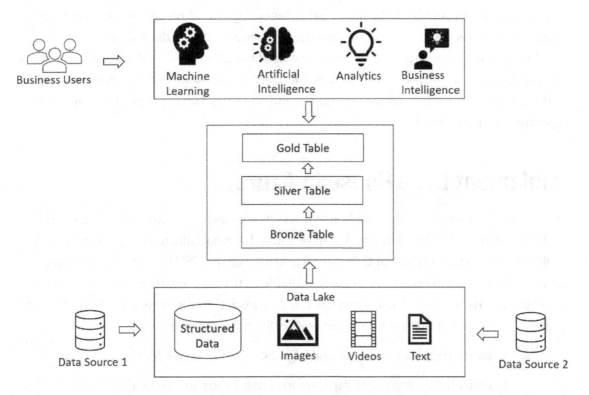

Figure 3-5. *Databricks lake house medallion architecture*

Data Lake, Storage, and Data Processing Engines Synergies and Dependencies

Data processing engines and pipelines play a pivotal role in the lake house. They facilitate data movements and ingest data into the data lake from external sources. The data ingested in the data lake is in raw format and, by default, cannot be used by the delta lake. Delta lakes are in the parquet format. You need data processing engines to format the data and convert them into delta lake parquet format. Even once the data is ready to be consumed from the lake house, you will need data processing engines to further enhance the data so that it can be ready for consumption as-is by the target data consumers.

Azure provides Azure Synapse pipelines and Azure Data Factory, which can connect to a variety of data stores and facilitate data processing and movements. AWS provides Glue, which helps you move and process data across a variety of data stores.

Data processing engines are an integral part of the lake house and accelerate solutions in the lake house platform. In subsequent sections, we will explore building a lake house on the cloud, where we will depend on these data processing engines and pipelines to a great extent.

Implement Lake House in Azure

By now we have seen how the lake house works as well as its architecture. Let us build a lake house in the Azure platform. We have a health-care platform that generates health data for patients daily in CSV format and ingests the CSV file into the data lake. We need to process the data and make it available in the lake house in Azure so that the target data-consuming platforms can use the data from the lake house database via SQL queries. To implement this scenario, we will perform the following steps:

- Create a data lake on Azure and ingest the health data CSV file.

- Create an Azure Synapse pipeline to convert the CSV file to a parquet file.

- Attach the parquet file to the lake database.

Create a Data Lake on Azure and Ingest the Health Data CSV File

Let us create an Azure data lake. On Azure, you can create a data lake on top of Azure Blob storage by enabling hierarchical namespaces. Azure Blob storage is highly robust and can store tons of structured data using hierarchical namespaces, and can serve as an Azure data lake. This is referred to as the Gen2 data lake on Azure. Let us go to the Azure portal and click on *Create a resource* as seen in Figure 3-6.

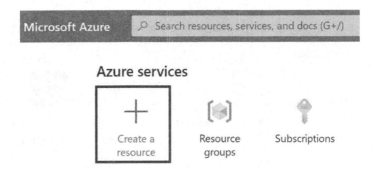

Figure 3-6. *Create a resource*

You will get navigated to the Marketplace, where you can search for *Storage Account* and then click on *Create* to spin up a storage account, as in Figure 3-7.

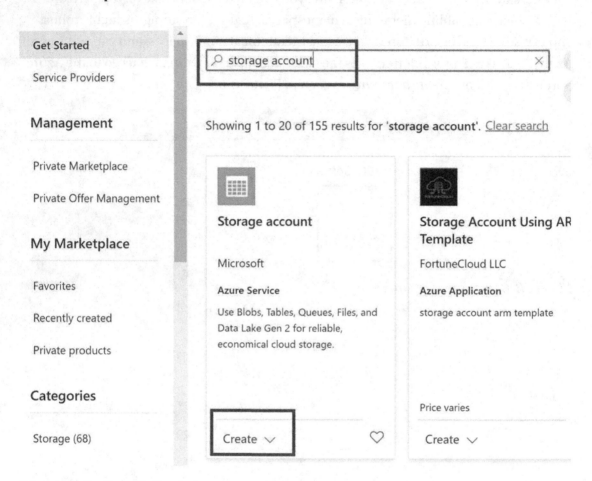

Figure 3-7. *Search for Azure storage account*

Provide the subscription, resource group, name, and region for the storage account, and then click on *Next: Advanced,* as in Figure 3-8.

Project details

Select the subscription in which to create the new storage account. Choose a new or existing r₁ manage your storage account together with other resources.

Subscription *

▔▔▔▔▔▔▔▔▔▔▔▔▔▔▔▔▔▔

|___
        Resource group *

(New) rg-lakehouse

Create new

Instance details

If you need to create a legacy storage account type, please click here.

Storage account name ⓘ *

healthidatalakenfo

Region ⓘ *

(US) East US

Review   < Previous   Next : Advanced >

Figure 3-8. *Provide basic details*

Check *Enable hierarchical namespace,* as in Figure 3-9. This will facilitate creating a data lake on top of Azure Blob storage. Click on *Review*.

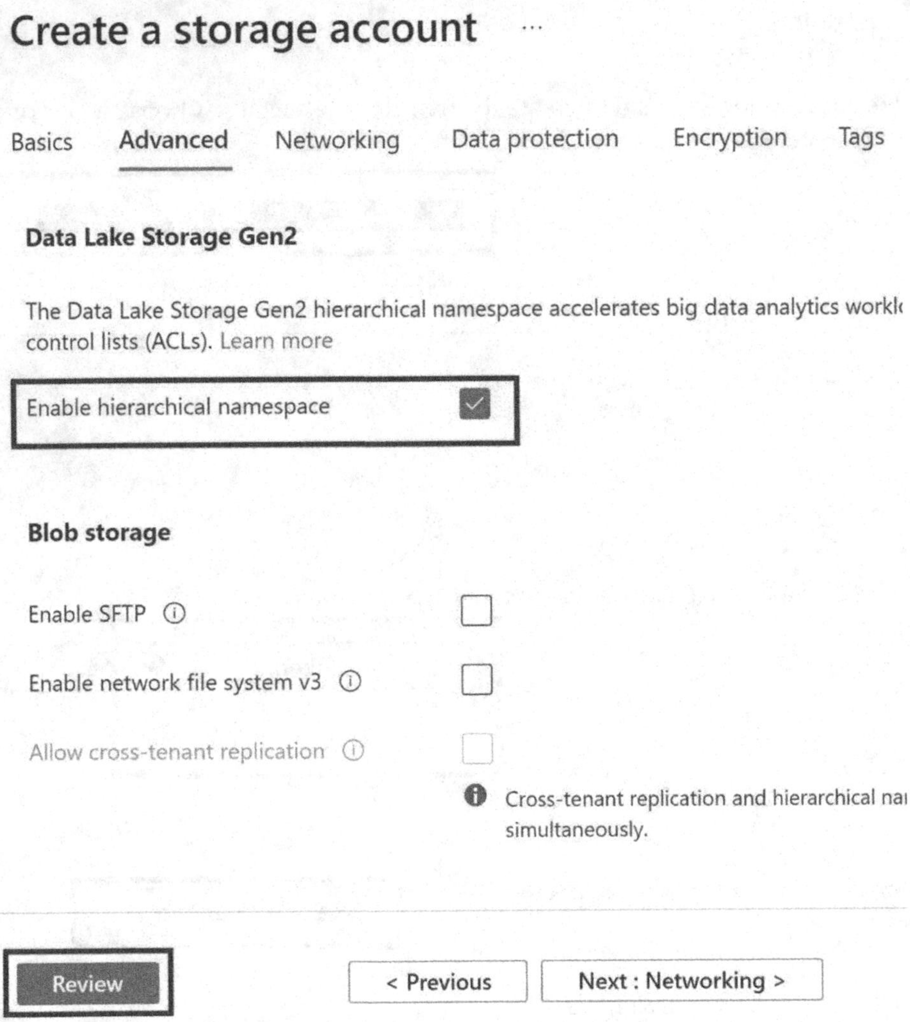

Figure 3-9. Enable hierarchical namespace

Click on *Create,* as in Figure 3-10. This will spin up an Azure data lake on top of Azure Blob storage.

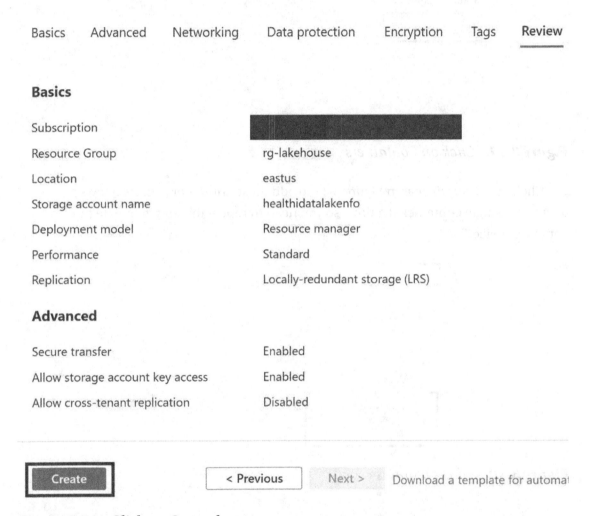

Figure 3-10. Click on Create button

Once the Azure storage account is created, navigate into it and click on *Containers* as in Figure 3-11. We need to add two containers named *raw* and *processed*. In the raw container, we will ingest the health data CSV file. We will process the CSV file in parquet format and keep it inside the processed folder.

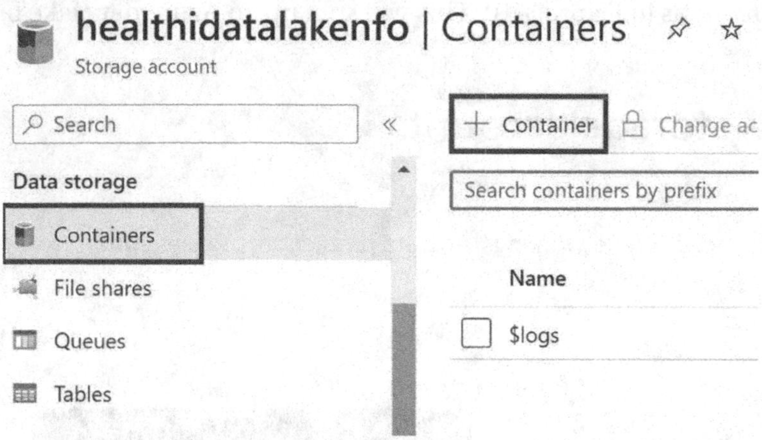

Figure 3-11. Click on Containers

Click on + *Container* as in Figure 3-12 to add these containers. Azure allows you to create a single container at a time, so you need to repeat this step to create the container twice.

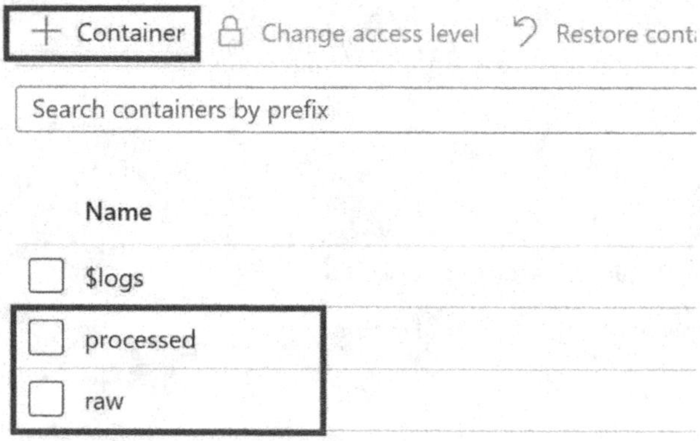

Figure 3-12. Add containers

Now we need to ingest the CSV file. Click on the *raw* container as in Figure 3-13.

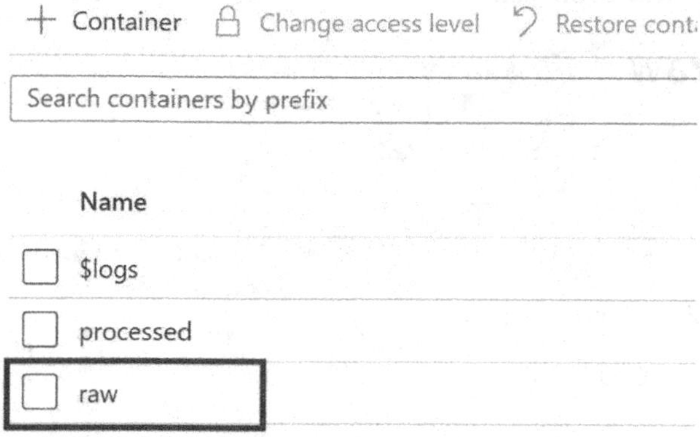

Figure 3-13. *Click on the raw container*

Click on *Upload* to upload the CSV file manually, as in Figure 3-14. In a real-world use case, data pipelines are used to ingest the data automatically. However, for simplicity, we are ingesting the data manually.

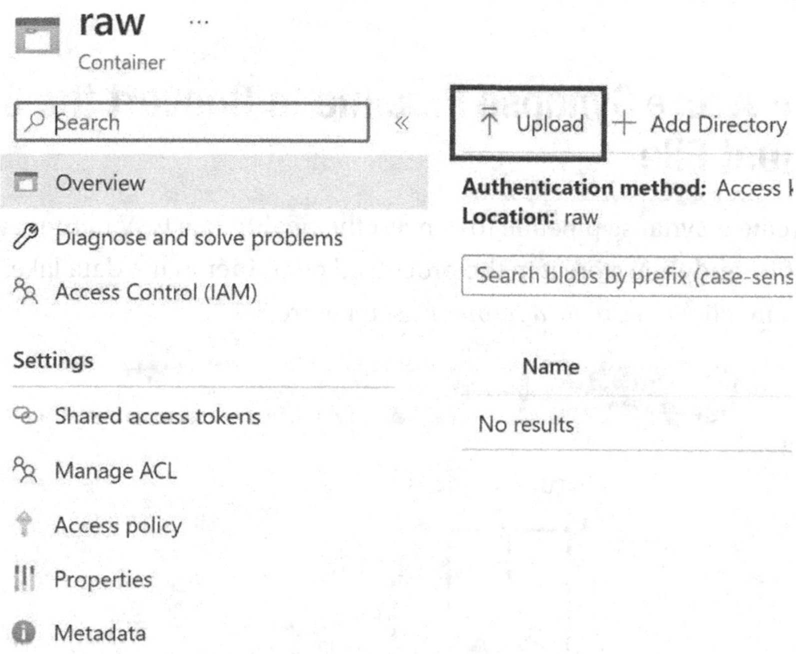

Figure 3-14. *Click on Upload*

Figure 3-15 depicts the uploaded CSV file. We will work on this file and move it to the lake house database after processing.

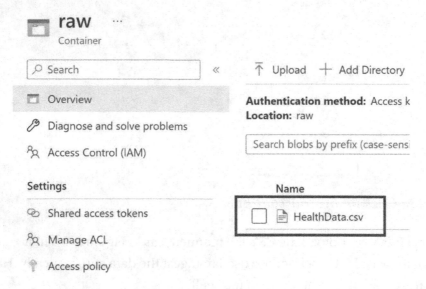

Figure 3-15. *Ingested health data CSV file*

Create an Azure Synapse Pipeline to Convert the CSV File to a Parquet File

Now let us create a Synapse pipeline to convert the health data CSV in the raw container to a parquet file, and then store it in the processed container in the data lake. Go to the Azure portal and click on *Create a resource* as in Figure 3-16.

Figure 3-16. *Create a resource*

You will get redirected to the Marketplace. Click on the *Analytics* tab and then click on *Azure Synapse Analytics,* as in Figure 3-17.

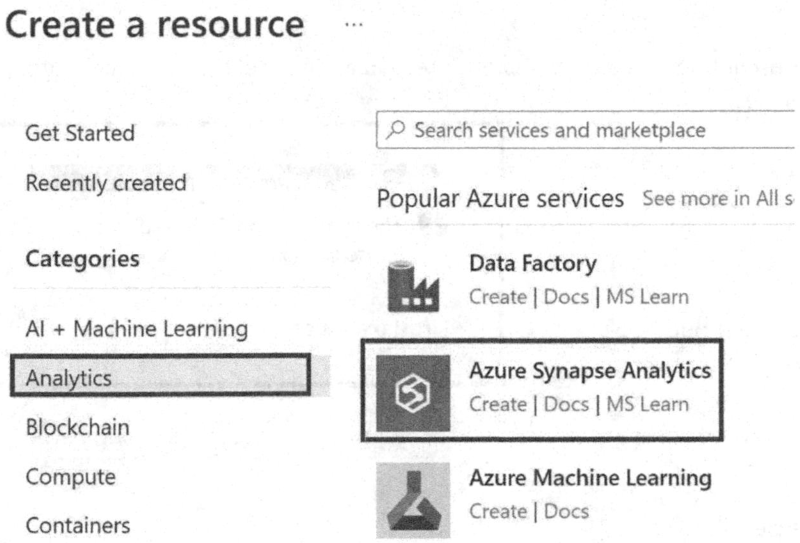

Create a resource   ⋯

Get Started

Recently created

Categories

AI + Machine Learning

Analytics

Blockchain

Compute

Containers

🔍 Search services and marketplace

Popular Azure services   See more in All s

Data Factory
Create | Docs | MS Learn

Azure Synapse Analytics
Create | Docs | MS Learn

Azure Machine Learning
Create | Docs

Figure 3-17. *Go to the Analytics tab*

Provide the basic details for the Synapse pipeline and the workspace, as in Figure 3-18.

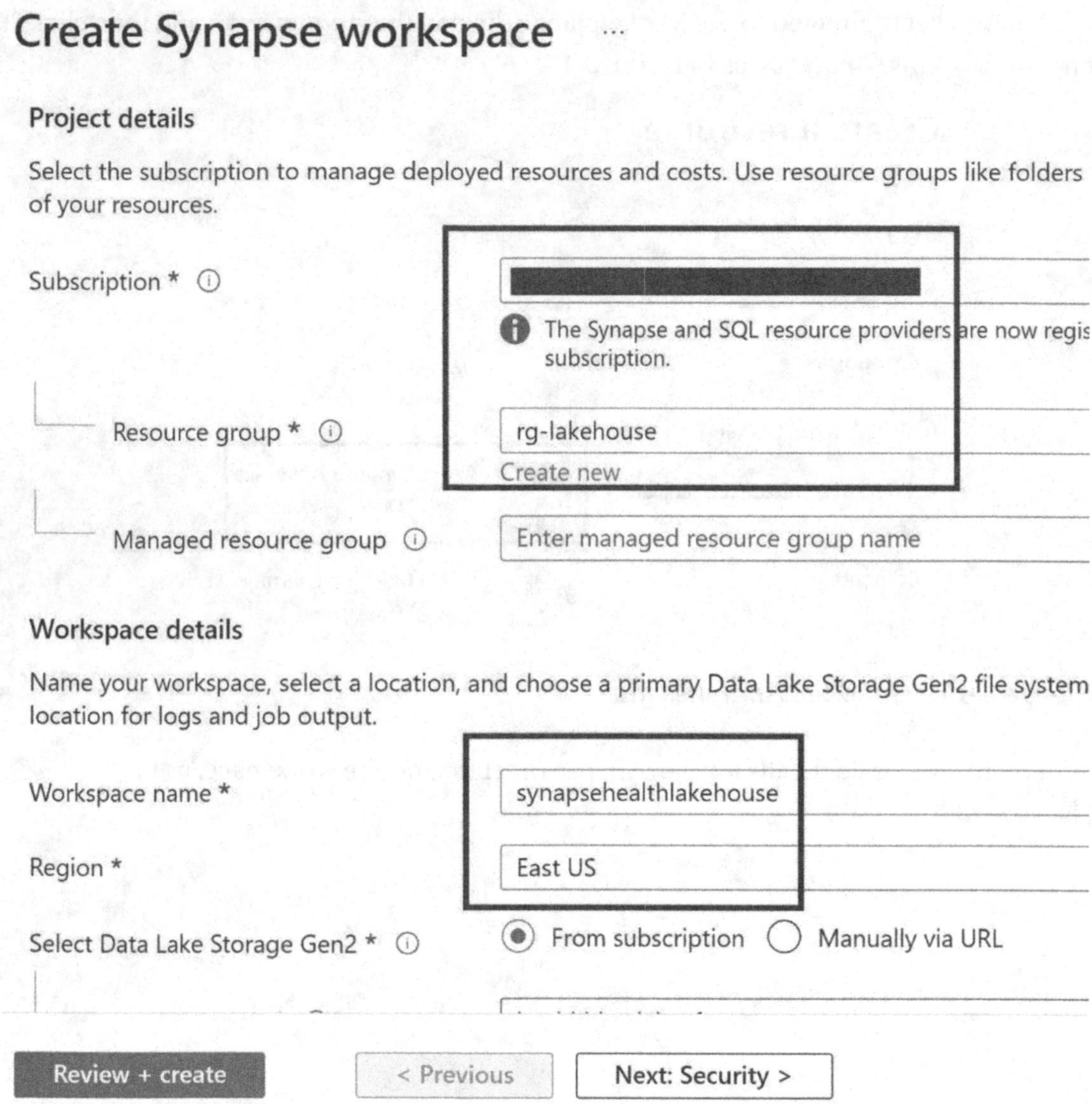

Create Synapse workspace   ...

Project details

Select the subscription to manage deployed resources and costs. Use resource groups like folders of your resources.

Subscription * ⓘ

       ⓘ The Synapse and SQL resource providers are now regis subscription.

└─── Resource group * ⓘ   rg-lakehouse
               Create new

└─── Managed resource group ⓘ   Enter managed resource group name

Workspace details

Name your workspace, select a location, and choose a primary Data Lake Storage Gen2 file system location for logs and job output.

Workspace name *   synapsehealthlakehouse

Region *   East US

Select Data Lake Storage Gen2 * ⓘ   ◉ From subscription   ○ Manually via URL

[Review + create]   [< Previous]   [Next: Security >]

Figure 3-18. *Provide basic details*

Scroll down and create a Gen2 container, as in Figure 3-19, in the same data lake and on the storage account that we created earlier.

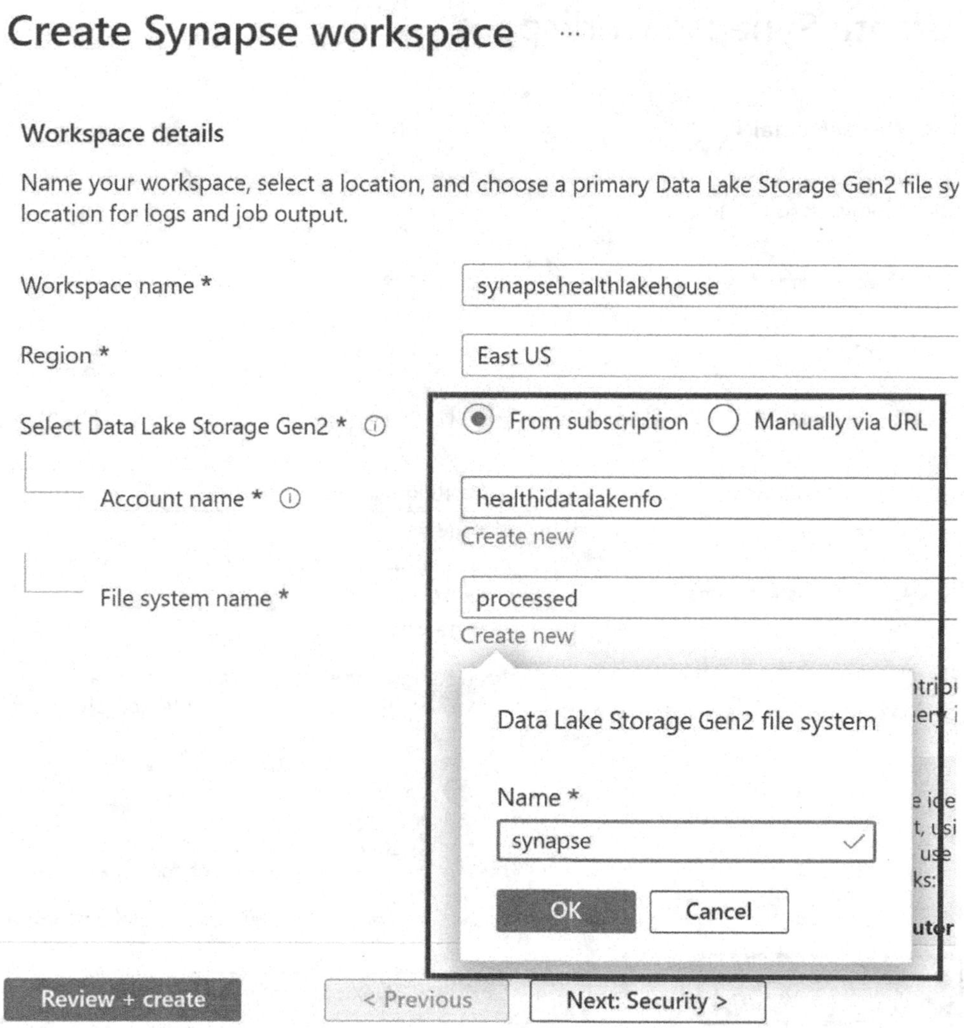

Create Synapse workspace   ...

Workspace details

Name your workspace, select a location, and choose a primary Data Lake Storage Gen2 file sy
location for logs and job output.

Workspace name *	synapsehealthlakehouse
Region *	East US
Select Data Lake Storage Gen2 * ⓘ	⦿ From subscription ◯ Manually via URL
└── Account name * ⓘ	healthidatalakenfo
	Create new
└── File system name *	processed
	Create new

Data Lake Storage Gen2 file system

Name *

synapse ✓

OK   Cancel

Review + create   < Previous   Next: Security >

Figure 3-19. *Provide data lake details*

Click on *Review + create* as in Figure 3-20 to spin up Azure Synapse Analytics, where
we can create the Synapse pipeline and the lake house database.

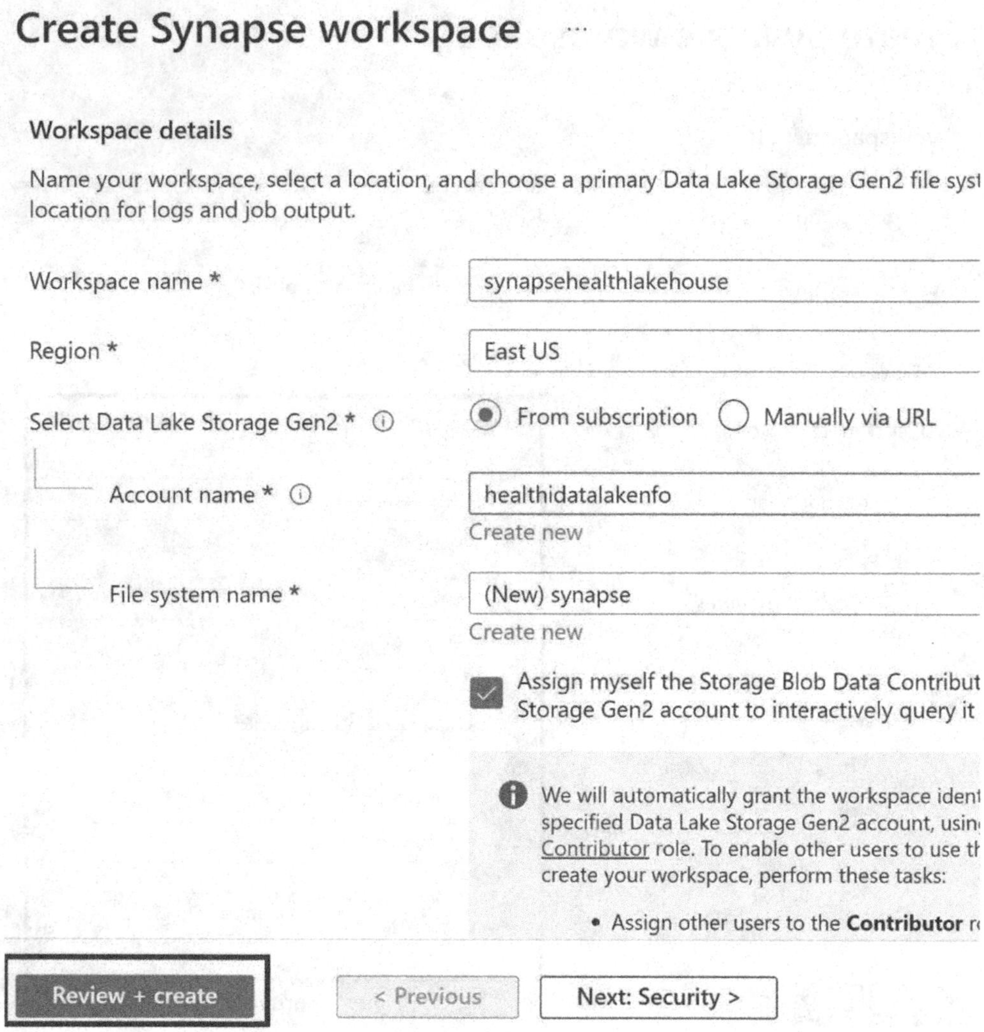

Create Synapse workspace   ···

Workspace details

Name your workspace, select a location, and choose a primary Data Lake Storage Gen2 file sys1
location for logs and job output.

Workspace name *	synapsehealthlakehouse
Region *	East US
Select Data Lake Storage Gen2 * ⓘ	● From subscription ○ Manually via URL
└─ Account name * ⓘ	healthidatalakenfo
	Create new
└─ File system name *	(New) synapse
	Create new

☑ Assign myself the Storage Blob Data Contribut
Storage Gen2 account to interactively query it

ⓘ We will automatically grant the workspace ident
specified Data Lake Storage Gen2 account, usin
Contributor role. To enable other users to use th
create your workspace, perform these tasks:

• Assign other users to the **Contributor** r

[Review + create]   [< Previous]   [Next: Security >]

Figure 3-20. *Review + create*

Click on *Create,* as in Figure 3-21. This will spin up an Azure Synapse Analytics
resource for you.

Figure 3-21. *Click on Create*

Once Synapse Analytics gets created, go to the *Overview* tab of Synapse Analytics and click on *Open,* as in Figure 3-22. We need to open the studio in Synapse Analytics to create pipelines and a lake database.

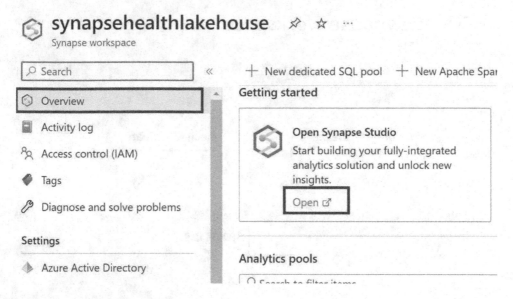

Figure 3-22. Open Synapse Studio

Once the Synapse Analytics studio opens, click on the *Integrate* tab, as in Figure 3-23. We will create the Synapse pipeline here that will convert the CSV file into a parquet file.

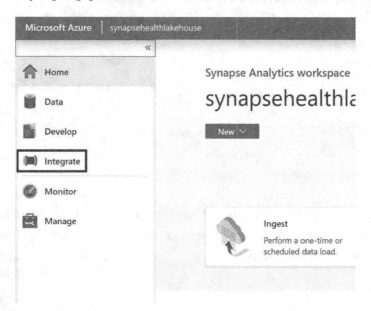

Figure 3-23. Integrate tab

Click on + and then on *Pipeline* in the context menu, as in Figure 3-24. This will create a new pipeline.

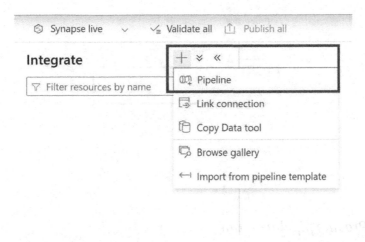

Figure 3-24. *Create new pipeline*

Search for the *Copy Data* activity and add it to the canvas, as in Figure 3-25. The copy activity will help us copy the CSV file from the raw folder, convert it to parquet, and put the parquet file back in the processed folder in the data lake.

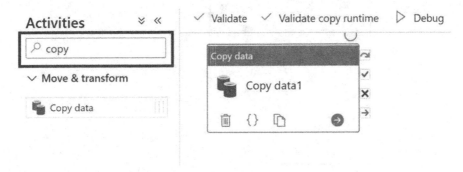

Figure 3-25. *Add Copy Data activity*

Provide a name for the pipeline, as in Figure 3-26. This will help you identify and maintain the pipeline.

Figure 3-26. *Provide pipeline name*

Click on the *Copy Data* activity and click on *Source*. We need to add the source dataset pointing to the CSV file in the raw folder. Click on *New,* as in Figure 3-27.

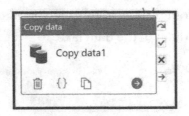

Figure 3-27. *Configure source*

Search for *Azure Data Lake Storage Gen2* and select it. Click on *Continue* as in Figure 3-28. We now have our source CSV in the Azure Data Lake Gen2 that is built on top of the storage blob.

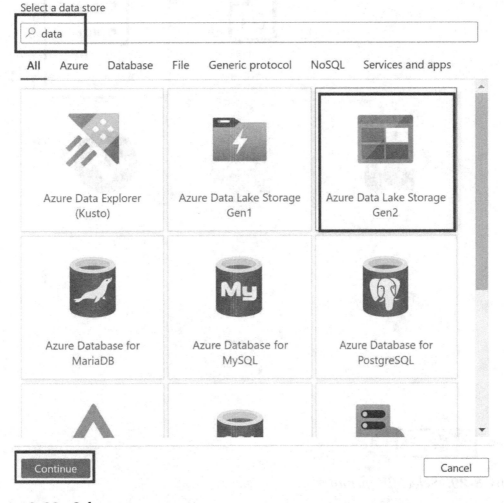

Figure 3-28. *Select source storage*

Selected the *DelimitedText* option as in Figure 3-29, as our data is in the CSV format in the data lake. Click on *Continue*.

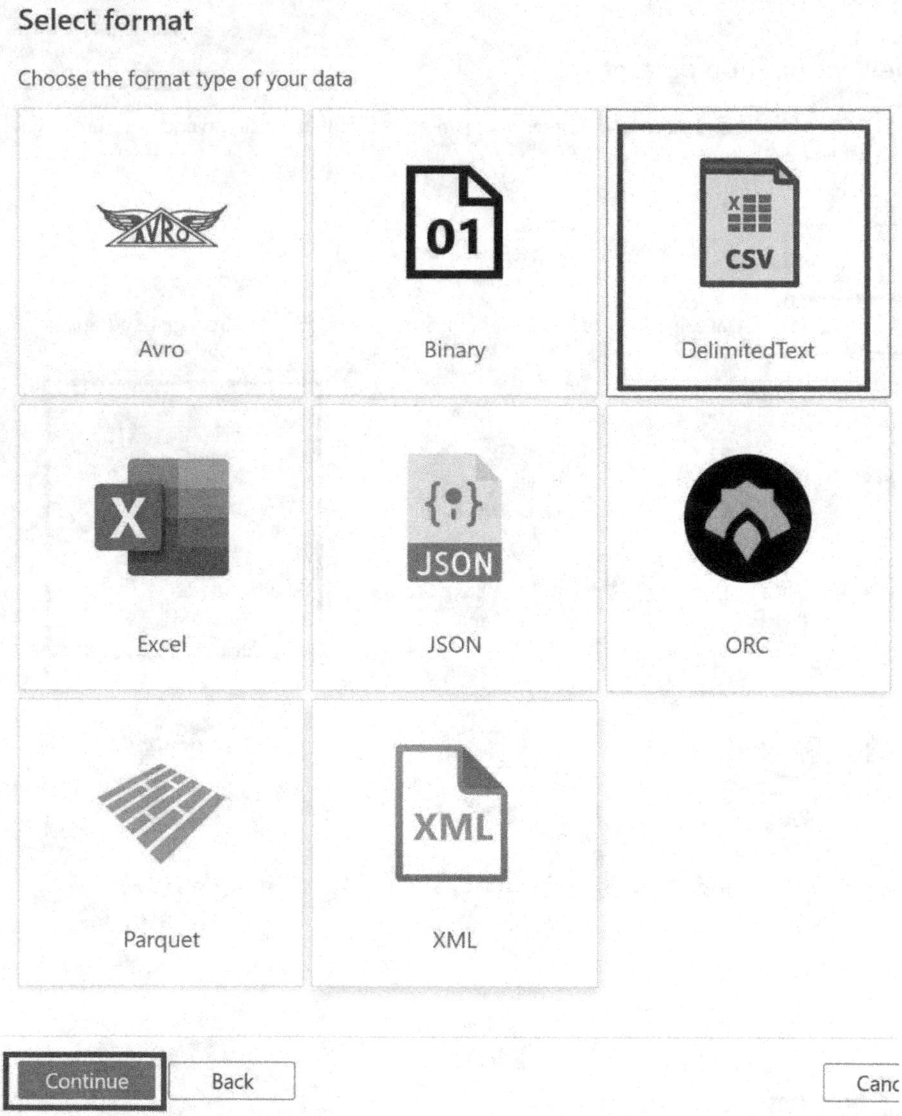

Select format

Choose the format type of your data

Avro	Binary	DelimitedText
Excel	JSON	ORC
Parquet	XML	

Continue   Back   Canc

Figure 3-29. *Select file format*

Create a new linked service, with which we will connect to the data lake, as in Figure 3-30. Click on +*New*.

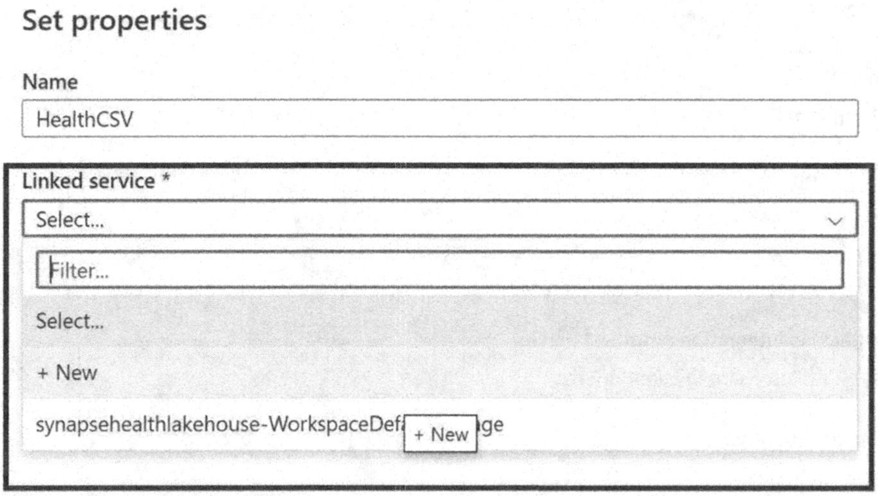

Set properties

Name

HealthCSV

Linked service *

Select...

Filter...

Select...

+ New

synapsehealthlakehouse-WorkspaceDef[+ New]ge

Figure 3-30. *Create a new linked service*

Select the data lake and test the connection to the data lake, as in Figure 3-31. Then click on *Create*.

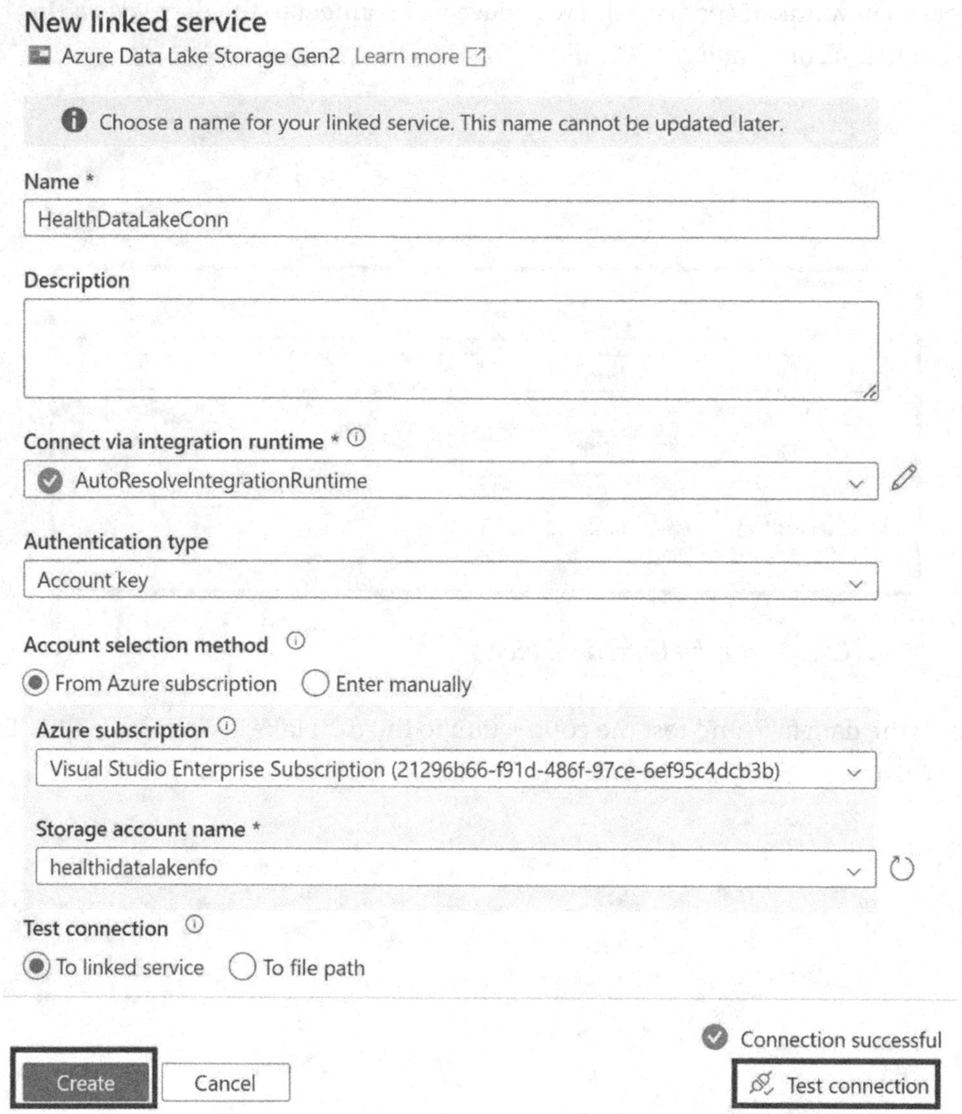

New linked service

■ Azure Data Lake Storage Gen2 Learn more ☐

ⓘ Choose a name for your linked service. This name cannot be updated later.

Name *

HealthDataLakeConn

Description

Connect via integration runtime * ⓘ

✓ AutoResolveIntegrationRuntime   ∨   ✎

Authentication type

Account key   ∨

Account selection method ⓘ

◉ From Azure subscription   ○ Enter manually

Azure subscription ⓘ

Visual Studio Enterprise Subscription (21296b66-f91d-486f-97ce-6ef95c4dcb3b)   ∨

Storage account name *

healthidatalakenfo   ∨   ↺

Test connection ⓘ

◉ To linked service   ○ To file path

✓ Connection successful

[Create]   [Cancel]   ✐ Test connection

Figure 3-31. *Test connection and click Create*

Provide the file path for the CSV file stored in the data lake raw folder, as in Figure 3-32, and then click on *OK*.

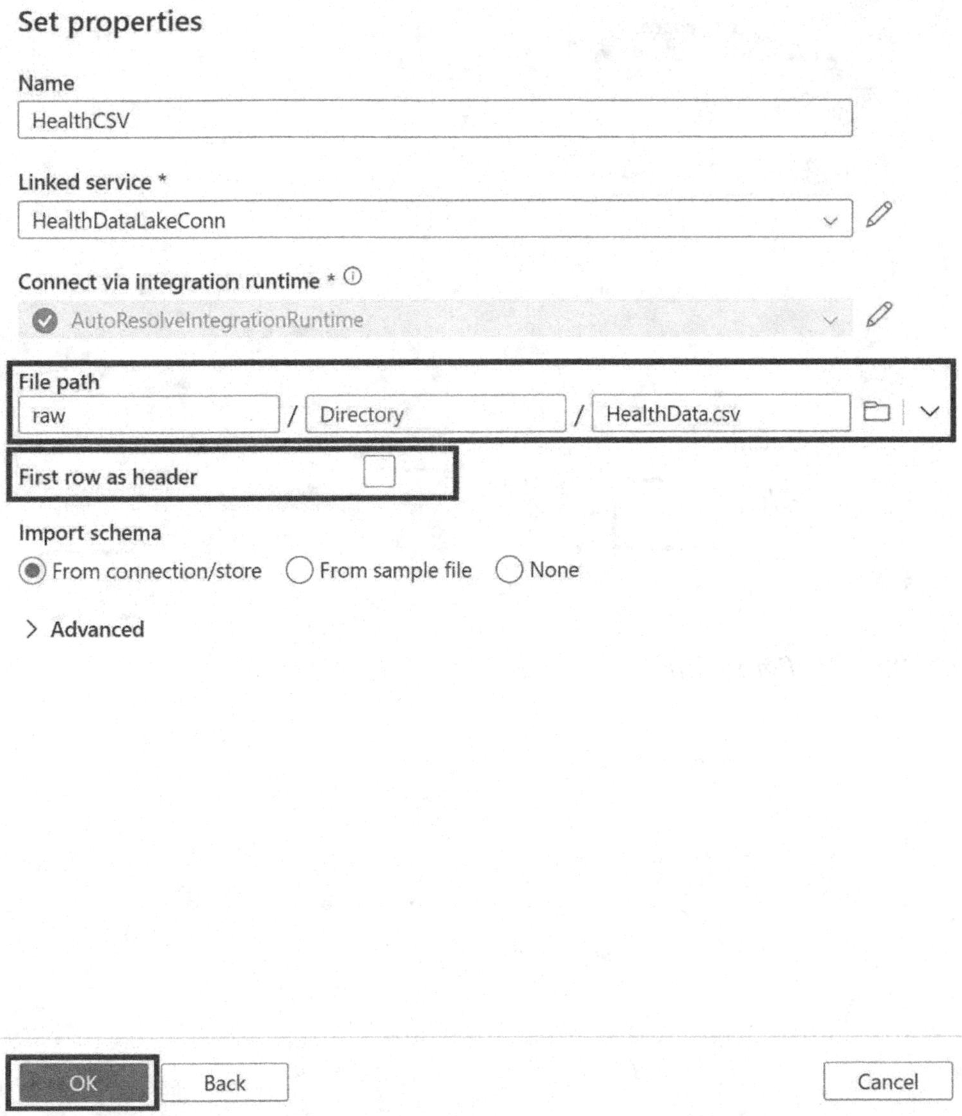

Set properties

Name

| HealthCSV |

Linked service *

| HealthDataLakeConn | ∨ | 🖉 |

Connect via integration runtime * ⓘ

| ✅ AutoResolveIntegrationRuntime | ∨ | 🖉 |

File path

| raw | / | Directory | / | HealthData.csv | 📁 | ∨ |

First row as header   ☐

Import schema

● From connection/store   ◯ From sample file   ◯ None

> Advanced

| OK | Back | | Cancel |

Figure 3-32. Provide file path

Now let us configure the sink. Go to the *Sink* tab and click on *+New* to add the destination dataset, as in Figure 3-33.

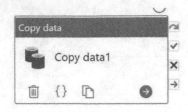

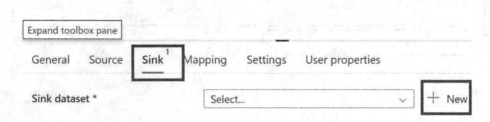

Figure 3-33. *Configure sink*

Search for *Azure Data Lake Storage Gen2* and select it. Click on *Continue* as in Figure 3-34. We need to have our processed data in the Azure Data Lake Gen2 that is built on top of the storage blob.

Figure 3-34. Select the destination data store

Selected the *Parquet* option, as in Figure 3-35, as we need to transform our data into the parquet format in the data lake. Click on *Continue*.

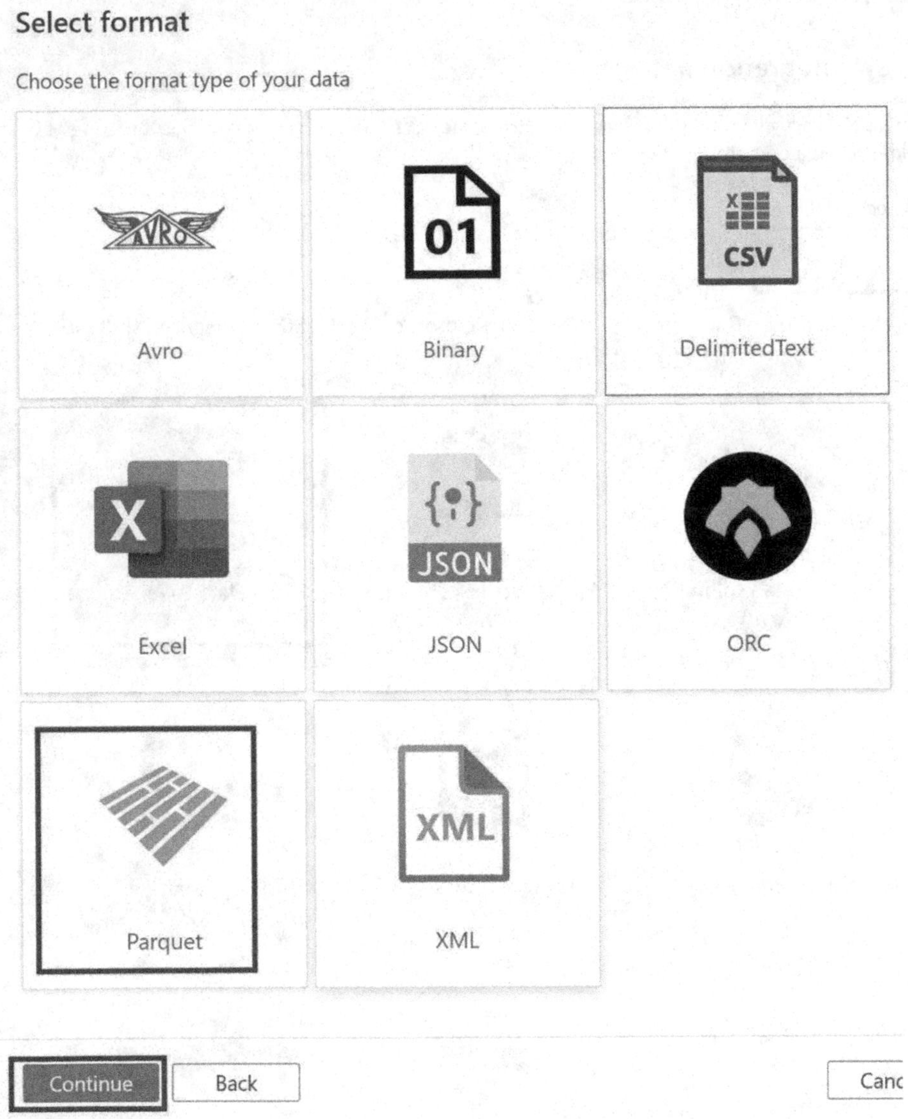

Select format

Choose the format type of your data

Figure 3-35. *Select destination data format*

Provide the file path for the processed folder, as in Figure 3-36. We need to keep the parquet file in this folder. Click on *OK*.

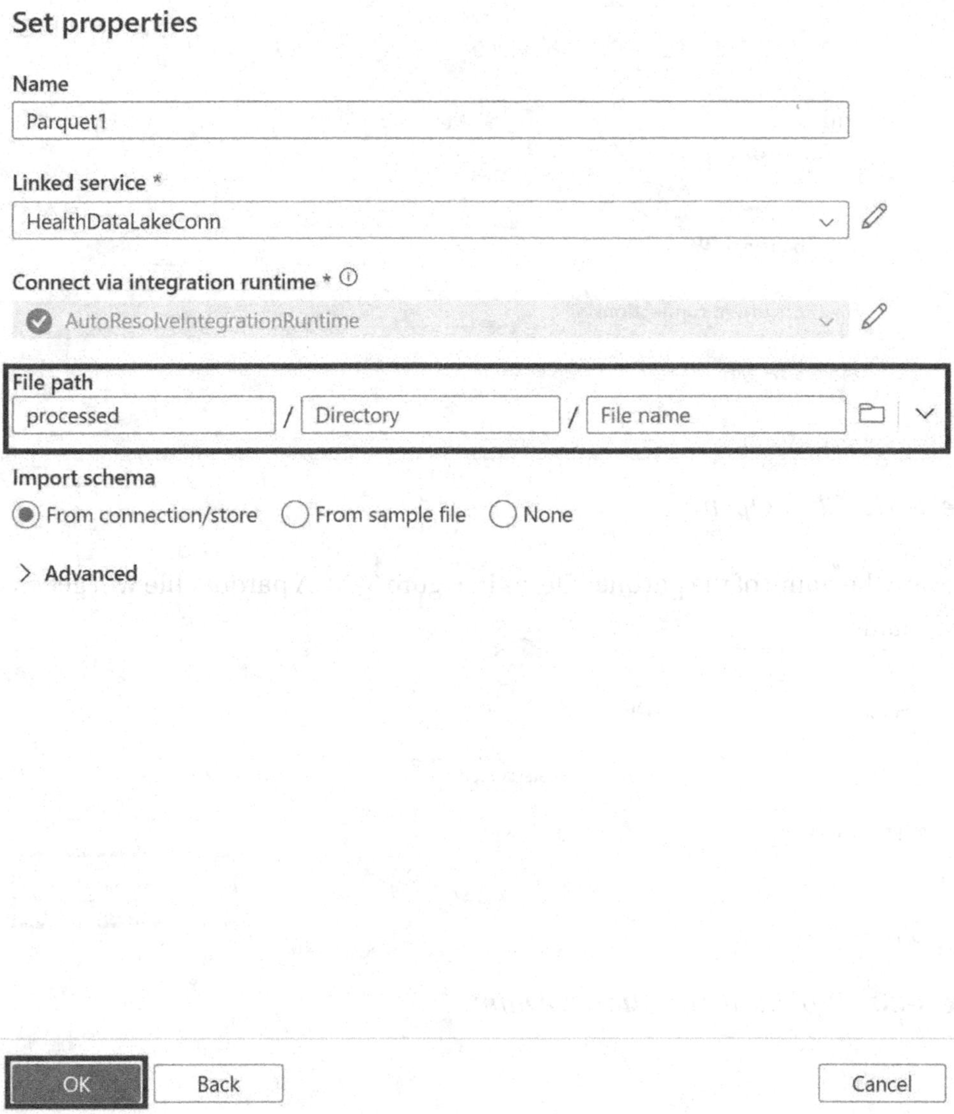

Set properties

Name

```
Parquet1
```

Linked service *

```
HealthDataLakeConn
```

Connect via integration runtime * ⓘ

✓ AutoResolveIntegrationRuntime

File path

processed	/	Directory	/	File name

Import schema

◉ From connection/store   ◯ From sample file   ◯ None

> Advanced

OK   Back   Cancel

Figure 3-36. *Provide file path*

Click on *Open,* as in Figure 3-37. We need to edit the destination dataset to meet our needs.

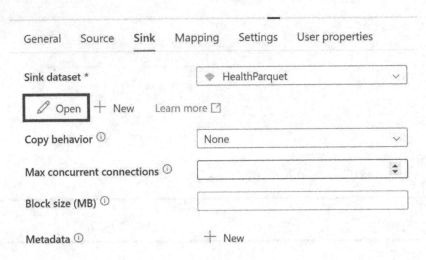

Figure 3-37. *Click Open*

Provide the name of the parquet file, as in Figure 3-38. A parquet file will get created with this name.

Figure 3-38. *Provide destination file name*

Scroll down and check the *First row as the header* option, as in Figure 3-39. We need to explicitly specify this. Click on *OK*.

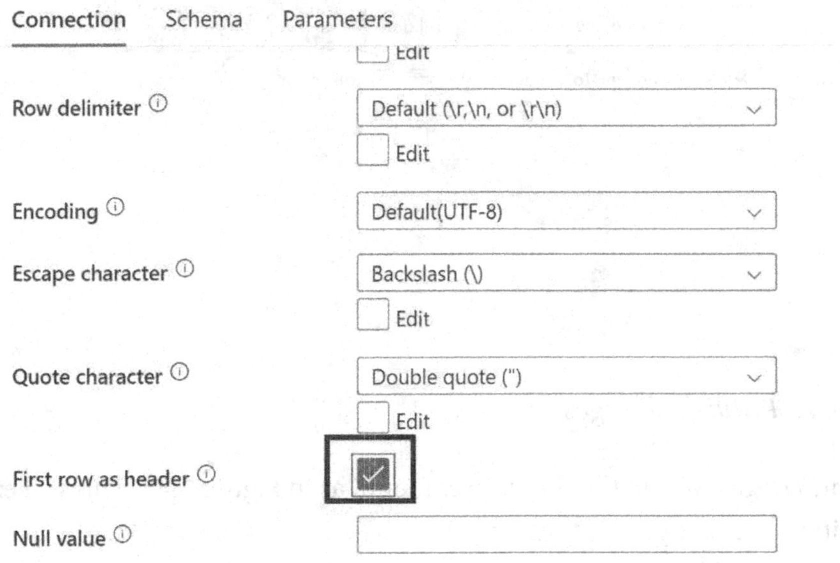

Figure 3-39. *Check the first row as the header*

Go to the *Mappings* tab and click on *Import Schemas,* as in Figure 3-40. Make changes to the data types if needed.

Figure 3-40. *Configure mapping*

Click on *Publish all,* as in Figure 3-41. This will publish the pipelines and all other work.

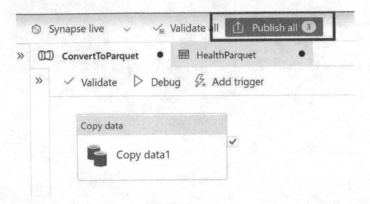

Figure 3-41. *Publish changes*

Click on *Trigger Now* in the *Add trigger* menu, as in Figure 3-42. This will execute the data pipeline.

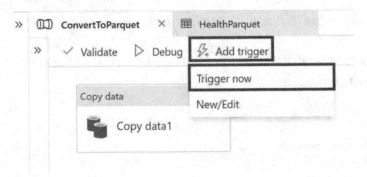

Figure 3-42. *Trigger pipeline*

Once the pipeline execution is complete, go to the *processed* container in the data lake, as in Figure 3-43. You can see the parquet file created.

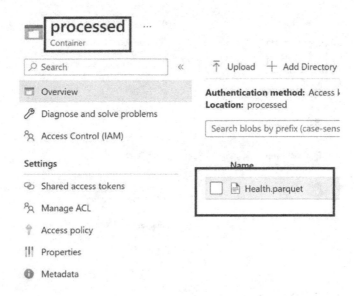

Figure 3-43. *Parquet file created in the processed container in data lake*

Attach the Parquet File to the Lake Database

Once the Synapse pipeline executes successfully, the parquet file gets generated in the processed folder. Now we need to create a lake database in Synapse and attach the parquet file. In the Synapse studio, go to the *Data* tab, as in Figure 3-44.

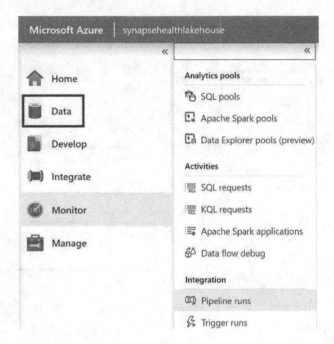

Figure 3-44. *Go to the Data tab*

Click on + as in Figure 3-45, and then click on *Lake database*. This will help us create a lake house on Synapse.

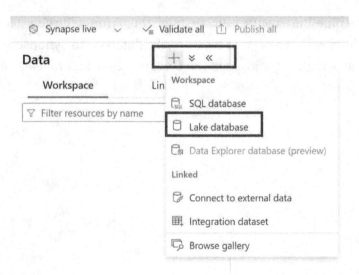

Figure 3-45. *Create lake database*

Provide the name of the lake database and all necessary details, like linked service, as in Figure 3-46.

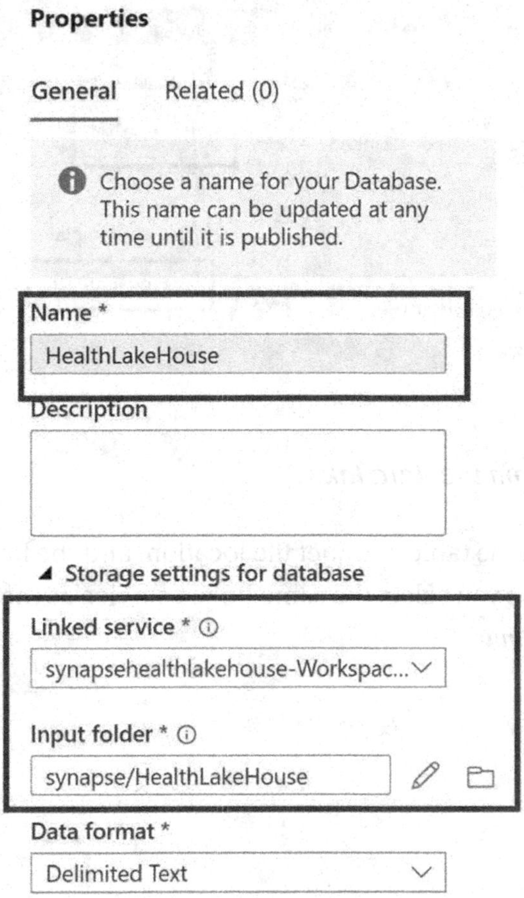

Properties

General   Related (0)

> ⓘ Choose a name for your Database. This name can be updated at any time until it is published.

Name *

HealthLakeHouse

Description

◢ Storage settings for database

Linked service * ⓘ

synapsehealthlakehouse-Workspac... ⌄

Input folder * ⓘ

synapse/HealthLakeHouse

Data format *

Delimited Text   ⌄

Figure 3-46. *Provide lake database details*

Click on *Table* and select the option *From data lake,* as in Figure 3-47. We need to select the parquet file in the processed folder in the data lake.

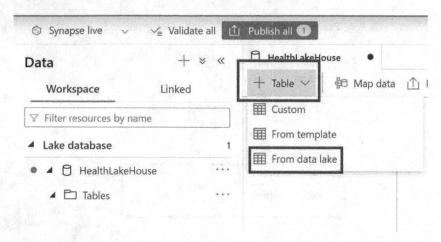

Figure 3-47. *Select from the data lake*

Provide the name of the table, parquet file location, and the linked service, as in Figure 3-48. Make sure you select the same linked service as the one for the lake database. Click on *Continue.*

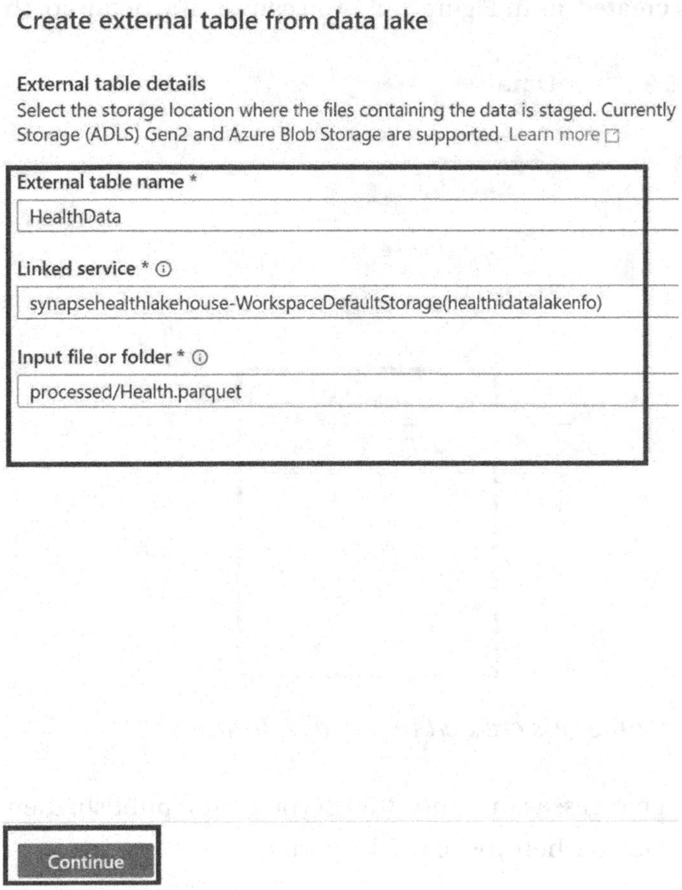

Create external table from data lake

External table details

Select the storage location where the files containing the data is staged. Currently Storage (ADLS) Gen2 and Azure Blob Storage are supported. Learn more

External table name *

HealthData

Linked service * ⓘ

synapsehealthlakehouse-WorkspaceDefaultStorage(healthidatalakenfo)

Input file or folder * ⓘ

processed/Health.parquet

Continue

Figure 3-48. *Click on Continue*

The table gets created, as in Figure 3-49. You can see the details of the columns.

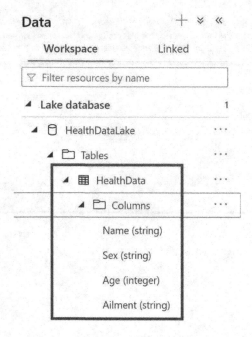

Figure 3-49. *The table gets created in the lake database*

Publish all the changes, as in Figure 3-50. If you do not publish, then the lake database will get deleted when you leave the portal.

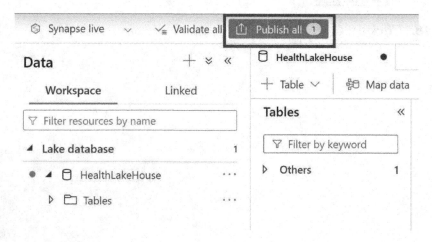

Figure 3-50. *Publish all changes*

Once the table is published, you can right-click on *Health Data* and then select *New SQL script*, as in Figure 3-51.

Figure 3-51. *New SQL script*

You can query the database, as in Figure 3-52.

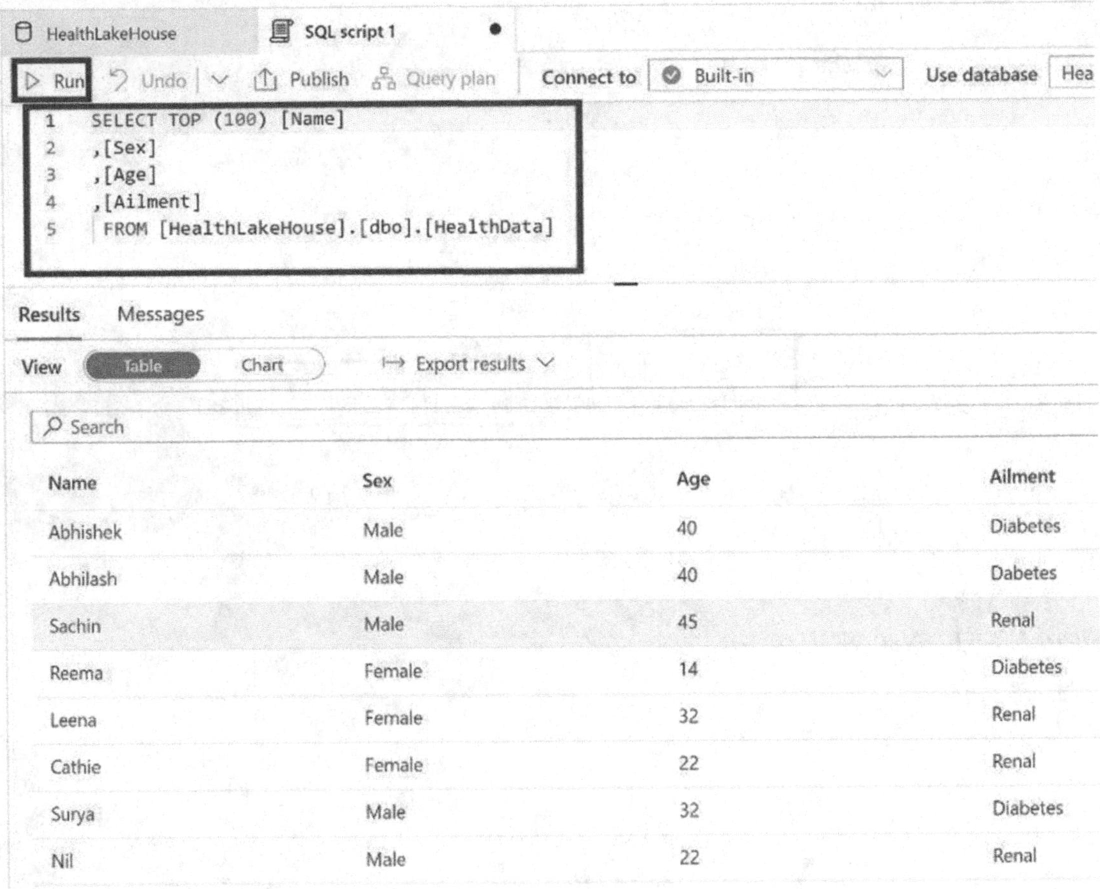

Figure 3-52. *Query lake database using SQL query*

Implement Lake House in AWS

Now, let us implement a lake house in AWS using the health data CSV file we used while building the lake house on Azure. We will go through the following steps to build the lake house in AWS:

- Create an S3 bucket to store the raw data.

- Create an AWS Glue job to convert the raw data into a delta table.

- Query the delta table using the AWS Glue job.

As a prerequisite, you should have permission for the IAM role, as in Figure 3-53.

Figure 3-53. *IAM permissions*

Create an S3 Bucket to Keep the Raw Data

Let us create an S3 bucket, as in Figure 3-54, to keep the raw data and the delta table. The AWS Glue job will transform the raw CSV data to a delta table in parquet format and keep it in the S3 bucket.

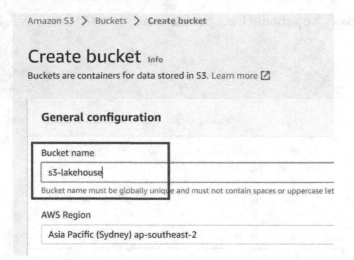

Figure 3-54. *Create bucket*

Click on the *Create folder,* as in Figure 3-55, to create a folder to keep the raw CSV file.

Figure 3-55. *Create folder*

Provide the name of the folder as *raw data,* as in Figure 3-56. Click on *Create folder*.

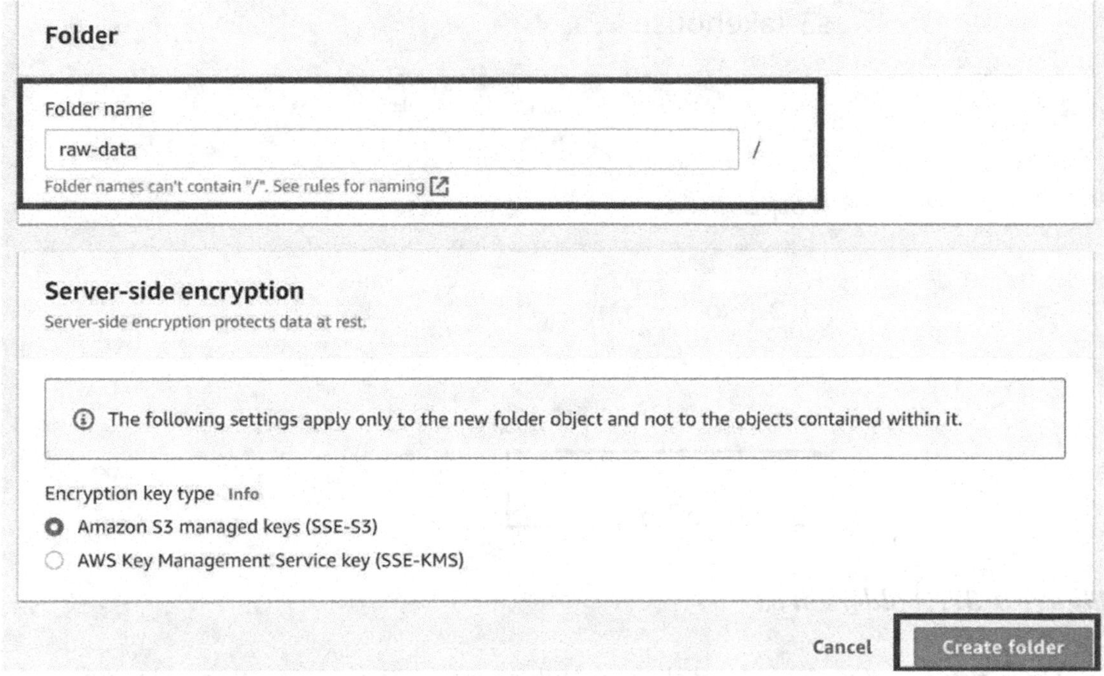

Folder

Folder name

raw-data   /

Folder names can't contain "/". See rules for naming ⬀

Server-side encryption
Server-side encryption protects data at rest.

    ⓘ   The following settings apply only to the new folder object and not to the objects contained within it.

Encryption key type Info

🔘 Amazon S3 managed keys (SSE-S3)

⭕ AWS Key Management Service key (SSE-KMS)

Cancel   **Create folder**

Figure 3-56. *Create folder*

Use the same steps to create another folder called *delta-lake,* as in Figure 3-57. We will keep the delta table here in this folder.

Figure 3-57. *Folders in S3*

Go to the *raw-data* folder and click on *Upload,* as in Figure 3-58. We need to upload the raw CSV file to this folder.

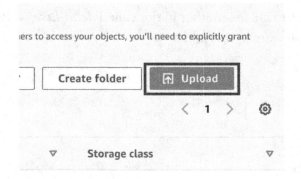

Figure 3-58. *Upload raw CSV file.*

Figure 3-59 depicts the uploaded CSV file in the S3 bucket. We will use the AWS Glue job to transform this CSV file into a delta table in parquet format.

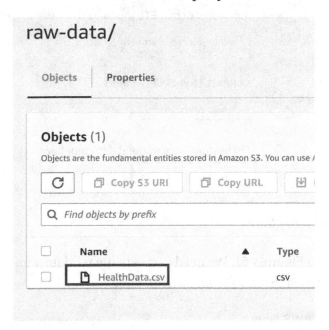

Figure 3-59. *Uploaded raw CSV file*

Create an AWS Glue Job to Convert the Raw Data into a Delta Table

Go to AWS Glue and click on *Go to workflows* as shown in Figure 3-60. We will get navigated to the AWS Glue studio, where we can create the AWS Glue job to convert the raw CSV file into a delta table.

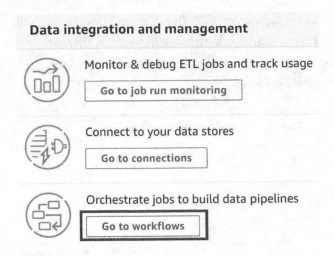

Data integration and management

Monitor & debug ETL jobs and track usage

Go to job run monitoring

Connect to your data stores

Go to connections

Orchestrate jobs to build data pipelines

Go to workflows

Figure 3-60. *Go to workflows*

Click on *Jobs* as in Figure 3-61. We need to create the workflow for the job and execute it to convert the raw CSV file into a delta table.

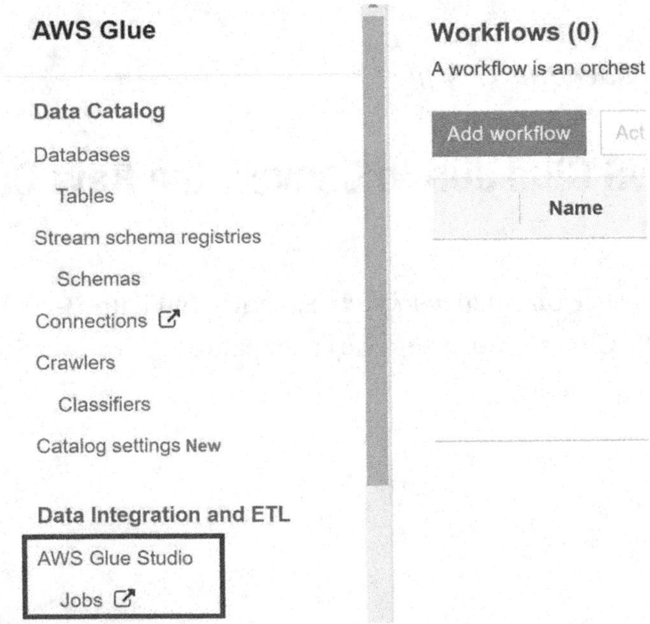

AWS Glue

Data Catalog
Databases
 Tables
Stream schema registries
 Schemas
Connections ☑
Crawlers
 Classifiers
Catalog settings New

Data Integration and ETL
AWS Glue Studio
 Jobs ☑

Workflows (0)
A workflow is an orchest

Add workflow   Act

Name

Figure 3-61. *Click on Jobs*

We will be using the delta lake connector in the AWS Glue job. We need to activate it. Go to the *Marketplace,* as in Figure 3-62.

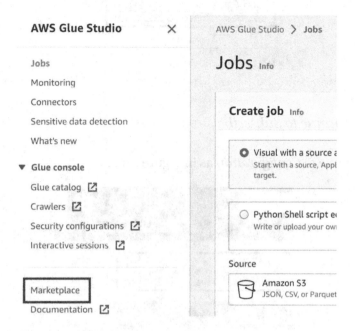

Figure 3-62. *Click on Marketplace*

Search for *delta lake* as in Figure 3-63, and then click on *Delta Lake Connector for AWS Glue.*

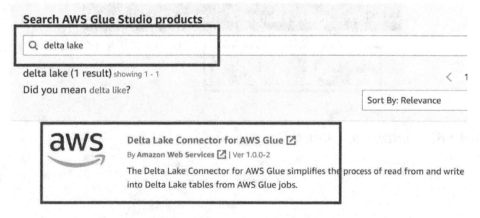

Figure 3-63. *Activate delta lake connector*

Click on *Continue to Subscribe* as in Figure 3-64.

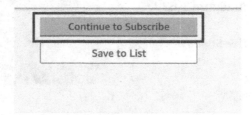

Figure 3-64. *Continue to Subscribe*

Click on *Continue to Configuration* as in Figure 3-65.

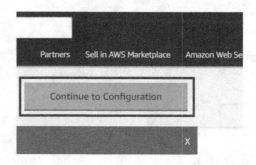

Figure 3-65. *Continue to Configuration*

Click on *Continue to Launch* as in Figure 3-66.

Figure 3-66. *Continue to Launch*

Click on *Usage instructions* as in Figure 3-67. The usage instructions will open up. We have some steps to perform on that page.

Figure 3-67. *Click Usage Instructions*

Read the usage instructions once and then click on *Activate the Glue connector from AWS Glue Studio,* as in Figure 3-68.

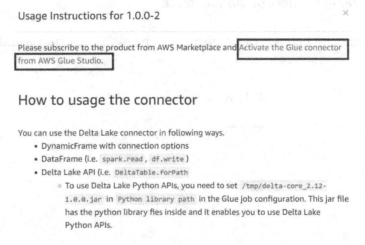

Figure 3-68. *Activate Glue connector*

Provide a name for the connection, as in Figure 3-69, and then click on *Create a connection and activate connector.*

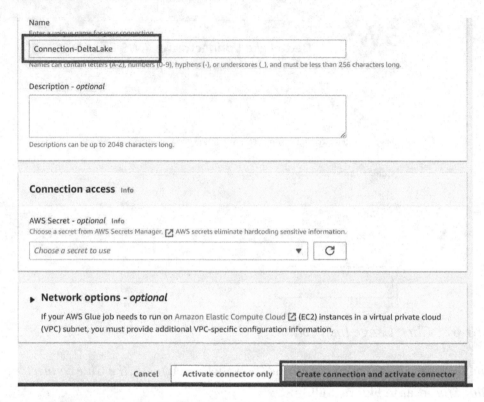

Figure 3-69. Create connection and activate connector

Once the connector gets activated, go back to the AWS Glue studio and click on *Jobs,* as in Figure 3-70.

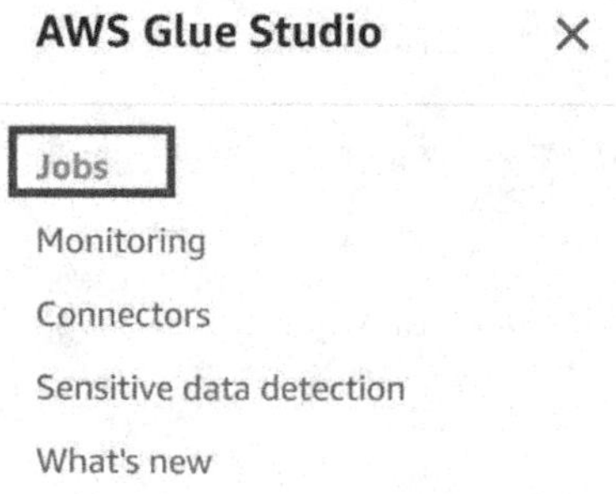

Figure 3-70. Click on Jobs

Select option *Visual with a source and target* and depict the source as *Amazon S3,* as in Figure 3-71.

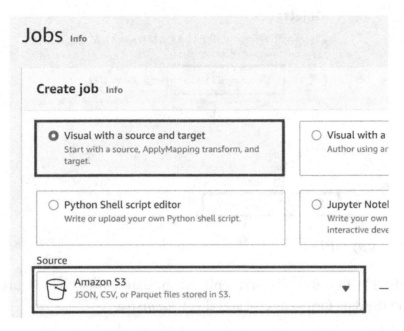

Figure 3-71. *Configure source*

Select the target as *Delta Lake Connector 1.0.0 for AWS Glue 3.0,* as in Figure 3-72. We activated the connector in the marketplace and created a connection earlier. Click on Create.

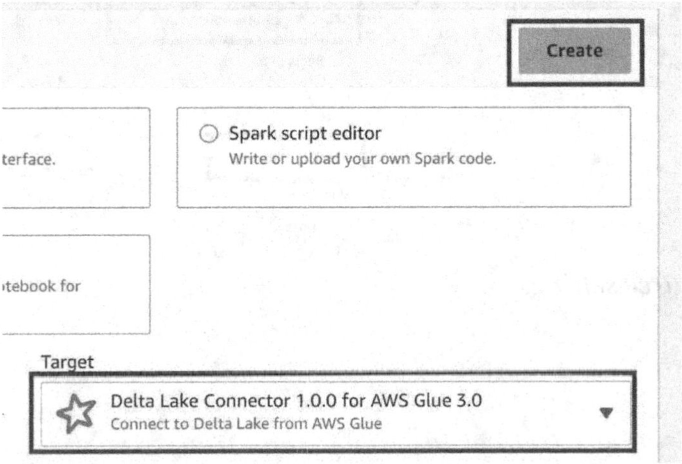

Figure 3-72. *Configure target*

Go to the S3 bucket and copy the S3 URI for the *raw-data* folder, as in *Figure 3-73*.

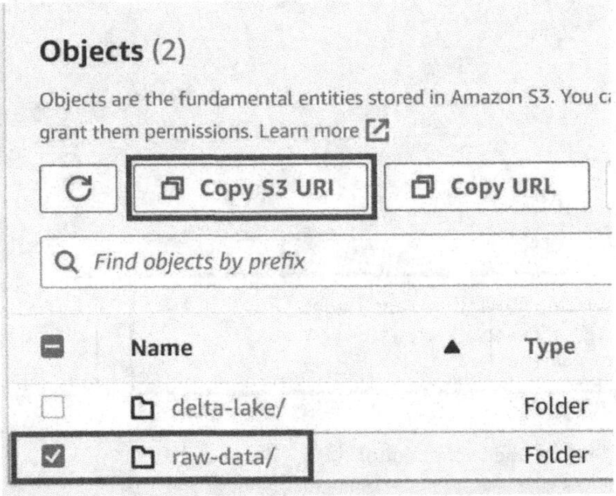

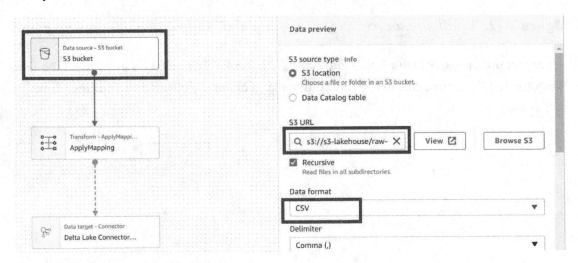

Figure 3-73. *Copy URI*

Provide the S3 URI you copied and configure the data source, as in Figure 3-74. Make sure you mark the data format as CSV and check *Recursive*.

Figure 3-74. *Source settings*

Scroll down and check the *First line of the source file contains column headers* option, as in Figure 3-75.

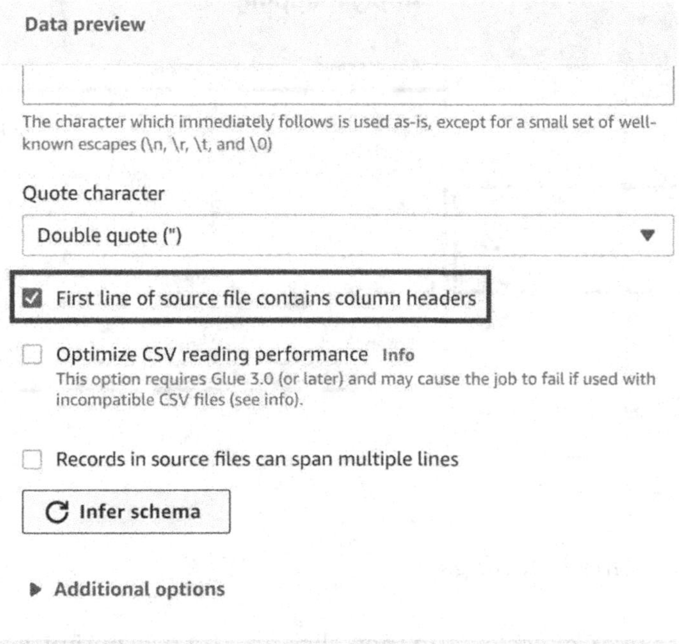

Data preview

The character which immediately follows is used as-is, except for a small set of well-known escapes (\n, \r, \t, and \0)

Quote character

Double quote (")   ▼

☑ First line of source file contains column headers

☐ Optimize CSV reading performance   Info
This option requires Glue 3.0 (or later) and may cause the job to fail if used with incompatible CSV files (see info).

☐ Records in source files can span multiple lines

⟳ Infer schema

▶ Additional options

Figure 3-75. Source settings

Click on *ApplyMapping* as in Figure 3-76 and provide the data mappings and correct data types. The target parquet file will be generated with these data types.

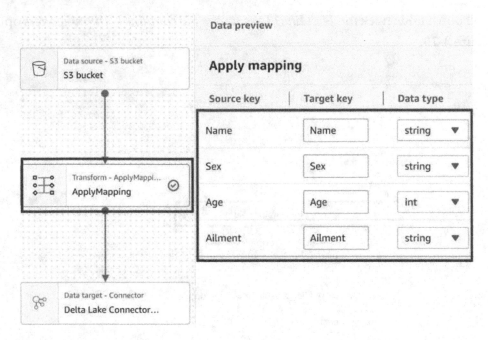

Figure 3-76. *Configure mappings*

Click on *Delta Lake Connector*, and then click on *Add new option,* as in Figure 3-77.

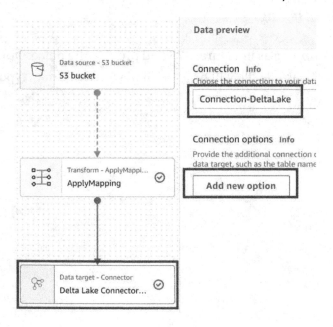

Figure 3-77. *Add new option*

Provide *Key* as *path* and *Value* as *URI* for the delta-lake folder in the S3 bucket, as in Figure 3-78.

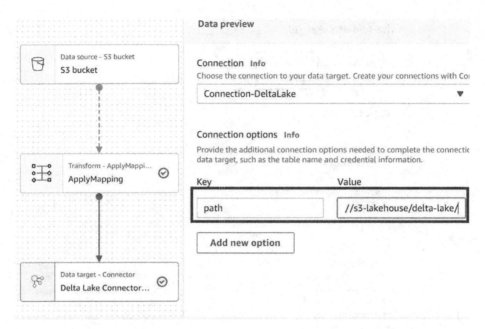

Figure 3-78.   *Configure target*

Go to the *Job details* as in Figure 3-79 and set IAM Role as the role we created as a prerequisite with all necessary permissions.

Figure 3-79. *Provide IAM role*

Click on *Save* as in Figure 3-80 and then run the job.

Figure 3-80. *Save and run*

Once the job runs successfully, go to the delta-lake folder in the S3 bucket. You can see the delta table parquet file generated in Figure 3-81.

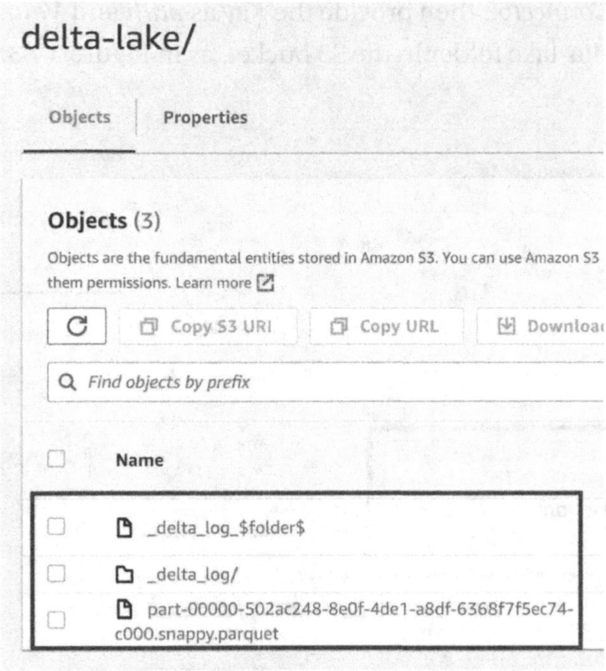

Figure 3-81. *Generated delta table in the delta-lake folder*

Query the Delta Table using the AWS Glue Job

Let us query the delta table using the AWS Glue job. Go to the job in AWS Glue studio, select *Visual with a blank canvas,* and then click on *Create,* as in Figure 3-82.

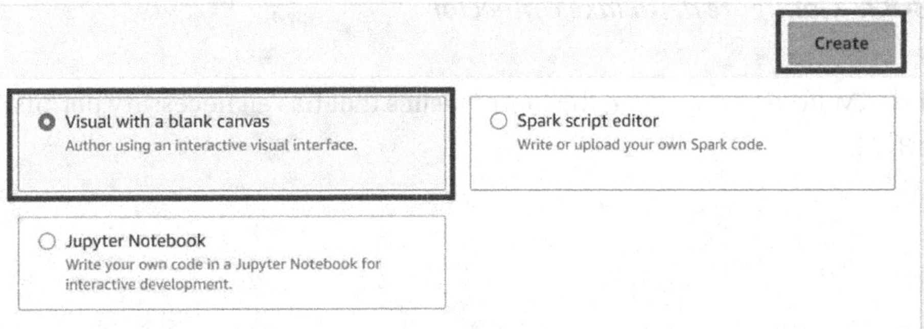

Figure 3-82. *Create new job*

Add *Delta Lake Connector,* then provide the *Key* as *path* and *Value* as *URI* for the parquet file in the delta-lake folder in the S3 bucket, as in Figure 3-83.

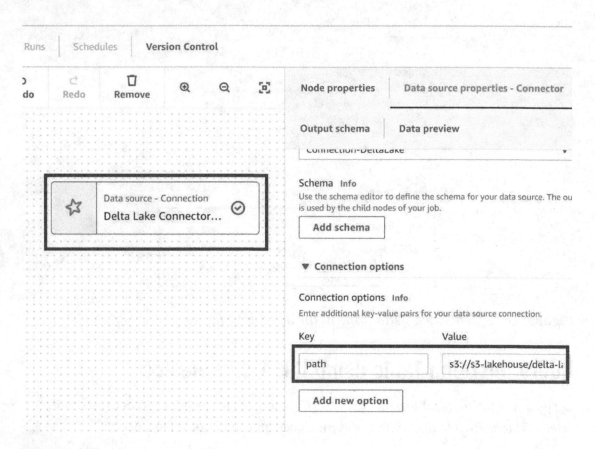

Figure 3-83. *Configure delta lake connector*

Set the IAM Role to the role in the prerequisites that has all necessary permissions, as in Figure 3-84.

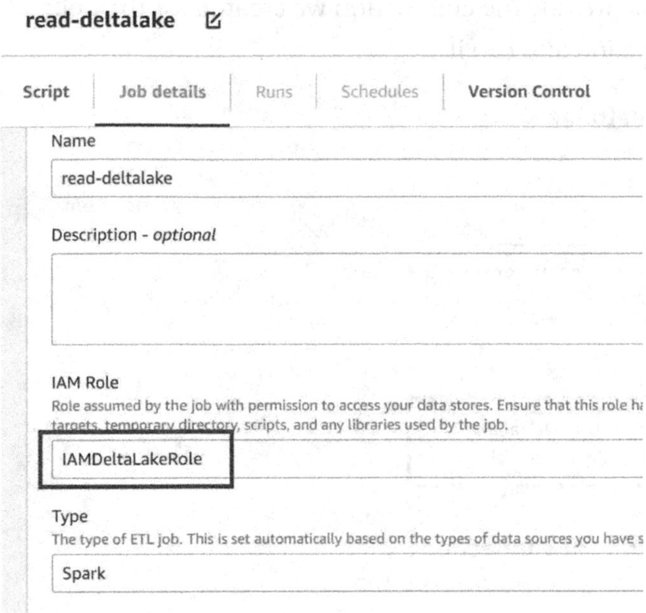

read-deltalake

Script | Job details | Runs | Schedules | Version Control

Name

read-deltalake

Description - *optional*

IAM Role
Role assumed by the job with permission to access your data stores. Ensure that this role ha
targets, temporary directory, scripts, and any libraries used by the job.

IAMDeltaLakeRole

Type
The type of ETL job. This is set automatically based on the types of data sources you have s

Spark

Figure 3-84. *Provide IAM role*

Expand Advanced properties, as in Figure 3-85.

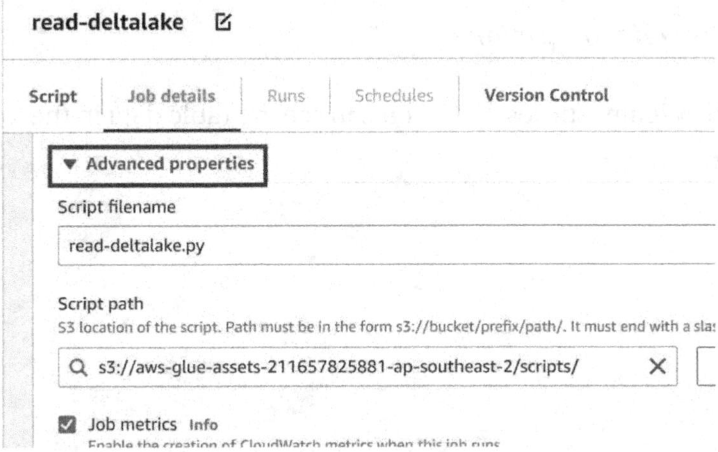

read-deltalake

Script | Job details | Runs | Schedules | Version Control

▼ Advanced properties

Script filename

read-deltalake.py

Script path
S3 location of the script. Path must be in the form s3://bucket/prefix/path/. It must end with a sla

s3://aws-glue-assets-211657825881-ap-southeast-2/scripts/   ✕

☑ Job metrics Info
Enable the creation of CloudWatch metrics when this job runs.

Figure 3-85. *Expand Advanced properties section*

157

Scroll down and provide the connection we created for the delta lake connector, as in Figure 3-86. Save the job and run it.

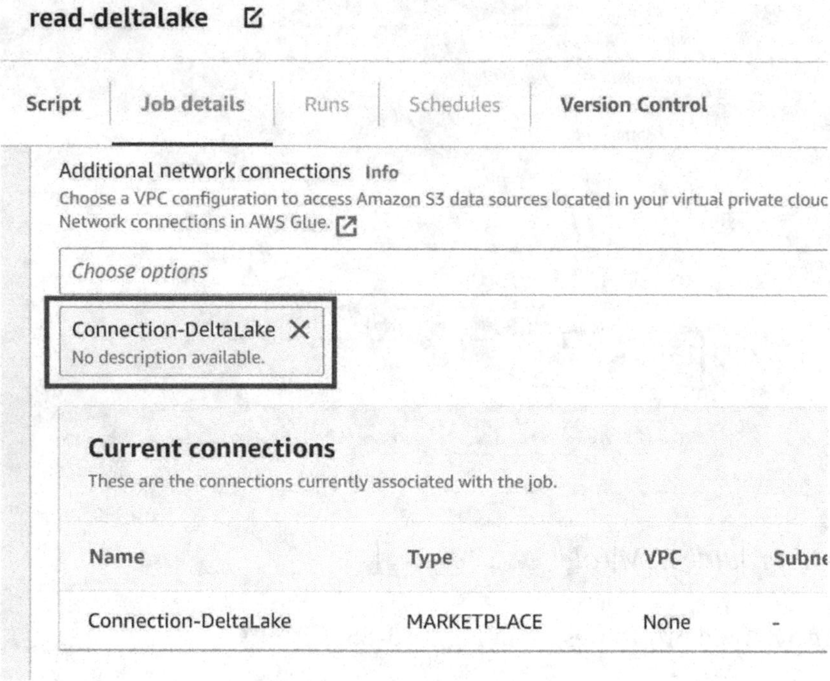

read-deltalake ☑

Script	Job details	Runs	Schedules	Version Control

Additional network connections Info
Choose a VPC configuration to access Amazon S3 data sources located in your virtual private cloud
Network connections in AWS Glue. ↗

Choose options

Connection-DeltaLake ✕
No description available.

Current connections
These are the connections currently associated with the job.

Name	Type	VPC	Subne
Connection-DeltaLake	MARKETPLACE	None	-

Figure 3-86. *Provode connection*

Once the job executes successfully, you can see the table data in the logs for the job, as in Figure 3-87.

You can use the filter bar below to search for and mat

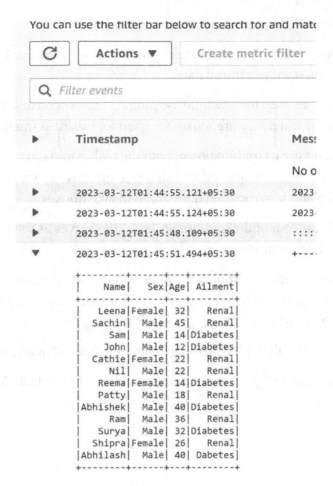

Figure 3-87. *Table data in logs*

Summary

In this chapter, we learned the basics of data lake, delta lake, and lake house. We explored the lake house architecture. We then created a lake house on Cloud using Azure and AWS. We learned orchestration tools, like AWS Glue and Synapse pipelines, that are used while building lake house architecture. In the next chapter, we will learn the basics of data meshes and implement a data mesh on the cloud.

The following are the key takeaways from this chapter:

- Data lakes store both structured and unstructured data. Data warehouses store structured data.

- Data lakes are used for machine learning and advanced analytics application, and data warehouses are used for business intelligence.

- Lake houses are a combination of both data lakes and data warehouses. You can query data using SQL queries for both structured and unstructured data stored in lake houses.

- Delta lakes are an optimized storage layer that serves as the metadata layer for the lake house.

- Delta lakes extend the underlying data stored in the data lake in raw format to support ACID transactions and querying capabilities using Apache Spark APIs or Spark SQL or anything similar.

- Delta lakes handle both streaming and batch data, all at one stop.

- Data processing engines and pipelines play a pivotal role in the lake house.

CHAPTER 4

Data Mesh

In the modern data landscape, the amount of data generated is huge. Data can be of varied formats, like XML or JSON files, relational data, images, videos, and many others. The generated data can be used in machine learning, analytics, and myriad other ways to derive meaningful insights. However, storing, organizing, retrieving, scaling, and consuming these data can be challenging. There needs to be a systematic pattern when dealing with data so that it is easy to store, manage, source, and consume. A data mesh comes to the rescue here.

In the previous chapter, we explored data lakes, lake houses, and delta lakes in detail. In this chapter, we will discuss the concept of a data mesh and learn how to design cloud-based data solutions using a data mesh.

Structure

In this chapter, we will explore the following areas.

- The Modern Data Problem and Data Mesh
- Data Mesh Principles
- Data Mesh Use Cases
- Design a Data Mesh Solution on Azure

Objectives

After studying this chapter, you should be able to do the folloing:

- Understand the fundamentals of the data mesh
- Design cloud-based solutions for a data mesh using Azure

© Anjani Kumar, Abhishek Mishra, and Sanjeev Kumar 2024
A. Kumar et al., *Architecting a Modern Data Warehouse for Large Enterprises*,
https://doi.org/10.1007/979-8-8688-0029-0_4

The Modern Data Problem and Data Mesh

Modern organizations keep data in centralized data platforms. Data get generated by multiple sources and are ingested into this data platform. This centralized data platform serves data for analytics and other data consumption needs for the data consumers in the organization. There are multiple departments in an organization, like sales, accounting, procurement, and many more, that can be visualized as domains. Each of these domains ingests data from this centralized data platform. There are data engineers, data administrators, data analysts, and other such roles that work from the centralized data platform. These data professionals work in silos and have very little knowledge of how these data relate to the domain functionality where they were generated. Managing the huge amount of data is cumbersome, and scaling the data for consumption is a big challenge. Making this data reusable and consumable for analytics and machine learning purposes is a big challenge. Storing, managing, processing, and serving the data centrally is monolithic in nature. Figure 4-1 represents the modern data problem. The data is kept in a monolithic centralized data platform that has limited scaling capability, and data is kept and handled in silos.

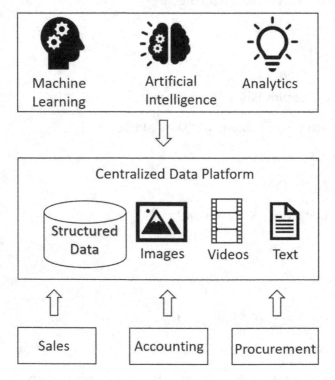

Figure 4-1. *Modern data problem*

The data mesh solves this modern data problem. It is a well-defined architecture or pattern that gives data ownership to the domains or the departments that are generating the data. The domains will generate, store, and manage the data and expose the data to the consumers as a product. This approach makes the data more scalable and discoverable as the data are managed by the domains, and these domains understand the data very well and know what can be done with them. The domains can enforce strict security and compliance mechanisms to secure the data. By adopting a data mesh, we are moving away from the monolithic centralized data platform to a decentralized and distributed data platform where the data are exposed as products and the ownership lies with the domains. Data are organized and exposed by the specific domain that owns the data generation.

Data Mesh Principles

There are four distinct principles when it comes to implementing DataMesh, as follows:

1. Domain-driven ownership

2. Data-as-a-product

3. Self-serve data platform

4. Federated computational governance

Let us discuss each of these areas in detail.

Domain-driven Ownership

As per the domain-driven ownership principle, the domain teams are owners of their respective data. For example, there can be different teams, like sales, human resources, information technology, and so on, in an enterprise. Each of these teams will generate, store, process, govern, and share their data. The ownership of the data will remain within the domain boundary. In other words, data is organized per domain. We get the following benefits by adopting this principle:

- The data is owned by domain experts who understand the data well. This process enhances the quality of data and the way it is stored, used, and shared.

- The data structure is modeled as per the needs of the domain. So, the data schema is realistic.

Data gets decentralized when it is being managed by the corresponding domain. This ensures better scalability and flexibility when it comes to management of data.

Data-as-a-Product

Data are often treated as a byproduct for the application. As a result, data are kept in silos, not stored properly, not utilized to the fullest, and thus the collaboration and sharing of the data is limited. However, when the data are treated as a product, they are treated at par with the application and are exposed for consumption to other teams and parties as a product. This process increases the data quality and makes data management efficient. A consumer-centric approach is followed that ensures that the data produced are consumable by the end consumers. This helps in maintaining well-defined data contracts that clearly define how the data will be accessed, shared, consumed, and integrated by other consumers in the enterprise. This makes the data teams autonomous, resulting in the team producing the data being responsible for that data and exposing it as a product.

Self-Serve Data Platform

Each of the domains exposing the data as products needs an infrastructure to host and operate the data. If we take a traditional approach, each of these domains will own their own infrastructure and have their own set of tooling and utilities to handle the data. This phenomenon is not cost effective and requires a lot of effort from the infrastructure engineers in the domains. This approach also leads to duplicity of efforts across the domain teams.

A better approach would be to build a self-serve platform to facilitate the domains' storing and exposing data as products. The platform will provide the necessary infrastructure to store and manage the data. The underlying infrastructure will be abstracted to the domain teams. It should expose necessary tooling that will enable the domain teams to manage their data and expose it as their domain's product to other domain teams. The self-serve platform should clearly define with whom the data should be shared. It should provide an interface to the domain teams so they can manage their data products by using either declarative code or some other convenient manner.

Federated Computational Governance

Data are exposed as products in a data mesh and are owned by the domain teams. The data life cycle is also maintained by the domain teams. However, there is a need for data interoperability across domains. For example, if an organization has a finance domain team and a sales domain team, the finance domain team will need data from the sales domain team, and vice versa. Governance must be defined as to how the data is exchanged, the format of the data, what data can be exposed, network resiliency, security aspects, and so forth. Here, we need Federated Computational Governance to help.

Federated computational governance helps in standardizing the message exchange format across the products. It also helps in automated execution of decisions pertaining to security and access. There will be a set of rules, policies, and standards that has been decided upon by all the domain teams, and there will be automated enforcement of these rules, policies, and standards.

Design a Data Mesh on Azure

Now, let us use the data mesh principles we discussed and design a data mesh on Azure. We will take a use case of an enterprise consisting of finance, sales, human resources, procurement, and inventory departments. Let us build a data mesh that can expose data for each of these departments. The data generated by these departments are consumed across each of them. The item details in the inventory department are used in the sales department while generating an invoice when selling items to a prospective customer. Human resources payroll data and rewards and recognition data are used in the finance department to build the balance sheet for the department. The sales data from the sales department and the procurement data from the procurement department are used in the finance department when building the balance sheet for the company.

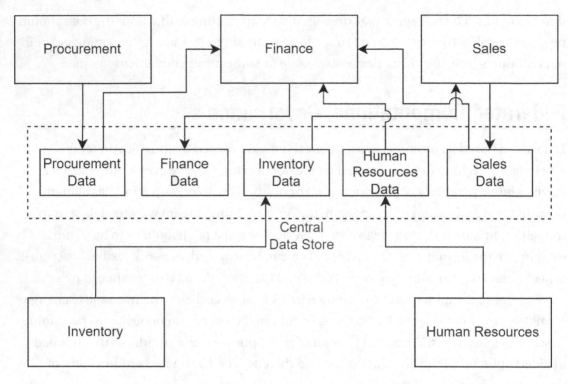

Figure 4-2. *As-is data architecture*

Figure 4-2 represents the as-is data architecture for the enterprise. The data are managed by a central data store. Each of the departments stores their data in the central data store. The finance department consumes data from human resources, sales, and procurement. Inventory data is consumed by the sales department. The central data team manages the data warehouse that stores and manages the central data. Each of these departments has a dependency on the central data team for data management, storage, and governance. The data engineers in the central data team are not experts for these domains. They do not understand how this data is produced or consumed. However, the engineers in the central data team are experts in storing and managing these data. The following are the steps to design a data mesh architecture on Azure:

1. Create data products for the domains.

2. Create self-serve data platform.

3. Create federated governance.

Create Data Products for the Domains

Let us design data products for each of the domains.

Create Data Product for Human Resources Domain

We can start with the human resources domain product.

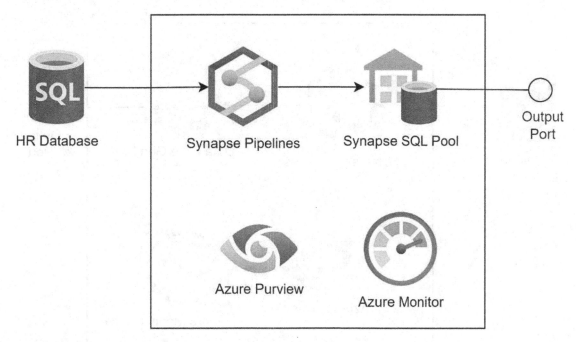

Figure 4-3. *Human resources domain product*

Figure 4-3 depicts the human resources domain product. The enterprise uses different human resources applications and portals that perform human resources tasks, like employee attendance, timecards, rewards and recognitions, performance management, and many more. All these human resources data are stored in the HR database built using Azure SQL. The Synapse pipeline reads the data from the HR database, transforms it into a consumable format, and then stores the data in the Synapse SQL pool. The Synapse pipeline can use the Copy activity to fetch the data from the HR database and put it in the Synapse SQL pool after processing the data. The Synapse SQL pool exposes the data to other domain products for consumption. Operational logs and metrics for Synapse are stored in Azure Monitor. Azure Monitor can be used to diagnose any run-time issues in the product. Azure Purview scans data capture and stores the data lineage, data schema, and other metadata information about the data that can help in discovering the data.

Create Data Product for Inventory Domain

Let us now design the inventory domain product.

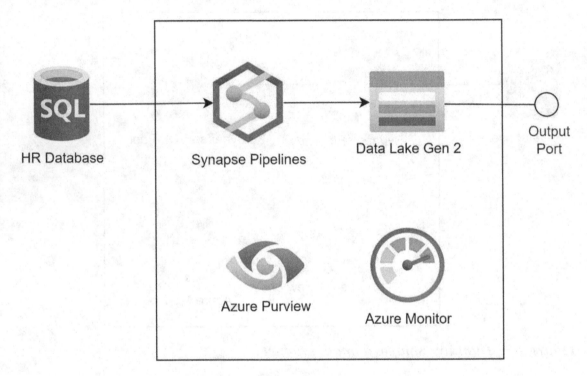

Figure 4-4. *Inventory resources domain product*

Figure 4-4 depicts the inventory domain product. The enterprise uses different inventory applications and portals that manage the inventory of the products that the enterprise develops. These applications add products' stock and information data, distribution details, and other necessary metadata information. All these inventory data are stored in the inventory database built using Azure SQL. The Synapse pipeline reads the data from the inventory database, transforms it into a consumable format, and then stores the data in an Azure Data Lake Gen2. The Synapse pipeline can use the Copy activity to fetch the data from the HR database and put it in the Azure Data Lake Gen2 after processing it. Azure Data Lake Gen2 exposes the data to other domain products for consumption. Operational logs and metrics for Synapse are stored in Azure Monitor. Azure Monitor can be used to diagnose the run-time issues in the product. Azure Purview scans data capture and stores the data lineage, data schema, and other metadata information about the data that can help in discovering the data.

Create Data Product for Procurement Domain

Let us now design the procurement domain product.

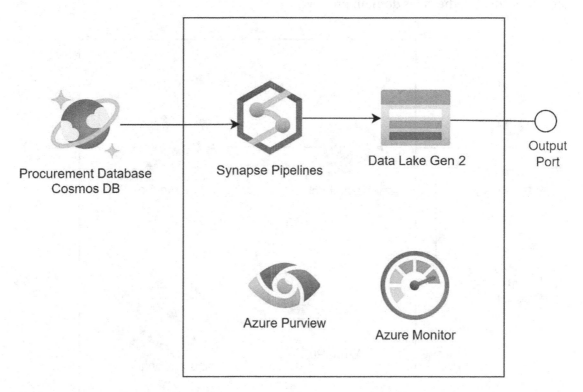

Figure 4-5. *Procurement domain product*

Figure 4-5 depicts the procurement domain product. There are different suppliers from whom the organization procures data. The data comprise procured product details, prices, and other necessary information. The data is directly ingested from the supplier system, and the data format varies from supplier to supplier. Cosmos DB database is used to store the supplier data. The Synapse pipeline reads the data from the supplier database, transforms the data into a consumable format, and then stores the data in an Azure Data Lake Gen2. Synapse pipeline can use the Copy activity to fetch the data from HR database and put it in the Azure Data Lake Gen2 after processing the data.

Azure Data Lake Gen2 exposes the data to other domain products for consumption. Operational logs and metrics for Synapse are stored in Azure Monitor. Azure Monitor can be used to diagnose the run-time issues in the product. Azure Purview scans data capture and stores the data lineage, data schema, and other metadata information that can help in discovering the data.

Create Data Product for Sales Domain

Let us now design the sales domain product.

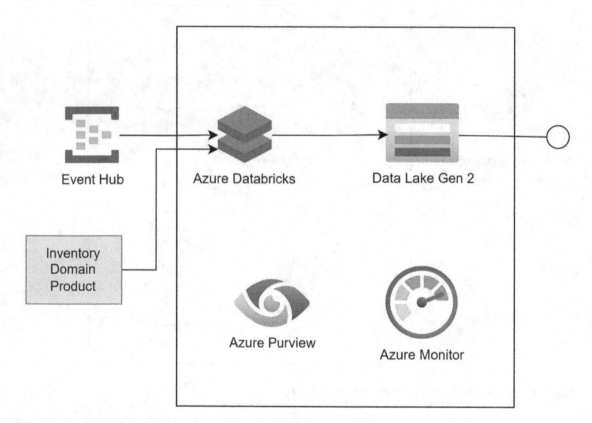

Figure 4-6. *Sales domain product*

Figure 4-6 depicts the sales domain product. There are different sales channels for the enterprise. There are distributors that sell the products. There are also B2C sales for the products in the enterprise e-commerce portal. The sales data from multiple channels are ingested into Azure Databricks through Event Hub. The volume of data that is getting ingested is huge. So, the data are stored in Azure Databricks. Data from the inventory domain droduct are consumed by the sales domain product. Spark pipelines transform the data and put the data in an Azure Data Lake Gen2, which exposes the data to other domain products for consumption. Operational logs and metrics for Synapse are stored in Azure Monitor. Azure Monitor can be used to diagnose the run-time issues in the product. Azure Purview scans data capture and stores the data lineage, data schema, and other metadata information that can help in discovering the data.

Create Data Product for Finance Domain

Let us now design the finance domain product.

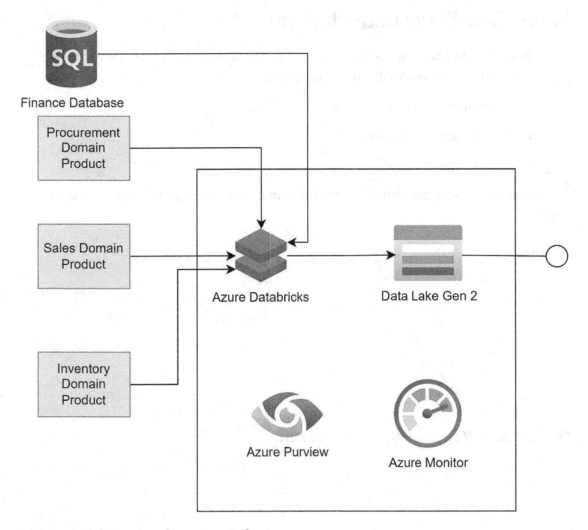

Figure 4-7. *Finance domain product*

171

Figure 4-7 depicts the finance domain product, which consumes data from the inventory, sales, and procurement domain products. The volume of data is huge. Azure Databricks is used to manage the huge amounts of data being ingested. Spark pipelines transform the data and put it in an Azure Data Lake Gen2, which exposes the data to other domain products for consumption. Operational logs and metrics for Synapse are stored in Azure Monitor. Azure Monitor can be used to diagnose the run-time issues in the product. Azure Purview scans data capture and stores the data lineage, data schema, and other metadata information that can help in discovering the data.

Create Self-Serve Data Platform

The self-serve data platform consists of the following components, which give data producers and consumers a self-service experience:

- Data mesh experience plane
- Data product experience plane
- Infrastructure plane

Figure 4-8 depicts the Azure services that can be used to build the self-serve data platform.

Azure Purview

Azure Monitor

Figure 4-8. *Self-serve platform components*

Data Mesh Experience Plane

The data mesh experience plane helps customers to discover the data products, explore metadata, see relationships among the data, and so on. The data mesh plane is used by the data governance team to ensure data compliance and best practices by giving them a way to audit and explore the data. Azure Purview can scan the data products and pull the data information from the products, like metadata, data schemas, data lineage, etc.

Data Product Experience Plane

The data product experience plane helps the data producers to add, modify, and delete data in the domain products. Azure Functions can be used in data products to allow data producers to add, modify, or delete the data in the domain product. The Purview catalog in the domain product will expose the data schema definitions and metadata, allowing the data producers to work with the data in the data domain.

Infrastructure Plane

The infrastructure plane helps in self-provisioning of the data domain infrastructure. You can use Azure Resource Manager APIs exposed through Azure Functions to create and destroy infrastructure for the data domain products.

Federated Governance

Azure Policies can be used to bring in federated governance. Data landing zones can be created using Azure Policies that can control and govern API access and activities for the data producers and consumers. Azure Functions and Azure Resource Manager APIs can also be used for governance purposes. Azure Monitor alerts can be used for generating governance alerts and notifications.

Summary

In this chapter, we learned the concept of a data mesh. We learned the data mesh principles, like domain-driven ownership, data-as-a-product, self-serve data platform, and federated computational governance. We explored each of these principles in detail. We explored a real-time scenario from an enterprise comprising inventory, human resources, sales, finance, and procurement domains and designed a data mesh for the enterprise.

In the next chapter, we will explore data orchestration techniques for the modern data warehouse.

CHAPTER 5

Data Orchestration Techniques

In today's world, businesses are generating and capturing more data than ever before. While this data is valuable, it can also be challenging to manage, integrate, and make sense of. This is where data orchestration comes in.

Data orchestration is the process of managing, organizing, and coordinating data from various sources to enable its efficient and effective use. It involves the utilization of various technologies, tools, and processes to ensure that data is collected, processed, and stored in a way that makes it accessible and usable for different purposes.

Data orchestration runs on three main components: data pipelines, data integration, and data governance. In this chapter, we will examine each of these components in detail and will also go through the tools and examples that help in effectively doing data orchestration at scale.

Structure

In this chapter, we will explore the following:

- Data Orchestration Concepts

- Data Integration

- Data Pipelines

- Data Governance Empowered by Data Orchestration

- Tools and Examples

© Anjani Kumar, Abhishek Mishra, and Sanjeev Kumar 2024
A. Kumar et al., *Architecting a Modern Data Warehouse for Large Enterprises*,
https://doi.org/10.1007/979-8-8688-0029-0_5

Objective

This chapter provides an overview of data orchestration and familiarizes readers with the terminologies and concepts. The chapter further focuses on the data orchestration tools, their purpose, and when to use what.

After studying this chapter, you should be able to do the following:

- Understand the basics of data orchestration, including the tools, processes, and techniques used in modern-day data processing and transformation using data pipelines built and scheduled over data orchestration tools.

- Understand and choose different cloud-based orchestration tools, such as Azure Data Factory, Azure Synapse Pipelines, AWS Glue, Snowflake, and Databricks, or even others not part of the example.

- Define better orchestration flow and set up governance around different phases and steps of data processing.

- Help your clients in decision-making toward choosing cloud tools that solve their current and future needs.

Data Orchestration Concepts

Data orchestration techniques are used to manage and coordinate the flow of data across various systems, applications, and processes within an organization. These techniques help ensure that data is collected, transformed, integrated, and delivered to the right place at the right time (Figure 5-1).

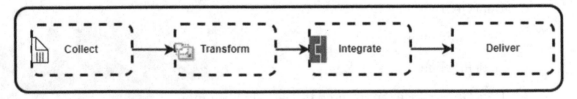

Figure 5-1. *Some of the data engineering activities where orchestration is required*

Data orchestration often involves data integration and extract, transform, load (ETL) processes. *Data integration* refers to combining data from different sources into a unified view, while ETL involves extracting data from source systems, transforming it to meet the target system's requirements, and loading it into the destination system.

Orchestration has evolved alongside advancements in data management technologies and the increasing complexity of data ecosystems. Traditional approaches involved manual and ad-hoc methods of data integration, which were time-consuming and error-prone. As organizations started adopting distributed systems, cloud computing, and Big Data technologies, the need for automated and scalable data orchestration techniques became evident.

In the early days, batch processing was a common data orchestration technique. Data was collected over a period, stored in files or databases, and processed periodically. Batch processing is suitable for scenarios where real-time data processing is not necessary, and it is still used in various applications today.

With the rise of distributed systems and the need for real-time data processing, message-oriented middleware (MOM) became popular. MOM systems enable asynchronous communication between different components or applications by sending messages through a middleware layer. This technique decouples the sender and the receiver, allowing for more flexible and scalable data orchestration.

Enterprise Service Bus (ESB) is a software architecture that provides a centralized infrastructure for integrating various applications and services within an enterprise. It facilitates the exchange of data between different systems using standardized interfaces, protocols, and message formats. ESBs offer features like message routing, transformation, and monitoring, making them useful for data orchestration in complex environments.

Modern data orchestration techniques often involve the use of data pipelines and workflow orchestration tools both on cloud and on-premises for batch processing and real-time systems involving event-driven and continuous data streaming. The major areas that it covers are as follows:

- **Data Pipelines and Workflow Orchestration:** Modern data orchestration techniques often involve the use of data pipelines and workflow orchestration tools. Data pipelines provide a structured way to define and execute a series of data processing steps, including data ingestion, transformation, and delivery. Workflow orchestration tools help coordinate and manage the execution of complex workflows involving multiple tasks, dependencies, and error handling.

- **Stream Processing and Event-Driven Architecture:** As the demand for real-time data processing and analytics increased, stream processing and event-driven architecture gained prominence. Stream processing involves continuously processing and analyzing data streams in real-time, enabling organizations to derive insights and take immediate action. Event-driven architectures leverage events and event-driven messaging to trigger actions and propagate data changes across systems.

- **Cloud-Based Data Orchestration:** Cloud computing has greatly influenced data orchestration techniques. Cloud platforms offer various services and tools for data ingestion, storage, processing, and integration. They provide scalable infrastructure, on-demand resources, and managed services, making it easier to implement and scale data orchestration workflows.

Modern Data Orchestration in Detail

Modern data orchestration encompasses a range of techniques and practices that enable organizations to manage and integrate data effectively in today's complex data ecosystems.

They go through cycles of data ingestion, data transformation, defining models and measures, and finally serving the data via different modes and tools based on latency, visibility, and accessibility requirements for representation (Figure 5-2).

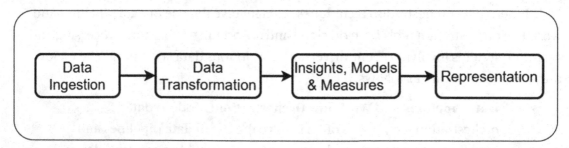

Figure 5-2. *Typical data orchestration flow in data analytics and engineering*

Here are key aspects to understand about modern data orchestration:

- **Data Integration and ETL:** Data integration remains a fundamental component of data orchestration. It involves combining data from disparate sources, such as databases, cloud services, and third-party APIs, into a unified and consistent format. Extract, transform, load (ETL) processes are commonly employed to extract data from source systems, apply transformations or cleansing, and load it into target systems.

- **Data Pipelines:** Data pipelines provide a structured and automated way to process and move data from source to destination. A data pipeline typically consists of a series of interconnected steps that perform data transformations, enrichment, and validation. Modern data pipeline solutions often leverage technologies like Apache Kafka, Apache Airflow, or cloud-based services such as AWS Glue, Google Cloud Dataflow, or Azure Data Factory.

- **Event-Driven Architectures:** Event-driven architectures have gained popularity in data orchestration. Instead of relying solely on batch processing, event-driven architectures enable real-time data processing by reacting to events or changes in the data ecosystem. Events, such as data updates or system notifications, trigger actions and workflows, allowing for immediate data processing, analytics, and decision-making.

- **Stream Processing:** Stream processing focuses on analyzing and processing continuous streams of data in real-time. It involves handling data in motion, enabling organizations to extract insights, perform real-time analytics, and trigger actions based on the data flow. Technologies like Apache Kafka, Apache Flink, and Apache Spark Streaming are commonly used for stream processing.

- **Data Governance and Metadata Management:** Modern data orchestration also emphasizes data governance and metadata management. Data governance ensures that data is properly managed, protected, and compliant with regulations. Metadata management involves capturing and organizing metadata, which provides valuable context and lineage information about the data, facilitating data discovery, understanding, and lineage tracking.

- **Cloud-Based Data Orchestration:** Cloud computing platforms offer robust infrastructure and services for data orchestration. Organizations can leverage cloud-based solutions to store data, process it at scale, and access various data-related services, such as data lakes, data warehouses, serverless computing, and managed ETL/ELT services. Cloud platforms also provide scalability, flexibility, and cost-efficiency for data orchestration workflows.

- **Automation and Workflow Orchestration:** Automation plays a vital role in modern data orchestration. Workflow orchestration tools, such as Apache Airflow, Luigi, or commercial offerings like AWS Step Functions or Azure Logic Apps, allow organizations to define, schedule, and execute complex data workflows. These tools enable task dependencies, error handling, retries, and monitoring, providing end-to-end control and visibility over data processing pipelines.

- **Data Quality and DataOps:** Data quality is a critical aspect of modern data orchestration. Organizations focus on ensuring data accuracy, consistency, completeness, and timeliness throughout the data lifecycle. DataOps practices, which combine data engineering, DevOps, and Agile methodologies, aim to streamline and automate data-related processes, improve collaboration between teams, and enhance data quality.

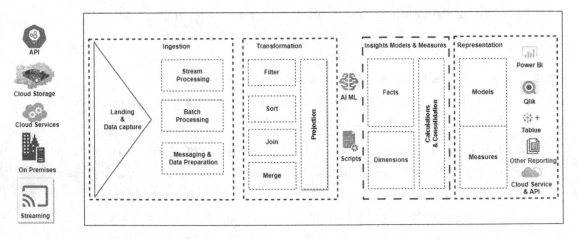

Figure 5-3. *A generic, well-orchestrated data engineering and analytics activity*

A well-orchestrated data engineering model for modern data engineering involves key components and processes (Figure 5-3). It begins with data ingestion, where data from various sources, such as databases, APIs, streaming platforms, or external files, is collected and transformed using ETL processes to ensure quality and consistency. The ingested data is then stored in suitable systems, like relational databases, data lakes, or distributed file systems. Next, data processing takes place, where the ingested data is transformed, cleansed, and enriched using frameworks like Apache Spark or SQL-based transformations. They are further segregated into models and measures, sometimes using OLAP or tabular fact and dimensions to be further served to analytic platforms such as power BI for business-critical reporting.

Data orchestration is crucial for managing and scheduling workflows, thus ensuring seamless data flow. Data quality and governance processes are implemented to validate, handle anomalies, and maintain compliance with regulations. Data integration techniques bring together data from different sources for a unified view, while data security measures protect sensitive information. Finally, the processed data is delivered to end users or downstream applications through various means, such as data pipelines, reports, APIs, or interactive dashboards. Flexibility, scalability, and automation are essential considerations in designing an effective data engineering model.

One of the key aspects to grasp in data orchestration is the cyclical nature of activities that occur across data layers. These cycles of activity play a crucial role in determining the data processing layers involved in the storage and processing of data, whether it is stored permanently or temporarily.

Data processing layers and their transformation in the ETL (extract, transform, load) orchestration process play a crucial role in data management and analysis. These layers, such as work area staging, main, OLAP (online analytical processing), landing, bronze, gold, silver, and zones, enable efficient data processing, organization, and optimization.

The evolution of data processing layers has had a significant impact on data orchestration pipelines and the ETL (extract, transform, load) process. Over time, these layers have become more sophisticated and specialized, enabling improved data processing, scalability, and flexibility.

Evolution of Data Orchestration

In traditional ETL processes, the primary layers consisted of extraction, transformation, and loading, forming a linear and sequential flow. Data was extracted from source systems, transformed to meet specific requirements, and loaded into a target system or data warehouse.

However, these traditional layers had limited flexibility and scalability. To address these shortcomings, the data staging layer was introduced. This dedicated space allowed for temporary data storage and preparation, enabling data validation, cleansing, and transformation before moving to the next processing stage.

The staging layer's enhanced data quality provided better error handling and recovery and paved the way for more advanced data processing. As data complexity grew, the need for a dedicated data processing and integration layer emerged. This layer focused on tasks like data transformation, enrichment, aggregation, and integration from multiple sources. It incorporated business rules, complex calculations, and data quality checks, enabling more sophisticated data manipulation and preparation.

With the rise of data warehousing and OLAP technologies, the data processing layers evolved further. The data warehousing and OLAP layer supported multidimensional analysis and faster querying, utilizing optimized structures for analytical processing. These layers facilitated complex reporting and ad-hoc analysis, empowering organizations with valuable insights.

The advent of big data and data lakes introduced a new layer specifically designed for storing and processing massive volumes of structured and unstructured data. Data lakes served as repositories for raw and unprocessed data, facilitating iterative and exploratory data processing. This layer enabled data discovery, experimentation, and analytics on diverse datasets, opening doors to new possibilities.

In modern data processing architectures, multiple refinement stages are often included, such as landing, bronze, silver, and gold layers. Each refinement layer represents a different level of data processing, refinement, and aggregation, adding value to the data and providing varying levels of granularity for different user needs. These refinement layers enable efficient data organization, data governance, and improved performance in downstream analysis, ultimately empowering organizations to extract valuable insights from their data.

The modern data processing architecture has made data orchestration efficient and effective with better speed, security, and governance. Here is the brief on the key impacts of modern data processing architecture on data orchestration and ETL:

- **Scalability:** The evolution of data processing layers has enhanced the scalability of data orchestration pipelines. The modular structure and specialized layers allow for distributed processing, parallelism, and the ability to handle large volumes of data efficiently.

- **Flexibility:** Advanced data processing layers provide flexibility in handling diverse data sources, formats, and requirements. The modular design allows for the addition, modification, or removal of specific layers as per changing business needs. This flexibility enables organizations to adapt their ETL pipelines to evolving data landscapes.

- **Performance Optimization:** With specialized layers, data orchestration pipelines can optimize performance at each stage. The separation of data transformation, integration, aggregation, and refinement allows for parallel execution, selective processing, and efficient resource utilization. It leads to improved data processing speed and reduced time to insight.

- **Data Quality and Governance:** The inclusion of data staging layers and refinement layers enhances data quality, consistency, and governance. Staging areas allow for data validation and cleansing, reducing the risk of erroneous or incomplete data entering downstream processes. Refinement layers ensure data accuracy, integrity, and adherence to business rules.

- **Advanced Analytics:** The availability of data warehousing, OLAP, and Big Data layers enables more advanced analytics capabilities. These layers support complex analytical queries, multidimensional analysis, and integration with machine learning and AI algorithms. They facilitate data-driven decision-making and insight generation.

Data Orchestration Layers

The amount of data orchestration required also depends on the needs of the data processing layers, and it's important to briefly understand each layer and its role in the orchestration and underlying ETL processes.

Here's a breakdown of the importance of each data layer and its role in the ETL flows and process:

- **Work area staging:** The staging area is used to temporarily store data before it undergoes further processing. It allows for data validation, cleansing, and transformation activities, ensuring data quality and integrity. This layer is essential for preparing data for subsequent stages.

- **Main layer:** The main layer typically serves as the central processing hub where data transformations and aggregations take place. It may involve joining multiple data sources, applying complex business rules, and performing calculations. The main layer is responsible for preparing the data for analytical processing.

- **Landing, bronze, gold, and silver layers:** These layers represent different stages of data refinement and organization in a data lake or data warehouse environment. The landing layer receives raw, unprocessed data from various sources. The bronze layer involves the initial cleansing and transformation of data, ensuring its accuracy and consistency. The gold layer further refines the data, applying additional business logic and calculations. The silver layer represents highly processed and aggregated data, ready for consumption by end users or downstream systems. Each layer adds value and structure to the data as it progresses through the ETL pipeline.

- **OLAP layer:** OLAP is designed for efficient data retrieval and analysis. It organizes data in a multidimensional format, enabling fast querying and slicing-and-dicing capabilities. The OLAP layer optimizes data structures and indexes to facilitate interactive and ad-hoc analysis.

Data Movement Optimization: OneLake Data and Its Impact on Modern Data Orchestration

One of the heavyweight tasks in data orchestration is around data movement through data pipelines. With the optimization of zones and layers on cloud data platforms, the new data architecture guidance emphasizes minimizing data movement across the platform. The goal is to reduce unnecessary data transfers and duplication, thus optimizing costs and improving overall data processing efficiency.

This approach helps optimize costs by reducing network bandwidth consumption and data transfer fees associated with moving large volumes of data. It also minimizes the risk of data loss, corruption, or inconsistencies that can occur during the transfer process.

Additionally, by keeping data in its original location or minimizing unnecessary duplication, organizations can simplify data management processes. This includes tracking data lineage, maintaining data governance, and ensuring compliance with data protection regulations.

A Strong Emphasis on Minimizing Data Duplicity

Overall, the trend of minimizing data movement aligns with the need for cost optimization, data efficiency, and streamlined data workflows in modern data architectures on cloud platforms. By leveraging the appropriate zone and layering strategies, organizations can achieve these benefits and optimize their data processing pipelines.

Zones (OneLake data or delta lake) are another advancement in data processing layers that refers to logical partitions or containers within a data lake or data storage system. They provide segregation and organization of data based on different criteria, such as data source, data type, or data ownership. Microsoft Fabric supports the use of OneLake and delta lakes as storage mechanisms for efficiently managing data zones.

By organizing data into different zones or layers based on its processing status and level of refinement, organizations can limit data movement to only when necessary. The concept of zones, such as landing zones, bronze/silver/gold layers, or trusted zones, allows for incremental data processing and refinement without requiring data to be moved between different storage locations, as well as effective management of data governance and security.

With the advancement of data architecture on cloud platforms, there is a growing emphasis on minimizing data movement. This approach aims to optimize costs and enhance speed in data processing, delivery, and presentation. Cloud platforms like Databricks and the newly introduced Microsoft Fabric support the concept of a unified data lake platform to achieve these goals.

By utilizing a single shared compute layer across services, such as Azure Synapse Analytics, Azure Data Factory, and Power BI, the recently introduced Microsoft Fabric (in preview at the time of writing this book) enables efficient utilization of computational resources. This shared compute layer eliminates the need to move data between different layers or services, reducing costs associated with data replication and transfer.

185

Furthermore, Microsoft Fabric introduces the concept of linked data sources, allowing the platform to reference data stored in multiple locations, such as Amazon S3, Google Cloud Storage, local servers, or Teams. This capability enables seamless access to data across different platforms as if they were all part of a single data platform. It eliminates the need for copying data from one layer to another, streamlining data orchestration, ETL processes, and pipelines.

Modern data orchestration relies on multiple concepts that work together in data integration to facilitate the acquisition, processing, storage, and delivery of data. Some of the key concepts depend on understanding ETL, ELT, data pipelines, and workflows. Before delving deeper into data integration and data pipelines, let's explore these major concepts, their origins, and their current usage:

- ETL and ELT are data integration approaches where ETL involves extracting data, transforming it, and then loading it into a target system, while ELT involves extracting data, loading it into a target system, and then performing transformations within the target system. ETL gained popularity in the early days of data integration for data warehousing and business intelligence, but it faced challenges with scalability and real-time processing. ELT emerged as a response to these challenges, leveraging distributed processing frameworks and cloud-based data repositories. Modern data integration platforms and services offer both ETL and ELT capabilities, and hybrid approaches combining elements of both are also common.

- *Data pipeline* refers to a sequence of steps that move and process data from source to target systems. It includes data extraction, transformation, and loading, and can involve various components and technologies, such as batch processing or stream processing frameworks. Data pipelines ensure the smooth flow of data and enable real-time or near-real-time processing.

- *Workflow* is a term used to describe the sequence of tasks or actions involved in a data integration or processing process. It defines the logical order in which the steps of a data pipeline or data integration process are executed. Workflows can be designed using visual interfaces or programming languages, and they help automate and manage complex data integration processes. Workflows can include data transformations, dependencies, error handling, and scheduling to ensure the efficient execution of the data integration tasks.

In summary, modern data orchestration encompasses data integration, pipelines, event-driven architectures, stream processing, cloud-based solutions, automation, and data governance. It emphasizes real-time processing, scalability, data quality, and automation to enable organizations to leverage their data assets effectively for insights, decision-making, and business outcomes, letting us understand it better through diving into data integration, data pipelines, ETL, supporting tools, and use cases.

Data Integration

Data integration is the process of combining data from multiple sources and merging it into a unified and coherent view. It involves gathering data from various systems, databases, files, or applications, regardless of their format, structure, or location, and transforming it into a standardized and consistent format. The goal of data integration is to create a consolidated and comprehensive dataset that can be used for analysis, reporting, and decision-making.

Data integration involves several steps, including data extraction, data transformation, and data loading. In the extraction phase, data is collected from different sources using various methods, such as direct connections, APIs, file transfers, or data replication. The extracted data is then transformed by cleaning, validating, and structuring it to ensure consistency and accuracy. This may involve performing data quality checks, resolving inconsistencies, and standardizing data formats. Finally, the transformed data is loaded into a central repository, such as a data warehouse or a data lake, where it can be accessed, queried, and analyzed.

Data integration is essential because organizations often have data stored in different systems or departments, making it difficult to gain a holistic view of their data assets. By integrating data, businesses can break down data silos, eliminate duplicate or redundant information, and enable a comprehensive analysis of their operations, customers, and performance. It provides a unified view of data, enabling organizations to make informed decisions, identify trends, and uncover valuable insights.

In the early days of data integration, manual methods such as data entry, file transfers, and manual data transformations were prevalent. These approaches were time-consuming, error-prone, and not scalable. Data integration has evolved significantly over the years to address the increasing complexity and diversity of data sources and systems. There are various approaches to data integration, including manual data entry, custom scripting, and the use of specialized data integration tools or platforms. These tools often provide features such as data mapping, data transformation, data cleansing, and data synchronization, which streamline the integration process and automate repetitive tasks.

With the rise of relational databases and structured data, batch processing emerged as a common data integration technique. It involved extracting data from source systems, transforming it, and loading it into a target system in batches. Batch processing was suitable for scenarios where real-time data integration was not necessary.

Middleware and ETL Tools

The advent of middleware and extract, transform, load (ETL) tools brought significant advancements in data integration. Middleware technologies, like message-oriented middleware (MOM), enabled asynchronous communication between systems, facilitating data exchange. ETL tools automated the process of extracting data from source systems, applying transformations, and loading it into target systems.

Middleware and ETL tools widely used include the following:

- **IBM WebSphere MQ:** This is a messaging middleware that enables communication between various applications and systems by facilitating the reliable exchange of messages.

- **Oracle Fusion Middleware:** This middleware platform from Oracle offers a range of tools and services for developing, deploying, and integrating enterprise applications. It includes components like Oracle SOA Suite, Oracle Service Bus, and Oracle BPEL Process Manager.

- **MuleSoft Anypoint Platform:** MuleSoft provides a comprehensive integration platform that includes Anypoint Runtime Manager and Anypoint Studio. It allows organizations to connect and integrate applications, data, and devices across different systems and APIs.

- **Apache Kafka:** Kafka is a distributed messaging system that acts as a publish-subscribe platform, providing high-throughput, fault-tolerant messaging between applications. It is widely used for building real-time streaming data pipelines.

ETL Tools include the following:

- **Informatica PowerCenter:** PowerCenter is a popular ETL tool that enables organizations to extract data from various sources, transform it based on business rules, and load it into target systems. It offers a visual interface for designing and managing ETL workflows.

- **IBM Infosphere DataStage:** DataStage is an ETL tool provided by IBM that allows users to extract, transform, and load data from multiple sources into target systems. It supports complex data transformations and provides advanced data integration capabilities.

- **Microsoft SQL Server Integration Services (SSIS):** SSIS is a powerful ETL tool included with Microsoft SQL Server. It provides a visual development environment for designing ETL workflows and supports various data integration tasks.

- **Talend Data Integration:** Talend offers a comprehensive data integration platform that includes Talend Open Studio and Talend Data Management Platform. It supports ETL processes, data quality management, and data governance.

These examples represent a subset of the wide range of middleware and ETL tools available in the market. Each tool has its own set of features and capabilities, allowing organizations to choose the one that best fits their specific integration and data processing requirements.

Enterprise Application Integration (EAI)

Enterprise application integration (EAI) emerged as a comprehensive approach to data integration. It aimed to integrate various enterprise applications and systems, such as ERP, CRM, and legacy systems, by providing a middleware layer and standardized interfaces. EAI solutions enabled seamless data sharing and process coordination across different applications.

EAI tools include the following:

- **IBM Integration Bus:** Formerly known as IBM WebSphere Message Broker, IBM Integration Bus is an EAI tool that enables the integration of diverse applications and data sources. It provides a flexible and scalable platform for message transformation, routing, and data mapping.

- **MuleSoft Anypoint Platform:** MuleSoft's Anypoint Platform offers EAI capabilities through components like Anypoint Studio and Anypoint Connectors. It allows organizations to connect and integrate applications, systems, and APIs, and provides features for data mapping, transformation, and orchestration.

- **Oracle Fusion Middleware:** Oracle's Fusion Middleware platform includes various tools and technologies for enterprise application integration, such as Oracle Service Bus, Oracle BPEL Process Manager, and Oracle SOA Suite. It enables organizations to integrate applications, services, and processes across different systems.

- **SAP NetWeaver Process Integration (PI):** SAP PI is an EAI tool provided by SAP that facilitates the integration of SAP and non-SAP applications. It offers features for message routing, transformation, and protocol conversion, and supports various communication protocols and standards.

- **TIBCO ActiveMatrix BusinessWorks:** TIBCO's ActiveMatrix BusinessWorks is an EAI platform that allows organizations to integrate applications, services, and data sources. It provides a graphical interface for designing and implementing integration processes and supports a wide range of connectivity options.

- **Dell Boomi:** Boomi, a part of Dell Technologies, offers a cloud-based EAI platform that enables organizations to connect and integrate applications, data sources, and devices. It provides features for data mapping, transformation, and workflow automation.

Service-Oriented Architecture (SOA)

Service-oriented architecture (SOA) brought a new paradigm to data integration. SOA allowed systems to expose their functionalities as services, which could be accessed and integrated by other systems through standardized interfaces (e.g., SOAP or REST). This approach enabled greater flexibility and reusability in integrating diverse systems and applications.

There are several tools available that can support the implementation and management of a service-oriented architecture (SOA). Here are some examples:

- **Apache Axis:** Axis is a widely used open-source tool for building web services and implementing SOA. It supports various protocols and standards, including SOAP and WSDL, and provides features like message routing, security, and interoperability.

- **Oracle Service Bus:** Oracle Service Bus is an enterprise-grade tool that facilitates the development, management, and integration of services in an SOA environment. It provides capabilities for service mediation, transformation, and routing, as well as message transformation and protocol conversion.

- **IBM Integration Bus (formerly IBM WebSphere Message Broker):** IBM Integration Bus is a powerful integration tool that supports the implementation of SOA and EAI solutions. It provides features for message transformation, routing, and protocol mediation, along with support for various messaging protocols.

- **MuleSoft Anypoint Platform:** Anypoint Platform by MuleSoft offers tools and capabilities for implementing SOA and API-based integrations. It includes Anypoint Studio for designing and building services, Anypoint Exchange for discovering and sharing APIs, and Anypoint Runtime Manager for managing and monitoring services.

- **WSO2 Enterprise Integrator:** WSO2 Enterprise Integrator is an open-source integration platform that supports building and managing services in an SOA environment. It provides features like message transformation, routing, and security, along with support for various integration patterns and protocols.

- **Microsoft Azure Service Fabric:** Azure Service Fabric is a distributed systems platform that can be used for building microservices-based architectures. It provides tools and services for managing and deploying services, as well as features like load balancing, scaling, and monitoring.

These tools offer features and functionalities that can simplify the development, deployment, and management of services in an SOA environment. The choice of tool depends on factors such as the specific requirements of the project, the technology stack being used, and the level of support needed from the vendor or open-source community.

Data Warehousing

Data warehousing became popular as a means of integrating and consolidating data from various sources into a centralized repository. Data was extracted, transformed, and loaded into a data warehouse, where it could be analyzed and accessed by business intelligence (BI) tools. Data warehousing facilitated reporting, analytics, and decision-making based on integrated data.

There are several popular tools and platforms available for data warehousing that facilitate the design, development, and management of data warehouse environments. Here are some examples:

- **Amazon Redshift:** Redshift is a fully managed data warehousing service provided by Amazon Web Services (AWS). It is designed for high-performance analytics and offers columnar storage, parallel query execution, and integration with other AWS services.

- **Snowflake:** Snowflake is a cloud-based data warehousing platform known for its elasticity and scalability. It separates compute and storage, allowing users to scale resources independently. It offers features like automatic optimization, near-zero maintenance, and support for structured and semi-structured data.

- **Microsoft Azure Synapse Analytics:** Formerly known as Azure SQL Data Warehouse, Azure Synapse Analytics is a cloud-based analytics service that combines data warehousing, Big Data integration, and data integration capabilities. It integrates with other Azure services and provides powerful querying and analytics capabilities.

- **Google BigQuery:** BigQuery is a fully managed serverless data warehouse provided by Google Cloud Platform (GCP). It offers high scalability, fast query execution, and seamless integration with other GCP services. BigQuery supports standard SQL and has built-in machine learning capabilities.

- **Oracle Autonomous Data Warehouse:** Oracle's Autonomous Data Warehouse is a cloud-based data warehousing service that uses artificial intelligence and machine learning to automate various management tasks. It provides high-performance, self-tuning, and self-securing capabilities.

- **Teradata Vantage:** Teradata Vantage is an advanced analytics platform that includes data warehousing capabilities. It provides scalable parallel processing and advanced analytics functions, and supports hybrid cloud environments.

- **Delta Lake:** A delta lake is an open-source storage layer built on top of Apache Spark that provides data warehousing capabilities. It offers ACID (Atomicity, Consistency, Isolation, Durability) transactions, schema enforcement, and data reliability for both batch and streaming data. Delta lakes enable you to build data pipelines with structured and semi-structured data, ensuring data integrity and consistency.

These tools offer a range of features and capabilities for data warehousing, including data storage, data management, query optimization, scalability, and integration with other systems. The choice of tool depends on specific requirements, such as the scale of data, performance needs, integration needs, and cloud provider preferences.

Real-Time and Streaming Data Integration

The need for real-time data integration emerged with the proliferation of real-time and streaming data sources. Technologies like change data capture (CDC) and message queues enabled the capture and integration of data changes as they occurred. Stream processing frameworks and event-driven architectures facilitated the real-time processing and integration of streaming data from sources like IoT devices, social media, and sensor networks.

Real-time and streaming data integration tools are designed to process and integrate data as it is generated in real-time or near real-time. These tools enable organizations to ingest, process, and analyze streaming data from various sources. Here are some examples:

- **Apache Kafka:** Kafka is a distributed streaming platform that provides high-throughput, fault-tolerant messaging. It allows for real-time data ingestion and processing by enabling the publishing, subscribing, and processing of streams of records in a fault-tolerant manner.

- **Confluent Platform:** Confluent Platform builds on top of Apache Kafka and provides additional enterprise features for real-time data integration. It offers features such as schema management, connectors for various data sources, and stream processing capabilities through Apache Kafka Streams.

- **Apache Flink:** Flink is a powerful stream processing framework that can process and analyze streaming data in real-time. It supports event-time processing and fault tolerance, and offers APIs for building complex streaming data pipelines.

- **Apache NiFi:** NiFi is an open-source data integration tool that supports real-time data ingestion, routing, and transformation. It provides a visual interface for designing data flows and supports streaming data processing with low-latency capabilities.

- **Amazon Kinesis:** Amazon Kinesis is a managed service by Amazon Web Services (AWS) for real-time data streaming and processing. It provides capabilities for ingesting, processing, and analyzing streaming data at scale. It offers services like Kinesis Data Streams, Kinesis Data Firehose, and Kinesis Data Analytics.

- **Google Cloud Dataflow:** Google Cloud Dataflow is a fully managed service for real-time data processing and batch processing. It provides a unified programming model and supports popular stream processing frameworks like Apache Beam.

- **Azure Stream Analytics:** Azure Stream Analytics is a fully managed real-time analytics service that makes it easy to process and analyze streaming data in real-time. It can be used to collect data from a variety of sources, such as sensors, applications, and social media, and then process and analyze that data in real-time to gain insights and make decisions.

- **Structured Streaming:** Databricks supports Apache Spark's Structured Streaming, a high-level streaming API built on Spark SQL. It enables you to write scalable, fault-tolerant stream processing applications. You can define streaming queries using dataframes and datasets, which seamlessly integrate with batch processing workflows.

- **Delta Live Tables:** Delta Live Tables is a feature in Databricks that provides an easy way to build real-time applications on top of Delta Lake. It offers abstractions and APIs for stream processing, enabling you to build and store data in delta tables underneath end-to-end streaming applications that leverage the reliability and scalability of delta lakes.

These tools are specifically designed to handle the challenges of real-time and streaming data integration, allowing organizations to process and analyze data as it flows in, enabling real-time insights and actions. The choice of tool depends on factors such as scalability requirements, integration capabilities, programming model preferences, and cloud platform preferences.

Cloud-Based Data Integration

Cloud computing has revolutionized data integration by offering scalable infrastructure and cloud-based integration platforms. Cloud-based data integration solutions provide capabilities such as data replication, data synchronization, and data virtualization, enabling seamless integration between on-premises and cloud-based systems.

There are several cloud-based data integration tools available that provide seamless integration and data management in cloud environments. Some popular examples include:

- **AWS Glue:** It is a fully managed extract, transform, and load (ETL) service provided by Amazon Web Services (AWS). It enables users to prepare and transform data for analytics, and it integrates well with other AWS services.

- **Microsoft Azure Data Factory:** This cloud-based data integration service by Microsoft Azure allows users to create data-driven workflows to orchestrate and automate data movement and transformation. It supports a wide range of data sources and destinations.

- **Google Cloud Data Fusion:** It is a fully managed data integration service on Google Cloud Platform (GCP) that simplifies the process of building and managing ETL pipelines. It provides a visual interface for designing data flows and supports integration with various data sources.

- **Informatica Cloud:** Informatica offers a cloud-based data integration platform that enables users to integrate and manage data across on-premises and cloud environments. It provides features like data mapping, transformation, and data quality management.

- **SnapLogic:** SnapLogic is a cloud-based integration platform that allows users to connect and integrate various data sources, applications, and APIs. It offers a visual interface for designing data pipelines and supports real-time data integration.

These cloud-based data integration tools provide scalable and flexible solutions for managing data integration processes in cloud environments, enabling organizations to leverage the benefits of cloud computing for their data integration needs.

Data Integration for Big Data and NoSQL

The emergence of Big Data and NoSQL technologies posed new challenges for data integration. Traditional approaches struggled to handle the volume, variety, and velocity of Big Data. New techniques, like Big Data integration platforms and data lakes, were developed to enable the integration of structured, semi-structured, and unstructured data from diverse sources.

When it comes to data integration for Big Data and NoSQL environments, there are several tools available that can help you streamline the process. Apart from Apache Kafka and Apache NiFi already described, some of the other tools that may be considered are the following:

- **Apache Spark and Databricks:** Spark is a powerful distributed processing engine that includes libraries for various tasks, including data integration. It provides Spark SQL, which allows you to query and manipulate structured and semi-structured data from different sources, including NoSQL databases.

- **Talend:** Talend is a comprehensive data integration platform that supports Big Data and NoSQL integration. It provides a visual interface for designing data integration workflows, including connectors for popular NoSQL databases like MongoDB, Cassandra, and HBase.

- **Pentaho Data Integration:** Pentaho Data Integration (PDI), also known as Kettle, is an open-source ETL (extract, transform, load) tool. It offers a graphical environment for building data integration processes and supports integration with various Big Data platforms and NoSQL databases.

- **Apache Sqoop:** Sqoop is a command-line tool specifically designed for efficiently transferring bulk data between Apache Hadoop and structured data stores, such as relational databases. It can be used to integrate data from relational databases to NoSQL databases in a Hadoop ecosystem.

- **StreamSets:** StreamSets is a modern data integration platform that focuses on real-time data movement and integration. It offers a visual interface for designing data pipelines and supports integration with various Big Data technologies and NoSQL databases.

Self-Service Data Integration

Modern data integration solutions often emphasize self-service capabilities that empower business users and data analysts to perform data integration tasks without heavy reliance on IT teams. Self-service data integration tools provide intuitive interfaces, visual data mapping, and pre-built connectors to simplify and accelerate the integration process.

The following are some of the examples of a self-service data integration tool:

- **Apache NiFi:** NiFi is an open-source data integration and workflow automation tool that allows users to design and execute data flows across various systems. It provides a web-based interface with a drag-and-drop visual interface, making it easy for users to create and manage data integration processes without extensive coding knowledge.

- Another example is **Talend Open Studio**, which is a comprehensive data integration platform that offers a graphical interface for designing and deploying data integration workflows. It supports various data integration tasks, such as data extraction, transformation, and loading (ETL), as well as data quality management.

The following are a few of the other newly introduced tools that are getting popular:

- **Hevo Data** is a cloud-based data integration platform that allows users to connect to and integrate data from over 149 data sources, including databases, cloud storage, Software as a Service (SaaS) applications, and more. Hevo Data offers a drag-and-drop interface that makes it easy to create data pipelines without writing any code.

- **SnapLogic** is another cloud-based data integration platform that offers a visual drag-and-drop interface for creating data pipelines. SnapLogic also offers a wide range of pre-built connectors for popular data sources, making it easy to connect to your data quickly.

- **Jitterbit** is a self-service data integration platform that offers a variety of features, including data mapping, data transformation, and data quality checking. Jitterbit also offers a wide range of pre-built connectors for popular data sources.

- **Celigo** is a self-service data integration platform that focuses on integrating data from SaaS applications. Celigo offers a variety of pre-built connectors for popular SaaS applications, as well as a drag-and-drop interface for creating data pipelines.

- **Zapier** is a no-code data integration platform that allows users to connect to and automate workflows between different apps and services. Zapier offers a wide range of pre-built integrations, as well as a visual interface for creating custom integrations.

One of the other tools to be understood is **Microsoft Fabric**, as it's a newly built end-to-end data analytics tool that is more like an ecosystem of data processing, storage, and sharing rather than just a data integration tool. These self-service data integration tools empower users to independently integrate data from multiple sources, apply transformations, and load it into target systems, all without relying heavily on IT or development teams.

Use Cases

In current usage, data integration is employed in various scenarios, including the following:

- **Business Intelligence and Analytics:** Data integration enables the consolidation of data from multiple sources to create a unified view for analysis, reporting, and decision-making.

- **Data Migration and System Consolidation:** When organizations undergo system upgrades, mergers, or acquisitions, data integration is crucial for migrating data from legacy systems to new platforms or consolidating data from multiple systems into a single unified system.

- **Data Governance and Master Data Management (MDM):** Data integration is essential for establishing data governance practices and implementing master data management strategies. It ensures data consistency, accuracy, and reliability by integrating and harmonizing data across different systems and applications.

- **Data Sharing and Collaboration:** Data integration enables seamless sharing and collaboration of data between different departments, teams, or partner organizations. It allows for real-time data exchange and synchronization, facilitating collaboration on shared datasets or joint projects.

- **Data Integration in the Cloud:** Cloud-based data integration solutions are widely used to integrate data across on-premises systems, cloud-based applications, and Software-as-a-Service (SaaS) platforms. It provides scalability, flexibility, and cost-efficiency, allowing organizations to leverage cloud-based infrastructure and services for data integration.

- **Real-time Data Integration and Stream Processing:** With the increasing availability of streaming data sources, real-time data integration and stream processing techniques are used to capture, process, and integrate data as it flows in real-time. This enables organizations to react quickly to events, make real-time decisions, and perform continuous analytics.

- **Internet of Things (IOT) Data Integration:** IOT devices generate vast amounts of data, and data integration is crucial for analyzing this data in real-time. Data integration techniques are employed to connect IoT devices, capture sensor data, and integrate it with other enterprise systems for real-time monitoring, predictive maintenance, and operational optimization.

- **Data Integration for Data Lakes and Big Data:** Data integration is used to ingest, process, and integrate diverse data sources into data lakes and Big Data platforms. It enables organizations to combine structured and unstructured data from various sources for advanced analytics, machine learning, and data exploration.

- **Data Integration for Data Science and AI:** Data integration plays a vital role in data science and AI initiatives by integrating and preparing data for model training, feature engineering, and predictive analytics. It involves integrating data from different sources, cleaning and transforming data, and creating curated datasets for analysis and modeling.

In summary, data integration has evolved to accommodate the complexities of modern data ecosystems. It is employed in various domains, including business intelligence, data migration, data governance, cloud-based integration, real-time processing, IOT, big data, and AI. These applications enable organizations to unlock the value of their data, make informed decisions, and drive business success.

Data Pipelines

Data pipelines are a series of interconnected steps that move data from one system to another, transforming it along the way to make it suitable for specific use cases. These pipelines can be built using a variety of technologies, including extract, transform, load (ETL) tools; data integration platforms; and cloud-based services, and they form an important component of any data orchestration.

The primary goal of data pipelines is to automate the movement of data, reducing the need for manual intervention and improving the speed and accuracy of data processing. Data pipelines can be used for a wide range of purposes, including data warehousing, data migration, data transformation, and data synchronization.

In today's digital landscape, data has become the lifeblood of businesses across industries. Organizations are collecting vast amounts of data from various sources, including customer interactions, transactions, sensors, social media, and more. This influx of data provides immense opportunities for extracting valuable insights and driving data-driven decision-making. However, it also presents significant challenges in terms of managing, processing, and deriving meaningful insights from this data.

Data pipelines have emerged as a crucial solution to address these challenges. A data pipeline is a systematic and automated approach to managing the flow of data from its source to its destination. It involves a series of steps, or stages, where data is ingested, processed, transformed, stored, and ultimately delivered to the intended recipients or systems. By establishing a well-designed data pipeline, organizations can streamline and accelerate their data processing workflows, enabling them to extract actionable insights and make informed decisions in a timely manner.

The significance of data pipelines lies in their ability to efficiently handle large volumes of data. With the explosion of data in recent years, organizations are faced with the daunting task of processing and analyzing massive datasets. Traditional manual data processing methods are no longer sufficient to meet the demands of today's data-driven world. Data pipelines provide a scalable and automated approach to handle these data volumes, ensuring that data processing is efficient, accurate, and timely.

Furthermore, data pipelines enable organizations to standardize and automate their data workflows. Instead of relying on ad-hoc and manual processes, data pipelines provide a structured framework for data processing, ensuring consistency and repeatability. This standardization not only reduces the chances of errors and inconsistencies but also allows for more efficient collaboration among teams working with the data.

Another significant advantage of data pipelines is their capability to enable real-time and near-real-time analytics. Traditional batch processing methods often involve delays between data collection and analysis. However, with data pipelines, organizations can process data in real-time or near real-time, allowing for immediate insights and rapid decision-making. This is particularly valuable in domains such as finance, e-commerce, and IOT, where timely actions based on fresh data can have a significant impact on business outcomes.

Moreover, data pipelines facilitate data integration and consolidation. Organizations often have data spread across multiple systems, databases, and applications. Data pipelines provide a means to efficiently gather, transform, and consolidate data from disparate sources into a unified and consistent format. This integrated view of data allows organizations to derive comprehensive insights and make better-informed decisions based on a holistic understanding of their data.

At its core, a data pipeline consists of the following key components:

- **Data sources:** The data sources are the places where the data comes from. They can be internal systems, external sources, or a combination of both.

- **Data Ingestion:** This is the initial stage of the data pipeline where data is collected from its source systems or external providers. It involves extracting data from various sources, such as databases, APIs, files, streaming platforms, or IOT devices. Data ingestion processes should consider factors like data volume, velocity, variety, and quality to ensure the efficient and reliable acquisition of data.

- **Data Processing:** Once the data is ingested, it goes through various processing steps to transform, clean, and enrich it. This stage involves applying business rules, algorithms, or transformations to manipulate the data into a desired format or structure. Common processing tasks include filtering, aggregating, joining, validating, and normalizing the data. The goal is to prepare the data for further analysis and downstream consumption.

- **Data Transformation:** In this stage, the processed data is further transformed to meet specific requirements or standards. This may involve converting data types, encoding or decoding data, or performing complex calculations. Data transformation ensures that the data is in a consistent and usable format for subsequent stages or systems. Transformations can be performed using tools, programming languages, or specialized frameworks designed for data manipulation.

- **Data Storage:** After transformation, the data is stored in a persistent storage system, such as a data warehouse, data lake, or a database. The choice of storage depends on factors such as data volume, latency requirements, querying patterns, and cost considerations. Effective data storage design is crucial for data accessibility, scalability, and security. It often involves considerations like data partitioning, indexing, compression, and backup strategies.

- **Data Delivery:** The final stage of the data pipeline involves delivering the processed and stored data to the intended recipients or downstream systems. This may include generating reports, populating dashboards, pushing data to business intelligence tools, or providing data to other applications or services via APIs or data feeds. Data delivery should ensure the timely and accurate dissemination of data to support decision-making and enable actionable insights.

Throughout these stages, data pipeline orchestration and workflow management play a critical role. Orchestration involves defining the sequence and dependencies of the different stages and processes within the pipeline. Workflow management tools, such as Apache Airflow or Luigi, facilitate the scheduling, monitoring, and coordination of these processes, ensuring the smooth and efficient execution of the pipeline.

It's important to note that data pipelines can vary in complexity and scale depending on the organization's requirements. They can range from simple, linear pipelines with a few stages to complex, branching pipelines with parallel processing and conditional logic. The design and implementation of a data pipeline should be tailored to the specific use case, data sources, processing requirements, and desired outcomes (Figure 5-4).

The stages of a data pipeline are as follows:

- **Ingestion:** The data is collected from the data sources and loaded into the data pipeline.

- **Cleaning:** The data is cleaned to remove errors and inconsistencies.

- **Transformation:** The data is transformed into a format that is useful for analysis.

- **Storage:** The data is stored in a central location.

- **Analysis:** The data is analyzed to extract insights.

- **Delivery:** The data is delivered to users.

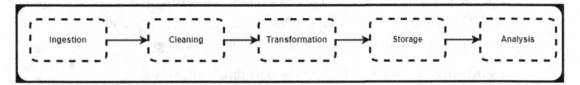

Figure 5-4. *Steps in a generic data pipeline*

Data Processing using Data Pipelines

There are two major types of data pipeline widely in use: batch and real-time data processing.

Batch processing is when data is collected over a period and processed all at once. This is typically done for large amounts of data that do not need to be processed in real-time. For example, a company might batch process their sales data once a month to generate reports.

Real-time processing is when data is processed as soon as it is received. This is typically done for data that needs to be acted on immediately, such as financial data or sensor data. For example, a company might use real-time processing to monitor their stock prices or to detect fraud.

The type of data processing that is used depends on the specific needs of the organization. For example, a company that needs to process large amounts of data might use batch processing, while a company that needs to process data in real-time might use real-time processing.

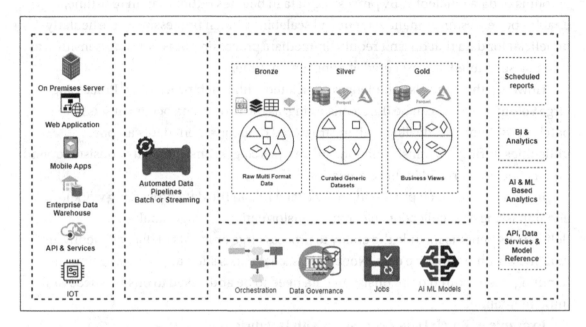

Figure 5-5. *A generic batch and stream-based data processing in a modern data warehouse*

Batch Processing in Detail

Batch processing is a key component of the data processing workflow, involving a series of stages from data collection to data delivery (Figure 5-5). The process begins with data collection, where data is gathered from various sources. Once collected, the data undergoes a data cleaning phase to eliminate errors and inconsistencies, ensuring its reliability for further analysis. The next step is data transformation, where the data is formatted and structured in a way that is suitable for analysis, making it easier to extract meaningful insights.

After transformation, the data is stored in a centralized location, such as a database or data warehouse, facilitating easy access and retrieval. Subsequently, data analysis techniques are applied to extract valuable insights and patterns from the data, supporting decision-making and informing business strategies. Finally, the processed data is delivered to the intended users or stakeholders, usually in the form of reports, dashboards, or visualizations.

One of the notable advantages of batch processing is its ability to handle large amounts of data efficiently. By processing data in batches rather than in real-time, it enables better resource management and scalability. Batch processing is particularly beneficial for data that doesn't require immediate processing or is not time-sensitive, as it can be scheduled and executed at a convenient time.

However, there are also challenges associated with batch processing. Processing large volumes of data can be time-consuming, as the processing occurs in sets or batches. Additionally, dealing with unstructured or inconsistent data can pose difficulties during the transformation and analysis stages. Ensuring data consistency and quality becomes crucial in these scenarios.

In conclusion, batch processing plays a vital role in the data processing workflow, encompassing data collection, cleaning, transformation, storage, analysis, and delivery. Its benefits include the ability to process large amounts of data efficiently and handle non-time-sensitive data. Nonetheless, challenges such as processing time and handling unstructured or inconsistent data need to be addressed to ensure successful implementation.

Example of Batch Data Processing with Databricks

Consider a retail company that receives sales data from multiple stores daily. To analyze this data, the company employs a batch data processing pipeline. The pipeline is designed to ingest the sales data from each store at the end of the day. The data is collected as CSV files, which are uploaded to a centralized storage system. The batch data pipeline is scheduled to process the data every night.

The pipeline starts by extracting the CSV files from the storage system and transforming them into a unified format suitable for analysis. This may involve merging, cleaning, and aggregating the data to obtain metrics such as total sales, top-selling products, and customer demographics. Once the transformation is complete, the processed data is loaded into a data warehouse or analytics database.

Analytics tools, such as SQL queries or business intelligence (BI) platforms, can then be used to query the data warehouse and generate reports or dashboards. For example, the retail company can analyze sales trends, identify popular products, and gain insights into customer behavior. This batch data processing pipeline provides valuable business insights daily, enabling data-driven decision-making.

In this use case, we will explore a scenario where batch processing of data is performed using CSV and flat files. The data will be processed and analyzed using Databricks, a cloud-based analytics platform, and stored in Blob storage.

Requirements:

- CSV and flat files containing structured data

- Databricks workspace and cluster provisioned

- Blob storage account for data storage

Steps:

Data Preparation:

- Identify the CSV and flat files that contain the data to be processed.

- Ensure that the files are stored in a location accessible to Databricks.

Databricks Setup:

- Create a Databricks workspace and provision a cluster with appropriate configurations and resources.

- Configure the cluster to have access to Blob storage.

Data Ingestion:

- Using Databricks, establish a connection to the Blob storage account.

- Write code in Databricks to read the CSV and flat files from Blob storage into Databricks' distributed file system (DBFS) or as Spark dataframes.

Data Transformation:

- Utilize the power of Spark and Databricks to perform necessary data transformations.

- Apply operations such as filtering, aggregations, joins, and any other required transformations to cleanse or prepare the data for analysis.

Data Analysis and Processing:

- Leverage Databricks' powerful analytics capabilities to perform batch processing on the transformed data.

- Use Spark SQL, DataFrame APIs, or Databricks notebooks to run queries, aggregations, or custom data processing operations.

Results Storage:

- Define a storage location within Blob storage to store the processed data.

- Write the transformed and processed data back to Blob storage in a suitable format, such as Parquet or CSV.

Data Validation and Quality Assurance:

- Perform data quality checks and validation on the processed data to ensure its accuracy and integrity.

- Compare the processed results with expected outcomes or predefined metrics to validate the batch processing pipeline.

Monitoring and Maintenance:

- Implement monitoring and alerting mechanisms to track the health and performance of the batch processing pipeline.

- Continuously monitor job statuses, data processing times, and resource utilization to ensure efficient execution.

Scheduled Execution:

- Set up a scheduled job or workflow to trigger the batch processing pipeline at predefined intervals.

- Define the frequency and timing based on the data refresh rate and business requirements.

Real-time Processing in Detail

Real-time processing is a crucial aspect of the data processing workflow, focusing on immediate data processing and delivery. The process begins with data collection, where data is gathered from various sources in real-time. Once collected, the data undergoes a data cleaning phase to eliminate errors and inconsistencies, ensuring its accuracy and reliability. The next step is data transformation, where the data is converted into a format that is suitable for real-time analysis, enabling prompt insights and actions.

After transformation, the data enters the data processing phase, where it is processed in real-time. This means that the data is acted upon immediately upon receipt, allowing for timely responses and decision-making. Finally, the processed data is delivered to the intended users or stakeholders in real-time, enabling them to take immediate action based on the insights derived from the data.

Real-time processing offers several benefits. It allows for data to be processed as soon as it is received, ensuring up-to-date and actionable information. It is particularly useful for data that requires immediate attention or action. Real-time processing also caters to data that is time sensitive, ensuring that it is analyzed and acted upon in a timely manner.

However, there are challenges associated with real-time processing. It can be expensive to implement and maintain the infrastructure and systems required for real-time processing. Scaling real-time processing to handle large volumes of data can also be challenging, as it requires robust and efficient resources. Additionally, ensuring the availability and reliability of real-time processing systems can be complex, as any downtime or interruptions can impact the timely processing and delivery of data.

In summary, real-time processing plays a vital role in the data processing workflow, emphasizing immediate data processing and delivery. Its benefits include prompt analysis and action based on up-to-date data, which is particularly useful for time-sensitive or critical information. Nevertheless, challenges such as cost, scalability, and system availability need to be addressed to ensure the effective implementation of real-time processing.

Example of Real-time Data Processing with Apache Kafka:

Consider a ride-sharing service that needs to track the real-time location of its drivers to optimize routing and improve customer service. In this scenario, a real-time data processing pipeline is employed. The pipeline continuously ingests and processes the driver location updates as they become available.

The ride-sharing service utilizes a messaging system, such as Apache Kafka, to receive real-time location events from drivers' mobile devices. The events are immediately processed by the pipeline as they arrive. The processing component of the pipeline may include filtering, enrichment, and aggregation operations.

For example, the pipeline can filter out events that are not relevant for analysis, enrich the events with additional information such as driver ratings or past trip history, and aggregate the data to calculate metrics like average driver speed or estimated time of arrival (ETA).

The processed real-time data can then be used to power various applications and services. For instance, the ride-sharing service can use this data to dynamically update driver positions on the customer-facing mobile app, optimize route calculations in real-time, or generate alerts if a driver deviates from the expected route.

Real-time data processing pipelines provide organizations with the ability to respond quickly to changing data, enabling immediate action and providing real-time insights that are essential for time-sensitive applications and services.

One of the ways to implement real-time processing is to design a data pipeline using tools like Apache Kafka, which involves several steps.

Here's a high-level overview of the process:

- **Identify Data Sources:** Determine the data sources you want to collect and analyze. These could be databases, logs, IOT devices, or any other system generating data.

- **Define Data Requirements:** Determine what data you need to collect and analyze from the identified sources. Define the data schema, formats, and any transformations required.

- **Install and Configure Apache Kafka:** Set up an Apache Kafka cluster to act as the backbone of your data pipeline. Install and configure Kafka brokers, Zookeeper ensemble (if required), and other necessary components.

- **Create Kafka Topics:** Define Kafka topics that represent different data streams or categories. Each topic can store related data that will be consumed by specific consumers or analytics applications.

- **Data Ingestion:** Develop data producers that will publish data to the Kafka topics. Depending on the data sources, you may need to build connectors or adapters to fetch data and publish it to Kafka.

- **Data Transformation:** If necessary, apply any required data transformations or enrichment before storing it in Kafka. For example, you may need to cleanse, aggregate, or enrich the data using tools like Apache Spark, Apache Flink, or Kafka Streams.

- **Data Storage:** Configure Kafka to persist data for a certain retention period or size limit. Ensure you have sufficient disk space and choose appropriate Kafka storage settings based on your data volume and retention requirements.

- **Data Consumption:** Develop data consumers that subscribe to the Kafka topics and process the incoming data. Consumers can perform various operations, such as real-time analytics, batch processing, or forwarding data to external systems.

- **Data Analysis:** Integrate analytics tools or frameworks like Apache Spark, Apache Flink, or Apache Storm to process and analyze the data consumed from Kafka. You can perform aggregations, complex queries, machine learning, or any other required analysis.

- **Data Storage and Visualization:** Depending on the output of your data analysis, you may need to store the results in a data store such as a database or a data warehouse. Additionally, visualize the analyzed data using tools like Apache Superset, Tableau, or custom dashboards.

- **Monitoring and Management:** Implement monitoring and alerting mechanisms to ensure the health and performance of your data pipeline. Monitor Kafka metrics, consumer lag, data throughput, and overall system performance. Utilize tools like Prometheus, Grafana, or custom monitoring solutions.

- **Scaling and Performance:** As your data volume and processing requirements grow, scale your Kafka cluster horizontally by adding more brokers, and fine-tune various Kafka configurations to optimize performance.

It's important to note that designing a data pipeline using Apache Kafka is a complex task, and the specifics will depend on your specific use case and requirements. It's recommended to consult the official Apache Kafka documentation and seek expert guidance when implementing a production-grade data pipeline.

Benefits and Advantages of Data Pipelines

Data pipelines offer numerous benefits and advantages that enable organizations to effectively manage and process their data. By leveraging data pipelines, organizations can unlock the full potential of their data assets and gain a competitive edge in the following ways:

- **Improved Data Processing Speed and Efficiency:** Data pipelines streamline the data processing workflow, automating repetitive tasks and reducing manual intervention. This leads to significant improvements in data processing speed and efficiency. By eliminating time-consuming manual processes, organizations can accelerate data ingestion, processing, and delivery, enabling faster insights and decision-making.

- **Scalability and Handling of Large Data Volumes:** With the exponential growth of data, organizations need scalable solutions to handle the increasing data volumes. Data pipelines provide a scalable architecture that can accommodate large amounts of data, ensuring efficient processing without compromising performance. They can handle data in various formats, such as structured, semi-structured, and unstructured, allowing organizations to process and analyze diverse data sources effectively.

- **Standardization and Automation of Data Workflows:** Data pipelines promote standardization and automation of data workflows, ensuring consistency and repeatability in data processing. By defining clear data pipeline stages, transformations, and validations, organizations can establish standardized processes for handling data. Automation reduces the risk of errors, improves data quality, and enhances productivity by eliminating manual intervention and enforcing predefined rules and best practices.

- **Enables Real-Time and Near-Real-Time Analytics:** Traditional batch processing methods often involve delays between data collection and analysis. Data pipelines enable real-time and near-real-time analytics by processing data as it arrives, allowing organizations to gain insights and make timely decisions. Real-time data processing is crucial in domains such as fraud detection, stock trading, IOT sensor data analysis, and customer engagement, where immediate action is required based on fresh data.

- **Facilitates Data Integration and Consolidation:** Organizations typically have data spread across multiple systems, databases, and applications. Data pipelines provide a mechanism for efficiently integrating and consolidating data from diverse sources into a unified view. This integration enables organizations to derive comprehensive insights, perform cross-system analysis, and make informed decisions based on a holistic understanding of their data.

- **Enhanced Data Quality and Consistency:** Data pipelines facilitate the implementation of data validation and cleansing techniques, improving data quality and consistency. By applying data quality checks, organizations can identify and address data anomalies, inconsistencies, and errors during the data processing stages. This ensures that downstream analytics and decision-making processes are based on accurate and reliable data.

- **Enables Advanced Analytics and Machine Learning:** Data pipelines play a critical role in enabling advanced analytics and machine learning initiatives. By providing a structured and automated process for data preparation and transformation, data pipelines ensure that data is the right format and quality for feeding into analytics models. This enables organizations to leverage machine learning algorithms, predictive analytics, and AI-driven insights to derive actionable intelligence from their data.

- **Cost Efficiency and Resource Optimization:** Data pipelines optimize resource utilization and reduce operational costs. By automating data processing tasks, organizations can minimize manual effort, streamline resource allocation, and maximize the utilization of computing resources. This helps to optimize costs associated with data storage, processing, and infrastructure, ensuring that resources are allocated efficiently based on actual data processing needs.

Common Use Cases for Data Pipelines

Data pipelines find applications in various industries and domains, enabling organizations to address specific data processing needs and derive valuable insights. Let's explore some common use cases where data pipelines play a pivotal role:

- **E-commerce Analytics and Customer Insights:** E-commerce businesses generate vast amounts of data, including customer interactions, website clicks, transactions, and inventory data. Data pipelines help collect, process, and analyze this data in real-time, providing valuable insights into customer behavior, preferences, and trends. These insights can be used for personalized marketing campaigns, targeted recommendations, inventory management, and fraud detection.

- **Internet of Things (IOT) Data Processing:** With the proliferation of IOT devices, organizations are collecting massive volumes of sensor data. Data pipelines are essential for handling and processing this continuous stream of data in real-time. They enable organizations to monitor and analyze IOT sensor data for predictive maintenance, anomaly detection, environmental monitoring, and optimizing operational efficiency.

- **Financial Data Processing and Risk Analysis:** Financial institutions deal with a vast amount of transactional and market data. Data pipelines streamline the processing and analysis of this data, enabling real-time monitoring of financial transactions, fraud detection, risk analysis, and compliance reporting. By leveraging data pipelines, financial organizations can make informed decisions, detect anomalies, and mitigate risks effectively.

- **Health Care Data Management and Analysis:** The health-care industry generates massive amounts of data, including patient records, medical imaging, sensor data, and clinical trial results. Data pipelines assist in collecting, integrating, and analyzing this data to support clinical research, patient monitoring, disease prediction, and population health management. Data pipelines can also enable interoperability among various health-care systems and facilitate secure data sharing.

- **Social Media Sentiment Analysis and Recommendation Engines:**
  Social media platforms generate vast amounts of user-generated
  content, opinions, and sentiments. Data pipelines play a critical role
  in collecting, processing, and analyzing this data to derive insights
  into customer sentiment, brand reputation, and social trends.
  Organizations can leverage these insights for sentiment analysis,
  social media marketing, personalized recommendations, and social
  listening.

- **Supply Chain Optimization:** Data pipelines are instrumental in
  optimizing supply chain operations by integrating data from various
  sources, such as inventory systems, logistics providers, and sales data.
  By collecting, processing, and analyzing this data, organizations can
  gain real-time visibility into their supply chain, optimize inventory
  levels, predict demand patterns, and improve overall supply chain
  efficiency.

- **Fraud Detection and Security Analytics:** Data pipelines are
  widely used in fraud detection and security analytics applications
  across industries. By integrating and processing data from multiple
  sources, such as transaction logs, access logs, and user behavior
  data, organizations can detect anomalies, identify potential security
  threats, and take proactive measures to mitigate risks.

- **Data Warehousing and Business Intelligence:** Data pipelines play
  a crucial role in populating data warehouses and enabling business
  intelligence initiatives. They facilitate the extraction, transformation,
  and loading (ETL) of data from various operational systems into a
  centralized data warehouse. By ensuring the timely and accurate
  transfer of data, data pipelines enable organizations to perform in-
  depth analyses, generate reports, and make data-driven decisions.

These are just a few examples of how data pipelines are utilized across industries.
The flexibility and scalability of data pipelines make them suitable for diverse data
processing needs, allowing organizations to leverage their data assets to gain valuable
insights and drive innovation.

In conclusion, data pipelines offer a wide range of benefits and advantages that empower organizations to efficiently manage and process their data. From improving data processing speed and scalability to enabling real-time analytics and advanced insights, data pipelines serve as a catalyst for data-driven decision-making and innovation. By embracing data pipelines, organizations can leverage the full potential of their data assets, derive meaningful insights, and stay ahead in today's data-driven landscape.

Data Governance Empowered by Data Orchestration: Enhancing Control and Compliance

Data governance plays a crucial role in ensuring the quality, integrity, and security of data within an organization. Data orchestration, with its ability to centralize and manage data workflows, can greatly support data governance initiatives. By implementing data orchestration practices, organizations can enhance their data governance strategies in the following ways:

- **Data Consistency:** Data orchestration enables organizations to establish standardized data workflows, ensuring consistent data collection, integration, and transformation processes. This consistency helps maintain data quality and integrity throughout the data lifecycle.

- **Data Lineage and Auditability:** With data orchestration, organizations can track and document the movement and transformation of data across various systems and processes. This lineage provides transparency and traceability, enabling data governance teams to understand the origin and history of data, facilitating compliance requirements and data audits.

- **Data Access Controls:** Data orchestration tools can enforce access controls and data security measures, ensuring that only authorized individuals or systems have appropriate access to sensitive data. This helps protect data privacy and ensure compliance with regulatory frameworks, such as GDPR or HIPAA.

- **Data Cataloging and Metadata Management:** Data orchestration platforms often include features for data cataloging and metadata management. These capabilities allow organizations to create a centralized repository of data assets, including metadata descriptions, data dictionaries, and data classifications. Such metadata management facilitates data governance efforts by providing comprehensive information about data sources, definitions, and usage.

- **Data Quality Monitoring:** Data orchestration tools can integrate with data quality monitoring solutions to continuously assess the quality and accuracy of data. By implementing data quality checks and validations at different stages of the orchestration process, organizations can proactively identify and address data quality issues, improving overall data governance practices.

- **Data Retention and Archiving:** Data orchestration can incorporate data retention policies and archiving mechanisms, ensuring compliance with legal and regulatory requirements for data retention. Organizations can define rules for data expiration, archival storage, and data disposal, thereby maintaining data governance standards for data lifecycle management.

In summary, data orchestration provides a foundation for effective data governance by enabling consistent workflows, ensuring data lineage and auditability, enforcing access controls, facilitating data cataloging and metadata management, monitoring data quality, and supporting data retention and archiving. By incorporating data orchestration practices into their data governance strategies, organizations can establish robust and compliant data management frameworks.

Achieving Data Governance through Data Orchestration

While a detailed discussion on data governance with supported tools has been covered in a separate chapter, this section aims to provide a concise overview of its implementation using data orchestration. Achieving data governance through data orchestration requires the implementation of specific practices and the effective utilization of data orchestration tools to enforce governance principles. Let's examine a step-by-step approach with an example:

217

- **Define Data Governance Policies:** Start by establishing data governance policies that align with your organization's goals and regulatory requirements. These policies may include data quality standards, data classification guidelines, access controls, and data retention policies.

- **Implement Data Orchestration Tools:** Choose a data orchestration tool that supports data governance capabilities, such as data lineage tracking, access control mechanisms, metadata management, and data quality monitoring.

- **Define Data Workflows:** Design data workflows within the data orchestration tool that adhere to the defined data governance policies. These workflows should include data integration, transformation, and validation steps, incorporating data governance controls at each stage.

- **Establish Data Lineage and Metadata Management:** Leverage the data orchestration tool's capabilities to capture and manage data lineage and metadata. This involves documenting the origin, transformations, and usage of data, as well as maintaining metadata descriptions and data dictionaries.

- **Enforce Access Controls:** Utilize the access control mechanisms provided by the data orchestration tool to enforce data governance policies. This includes role-based access control, authentication mechanisms, and data masking techniques to protect sensitive data.

- **Monitor and Validate Data Quality:** Implement data quality monitoring within the data orchestration tool to continuously assess the quality of data. Set up automated checks and validations to detect and address data quality issues in real-time.

- **Regular Auditing and Compliance:** Conduct regular audits to ensure compliance with data governance policies and regulatory requirements. Use the data lineage, metadata, and access control information captured by the data orchestration tool to facilitate audits and demonstrate compliance.

By following these steps and leveraging the capabilities of a data orchestration tool, organizations can achieve effective data governance. The example provided illustrates how data governance policies can be implemented and enforced through data orchestration, promoting data quality, security, and compliance throughout the data lifecycle.

Example

For instance, let's consider a generic organization implementing data governance through data orchestration. The organization establishes a policy that mandates the classification of all customer data as sensitive and restricts access to authorized personnel only. They do the following:

- To support their data governance initiatives, the organization selects a data orchestration tool that seamlessly integrates with their existing data management infrastructure. The chosen tool offers robust features, such as data lineage tracking, access control mechanisms, metadata management, and data quality checks. While most of the cloud tools for data orchestration now support these features, some of the common cloud tools that an organization can select is Azure Data Factory, an AWS data pipeline, a Google cloud dataflow, a Snowflake data cloud, and so forth.

- They create a comprehensive data workflow within the data orchestration tool that encompasses the integration of customer data from various sources, data transformations with a focus on maintaining data quality, and validation of access permissions before storing the data.

- Utilizing the data orchestration tool, the organization automates the capture of vital information such as source systems, applied transformations, and destination storage for each customer data record. Additionally, they leverage the tool's capabilities to assign metadata descriptions and data classifications to the data, providing valuable context and organization.

- By leveraging the access control mechanisms inherent to the data orchestration tool, the organization ensures that only users with the appropriate roles and permissions can access and modify customer data. Furthermore, sensitive information is safeguarded through data masking techniques, anonymizing it for users with restricted access.

- Data quality is a top priority, and the data orchestration tool incorporates data quality checks throughout the integration and transformation processes. These checks validate the accuracy, completeness, and consistency of customer data. Whenever data quality thresholds are not met, the tool generates alerts or notifications to address any issues promptly.

- The organization conducts periodic reviews of the data lineage, metadata, and access logs generated by the data orchestration tool. These reviews serve to validate compliance with their data governance policies and enable the creation of audit reports that demonstrate adherence to regulatory requirements.

In summary, through the implementation of data orchestration, this generic organization successfully enforces data governance by classifying customer data as sensitive, selecting a suitable data orchestration tool, creating a comprehensive data workflow, capturing essential metadata, enforcing access controls, conducting data quality checks, and conducting regular reviews to ensure compliance and demonstrate adherence to regulatory requirements.

Tools and Examples

Various tools and platforms facilitate data orchestration, offering features such as data integration, transformation, and workflow automation. Here are some tools and examples of data orchestration:

Azure Data Factory

Azure Data Factory is a comprehensive data integration and orchestration service with a range of key features and capabilities. It allows you to integrate data from various sources, including on-premises systems, cloud platforms, relational databases, Big Data sources, and SaaS applications. Data workflows can be defined and executed using visual tools or code-based configurations, with pipelines consisting of activities for data ingestion, transformation, and movement. The service offers built-in data transformation capabilities through Mapping Data Flow, providing a code-free approach for designing and executing data transformations. Data movement between different data stores is efficient and supports both batch and real-time scenarios. Azure Data Factory also includes data governance and security features, such as encryption, RBAC, and integration with Azure Active Directory. It seamlessly integrates with other Azure services, enabling you to leverage their capabilities within your data integration pipelines. Monitoring and management features allow for tracking pipeline execution, monitoring activity performance, and troubleshooting, with integration options for advanced monitoring and alerting. The service is scalable, cost-efficient, and provides auto-scaling capabilities to optimize resource allocation. Azure Data Factory empowers organizations to build scalable and efficient data pipelines, making it a powerful tool for managing data workflows in the cloud.

Azure Data Factory consists of several important components that contribute to its data integration and orchestration capabilities. These components include linked services, datasets, pipelines, activities, triggers, and integration runtimes (Figure 5-6).

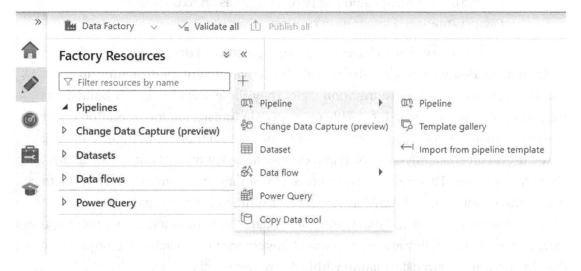

Figure 5-6. *Azure Data Factory panel depicting different features*

- **Linked Services** represent connections to various data sources and destinations, such as Azure Storage, Azure SQL Database, and on-premises systems. They are configured to establish connectivity and enable data movement.

- **Datasets** define the data structures in the source and destination data stores. They specify the format, schema, and location of the data. Datasets serve as the foundation for data integration and transformation operations.

221

- **Pipelines** are the core building blocks of Azure Data Factory. They define the workflow and sequence of activities to be executed. Activities can include data ingestion, transformation, movement, or processing tasks. Pipelines are created using a visual designer or JSON code.

- **Triggers** are used to schedule or initiate the execution of pipelines. Time-based schedules and event-based triggers, such as Azure Blob storage events or Azure Logic Apps, can be configured to start the execution of pipelines at specific intervals or based on specific events.

- **Integration runtimes** provide the execution environment for data integration tasks. They can be used to run pipelines on Azure infrastructure, self-hosted infrastructure, or as an Azure Data Factory–managed integration runtime.

Azure Data Factory also includes the powerful feature of **data flows**. Data flows in Azure Data Factory provide a visual, code-free environment for designing and executing complex data transformation logic. They allow users to visually build data transformation workflows using a wide range of data transformation operations, such as data cleansing, filtering, aggregation, joins, and custom transformations. With data flows, users can efficiently transform and cleanse large volumes of data in a scalable and serverless manner. This feature empowers organizations to streamline and automate their data preparation and transformation tasks, ultimately enabling them to derive valuable insights from their data. By integrating data flows into their data pipelines, users can leverage the flexibility and ease of use of this component to achieve comprehensive data integration and transformation within Azure Data Factory.

Working with Azure Data Factory (ADF) involves designing and orchestrating data workflows, ingesting data from various sources, transforming and processing it, and loading it into target destinations. Azure Data Factory is a cloud-based data integration service that allows you to create, schedule, and manage data pipelines.

Here is a step-by-step guide to working with Azure Data Factory:
Set Up Azure Data Factory

- Create an Azure Data Factory instance in the Azure portal.

- Select the appropriate subscription, resource group, and region for your data factory.

- Configure Linked Services to connect to various data sources, like Azure Storage, Azure SQL Database, Azure Data Lake Storage, on-premises systems, or other cloud services.

Define Datasets

Datasets represent the data structures in your data sources and destinations.

- Define the structure and properties of datasets, including file formats, schema, and location.

Create Pipelines

Pipelines define the workflow and activities to be executed in a specific sequence.

- Create pipelines in ADF using a visual designer or by writing JSON code.

- Add activities to the pipeline, such as data ingestion, data transformation, data movement, or data processing activities.

Configure Activities

- Configure each activity in the pipeline according to its purpose.

- For data ingestion, specify the source dataset and linked service.

- For data transformation (i.e., filter, sort, join, merge, etc.), use data transformation tools like ADF Dataflow, Azure Databricks, Azure HDInsight, or Azure Synapse Analytics.

- For data movement, specify the source and destination datasets and linked services.

- For data processing, define the necessary operations or computations to be performed.

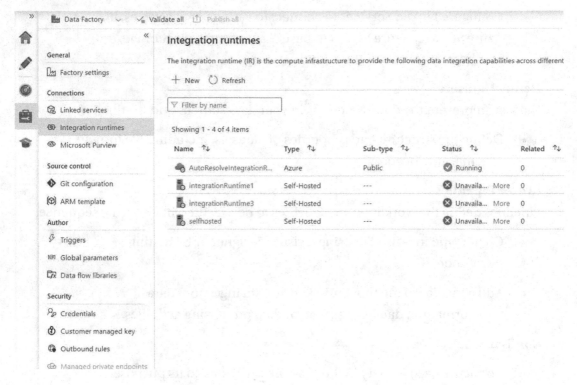

Figure 5-7. Azure integration runtime

Note: "Auto-resolve integration runtime" is always active, which interacts with other Azure sources. Inactive runtimes are self-hosted integration runtimes installed on an on-premises instance.

Schedule and Trigger Pipelines

- Set up a schedule or trigger to execute the pipeline at specific intervals or based on events.

- Use ADF's built-in triggers, such as time-based schedules or event-based triggers, like Azure Blob storage events or Azure Logic Apps.

Monitor and Troubleshoot

- Monitor the execution of your pipelines using Azure Data Factory monitoring capabilities (Figure 5-8).

- Monitor pipeline runs, track activity statuses, and review diagnostic logs for troubleshooting.

- Utilize ADF's integration with Azure Monitor and Azure Log Analytics for advanced monitoring and alerting.

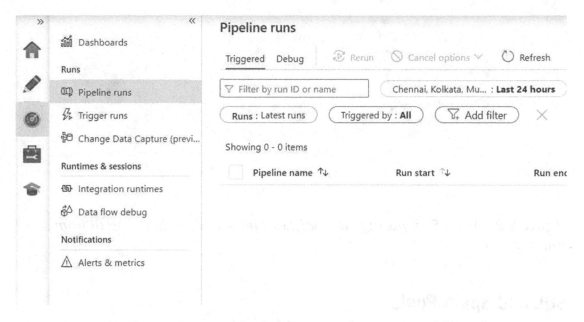

Figure 5-8. *Pipeline, triggers, and other runs can be monitored from the section in the screenshot gatherd from a live Azure Data Factory instance*

Data Integration and Transformation

- Use ADF's data integration capabilities to perform data cleansing, filtering, aggregation, joins, or custom transformations, or use Notebook from Databricks or Synapse analytics to transform and shape the data as required.

Azure Data Factory provides a flexible and scalable platform for building and managing data integration workflows. By following these steps, you can design, schedule, monitor, and optimize data pipelines to efficiently integrate, transform, and move data across various sources and destinations within the Azure ecosystem.

Azure Synapse

Azure Synapse is a powerful data analytics platform that offers a range of features and services to streamline data processing and integration (Figure 5-9).

Figure 5-9. *Azure Synapse ingests, analyzes, and visualizes In Power BI from a single platform*

SQL and Spark Pools

One of its key components is the SQL Analytics engine, which supports both traditional data warehousing and Big Data analytics. This engine allows users to run complex SQL queries on large datasets stored in Azure Data Lake Storage or dedicated SQL pools.

Azure Synapse also integrates with Apache Spark, an open-source analytics engine known for its speed and scalability. By leveraging Spark capabilities, users can perform Big Data processing, machine learning, and data exploration tasks within the Azure Synapse environment with its Spark pool.

Data Integration Features

Data integration is another important aspect of Azure Synapse, offering the ability to ingest data from various sources such as Azure Blob storage, Azure Data Lake Storage, and on-premises data sources. The platform provides connectors, data movement activities, and data mapping features to facilitate the data ingestion process.

For structured and semi-structured data storage and analysis, Azure Synapse includes Synapse SQL Pools, a fully managed and scalable data warehousing solution. This feature utilizes a massive parallel processing architecture to efficiently handle large volumes of data.

To support Big Data workloads, Azure Synapse integrates with Azure Data Lake Storage Gen2, a secure and scalable storage solution. This integration allows users to centrally store and manage structured and unstructured data within the platform.

Analytics and Power BI

Furthermore, Azure Synapse seamlessly integrates with Microsoft's Power BI, a popular business intelligence and visualization tool. This integration enables users to create compelling visualizations and dashboards, extracting valuable insights from their data.

Governance

Security and governance are prioritized in Azure Synapse, with features such as Azure Active Directory authentication, role-based access control (RBAC), and data encryption at rest and in transit. The platform also includes auditing, monitoring, and data classification capabilities to ensure compliance and effective data governance.

Synapse Studio

Synapse Studio serves as the unified development environment for Azure Synapse, providing a comprehensive suite of tools and features for managing data integration, analytics, and data warehousing workflows. It offers a user-friendly interface to develop, monitor, and manage data processes within the Azure Synapse environment.

Synapse Serverless

Azure Synapse Serverless is a valuable offering within Synapse Analytics that eliminates the need for a dedicated SQL or Spark pool. With Synapse Serverless, users can seamlessly work with external sources and popular formats like Delta and Parquet. This capability allows for the creation of views that can be easily and efficiently utilized with various analytics tools. By leveraging Synapse Serverless, organizations can achieve greater flexibility and cost efficiency in their data analytics workflows, as they can access and analyze data from external sources without the need for dedicated resources. This feature enhances the versatility of Synapse Analytics, enabling users to leverage external data and industry-standard formats to derive insights and make data-driven decisions using tools like Power BI.

Overall, Azure Synapse empowers organizations to streamline their data analytics and integration processes, enabling faster insights and informed decision-making. With its robust set of tools and services, users can handle data at scale and extract meaningful insights from diverse and large datasets.

Azure Synapse and Its ETL Features

Azure Synapse Workspace:

- Start by creating an Azure Synapse workspace in the Azure portal. This workspace serves as the central hub for all your data and analytics activities in Azure Synapse.

Data Integration:

- Azure Synapse supports data integration from various sources, including Azure Blob storage, Azure Data Lake Storage, Azure SQL Database, Azure SQL Data Warehouse, and more.

- Use the Synapse Studio interface within the workspace to configure and manage data connections.

Data Flow:

- Azure Synapse Data Flow provides a visual, code-free environment for designing and executing ETL processes.

- Within Synapse Studio, create a data flow to define your data transformation logic using a visual interface.

- Use built-in transformations, such as aggregations, joins, pivots, filters, and data mapping, to transform the data.

Mapping Data Flows:

- Mapping data flows within Azure Synapse provides a code-free environment for data transformation.

- Use the visual interface to design and build complex data transformations, combining sources, transformations, and sinks in a pipeline-like manner.

Wrangling Data Flows:

- Azure Synapse also offers wrangling data flows, which provide an interactive and exploratory approach to data preparation.

- Use data-wrangling capabilities to cleanse, shape, and transform the data interactively using a visual interface.

Data Movement:

- Azure Synapse provides efficient data movement capabilities to load data into the target destination.

- Use Copy Activity to move data between different data stores, including Azure Blob storage, Azure Data Lake Storage, and Azure Synapse Analytics.

Data Lake Integration:

- Azure Synapse integrates seamlessly with Azure Data Lake Storage Gen2, which serves as the primary storage for large volumes of structured and unstructured data.

- Utilize the power of Data Lake Storage Gen2 for scalable storage and processing of your ETL data.

Performance and Scalability:

- Azure Synapse is designed for high performance and scalability, enabling you to process large volumes of data efficiently.

- Leverage the underlying distributed processing architecture to achieve parallelism and optimize ETL performance.

Monitoring and Management:

- Azure Synapse provides monitoring and management capabilities to track the execution of your ETL processes.

- Utilize the built-in monitoring tools and features within the Synapse Studio interface to monitor pipeline runs, view execution history, and troubleshoot issues.

By leveraging Azure Synapse's ETL features, you can design and execute efficient data integration and transformation processes to prepare your data for analysis and reporting. The unified nature of Azure Synapse allows you to seamlessly integrate data warehousing, Big Data processing, and advanced analytics capabilities in a single platform, enabling powerful insights and data-driven decision-making.

AWS Glue

AWS Glue is a fully managed extract, transform, and load (ETL) service provided by Amazon Web Services (AWS). AWS Glue automates the discovery, cataloging, and transformation of data, reducing the manual effort required for data integration (Figure 5-10).

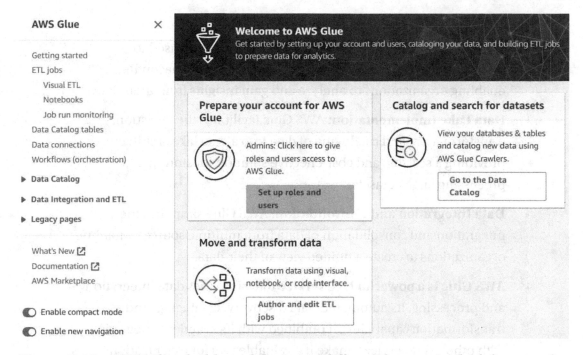

Figure 5-10. *AWS Glue dashboard depicting different features in the left pane of this screenshot*

Some of the key benefits of using AWS Glue are as follows:

- **Scalability and Performance:** AWS Glue can handle large volumes of data and scale resources dynamically to meet processing demands, ensuring optimal performance.

- **Serverless Architecture:** With its serverless design, AWS Glue eliminates the need for infrastructure management, allowing users to focus on their data and ETL logic.

- **Integration with Other AWS Services:** AWS Glue seamlessly integrates with other AWS services, such as Amazon S3, AWS Glue DataBrew, and AWS Glue Streaming, enabling end-to-end data workflows.

- **Cost-Effective:** AWS Glue offers a pay-as-you-go pricing model, allowing users to pay only for the resources and services they use, without any upfront costs or long-term commitments.

Use Cases for AWS Glue

- **Data Warehousing and Analytics:** AWS Glue can be used to transform and load data into data warehouses like Amazon Redshift, enabling organizations to analyze and gain insights from their data.

- **Data Lake Implementation:** AWS Glue facilitates the ingestion, transformation, and cataloging of data into a data lake architecture, providing a scalable and cost-effective solution for storing and processing large datasets.

- **Data Integration and Consolidation:** AWS Glue simplifies the integration and consolidation of data from multiple sources, enabling organizations to create a unified view of their data.

- **AWS Glue is a powerful ETL service** that simplifies data integration and processing. Its automated data discovery, cataloging, and transformation capabilities, combined with its seamless integration with other AWS services, make it a valuable tool for organizations seeking to leverage their data effectively. By leveraging AWS Glue, organizations can accelerate their data-driven initiatives and gain actionable insights from their data without the hassle of infrastructure management.

Key Components of AWS Glue

- **Data Catalog:** The Data Catalog is a centralized metadata repository that stores and organizes metadata information about various data sources. It provides a consistent view of the data assets and their structures, making it easier to discover, search, and understand the data within an AWS environment.

- To access the Data Catalog in AWS Glue, log in to the AWS Management Console, navigate to AWS Glue, and click on "Data Catalog." Create a new database or populate the catalog with metadata using AWS Glue crawlers. Configure the crawler by specifying the data source and schedule. Once completed, the crawler scans the data source and populates the catalog. With the Data Catalog, manage metadata, explore tables, and modify properties. The Data Catalog is essential for AWS Glue jobs, automating ETL operations and integrating with various AWS services. AWS Glue crawlers automate data discovery, infer schemas, and populate the catalog. Manage and monitor crawlers through the AWS Glue console.

- **Crawlers:** Crawlers are used to automatically discover and infer the schema and metadata of various data sources. They scan data stores such as Amazon S3, Amazon RDS, and Amazon Redshift, and create or update table definitions in the Data Catalog.

- **ETL (Extract, Transform, Load) Engine:** The ETL engine allows you to create and manage data transformation workflows. It provides a visual interface for building ETL jobs and allows you to write custom code using Apache Spark. The ETL engine can efficiently process large volumes of data and perform transformations on the data before loading it into the target destination.

- AWS Glue ETL scripts provide a powerful solution for custom data transformations in AWS Glue jobs. To use them, access the AWS Glue console, create or select a job, and locate the "Script" section. Choose Python or Scala, write your custom logic, and leverage AWS Glue libraries and APIs. Integrate the script into the job by mapping source and target columns. Save the configuration, execute or schedule the job, and monitor its progress and logs in the console. AWS Glue ETL scripts offer flexibility and enable tailored data transformations according to specific requirements.

- **Jobs:** Jobs in AWS Glue are used to execute ETL workflows. You can create and schedule jobs to run at specific intervals or trigger them based on events. Jobs can leverage the power of the underlying Spark engine to process and transform data at a scale.

- To create an AWS Glue job, access the AWS Glue console by logging into the AWS Management console and navigating to the AWS Glue service. Click on "Jobs" and then "Add job" to create a new job. Specify parameters such as source and target connections, ETL transformations, and mapping data. Configure execution settings, leverage AWS Glue ETL scripts for complex transformations, save the job, and execute or schedule it. Monitor progress, access logs and metrics, and manage and update jobs as needed. AWS Glue jobs offer a scalable and automated solution for data transformation, leveraging the metadata in the AWS Glue Data Catalog.

- **Data Lake Formation:** Data lake formation is a feature within AWS Glue that simplifies the process of setting up and managing a data lake. It provides capabilities for data ingestion, data cataloging, and data access control, making it easier to build and manage a data lake environment.

- **ML Transformations:** AWS Glue also offers machine learning (ML) capabilities for data transformation tasks. You can use ML transformations to generate code for data preparation tasks, such as data cleaning, normalization, and feature engineering, using machine learning techniques.

- **DataBrew Integration:** AWS Glue integrates with AWS Glue DataBrew, a visual data preparation tool. DataBrew allows you to visually explore, clean, and transform your data using a point-and-click interface. It simplifies the process of data preparation and can be used in conjunction with AWS Glue to enhance data transformation workflows.

AWS Glue Best Practices

- **Consistent Data Catalog Management:** Maintain a well-organized and up-to-date AWS Glue Data Catalog. Regularly update metadata and schemas as data sources evolve. This ensures that your data catalog reflects the current state of your data assets accurately.

- **Utilize Partitioning and Classification:** Leverage partitioning in your data catalog to improve query performance, especially when dealing with large datasets. Additionally, utilize classifications to categorize and organize your data assets based on their characteristics, enabling easier data discovery and access.

- **Custom Metadata and Descriptions:** Enhance the understanding of your data assets by adding custom metadata and descriptions. This additional information provides context and aids in the interpretation and usage of the data.

- **Schema Evolution Management:** As your data sources evolve and schema changes occur, update and manage the corresponding schema definitions in the AWS Glue Data Catalog. This ensures that downstream processes and applications can adapt to the changes seamlessly.

- Versioning and Change Control: Implement versioning and change control mechanisms for your metadata and schemas. This allows you to track and manage changes over time, providing a historical record of schema evolution and facilitating collaboration among data stakeholders.

- Integration with Data Pipeline Workflows: Integrate the AWS Glue Data Catalog with your data pipeline workflows, ensuring that metadata changes and schema updates are synchronized across the pipeline. This guarantees consistent and accurate data processing throughout the pipeline.

- Monitoring and Alerting: Monitor the usage, quality, and performance of your data assets through metrics and logs provided by AWS Glue. Set up appropriate alerts and notifications to be informed of any anomalies, errors, or issues related to metadata and schema evolution.

To effectively manage your data schema in AWS Glue Data Catalog, follow these best practices:

- Establish a strategy for schema evolution to handle changes over time.

- Implement schema versioning to track and manage schema changes.

- Capture and store metadata in the Data Catalog for all data sources and tables.

- Automate metadata extraction using AWS Glue crawlers to keep metadata up to date.

- Leverage classification and schema inference features to categorize and infer schema.

- Utilize custom metadata and tags to add additional information or annotations.

- Plan for schema changes, document them, and communicate with stakeholders.

- Monitor and track changes in metadata and schema using version control or change management tools.

- Implement backup and recovery mechanisms for the Data Catalog to ensure data integrity.

By following these practices, you can effectively manage your data schema and metadata in the AWS Glue Data Catalog, enabling efficient data processing and ensuring data consistency and reliability.

By leveraging the AWS Glue Data Catalog and following these best practices, you can effectively manage metadata and schema evolution, ensure data consistency, and facilitate efficient data discovery and analysis. It simplifies the process of preparing and loading data for analytics by automating tasks like data discovery, schema inference, and data transformation. Users can create and manage data catalogs, extract data from various sources, transform it to meet their specific requirements, and load it into data lakes, data warehouses, or other analytical storage systems. The service is designed to be highly scalable, enabling users to process large volumes of data efficiently. By eliminating the need for manual coding and providing a visual interface for ETL workflows, AWS Glue enables organizations to accelerate their data preparation processes and derive valuable insights from their data in a faster and more efficient manner.

Snowflake and Its ETL Features

The Snowflake ETL pipeline provides organizations with a scalable, flexible, and high-performance solution for processing and transforming data. This whitepaper explored the architectural considerations, best practices, and real-world use cases of working with Snowflake in ETL workflows. By leveraging Snowflake's unique capabilities, organizations can build efficient and scalable ETL pipelines, enabling them to unlock the full potential of their data and drive data-driven insights and decision-making. With its cloud-native architecture and comprehensive feature set, Snowflake empowers businesses to harness the power of data and stay competitive in the rapidly evolving digital landscape.

About Snowflake

Snowflake is a cloud-based data warehousing platform designed to handle large-scale data processing and analytics workloads. Its architecture is built on a unique combination of distributed systems and cloud computing principles.

Snowflake Architecture

At the core of Snowflake's architecture is the Snowflake account, which serves as the top-level entity and container for all resources within the Snowflake ecosystem. When you sign up for Snowflake, a Snowflake account is created, providing a centralized location to manage and organize your data.

Virtual Warehouse

One of the key components of Snowflake's architecture is the concept of virtual warehouses. These compute clusters execute queries and perform data processing tasks. They can dynamically scale up or down based on workload requirements, ensuring optimal performance and concurrency. By isolating workloads from each other, virtual warehouses enable efficient resource utilization and workload management.

Database and Schemas

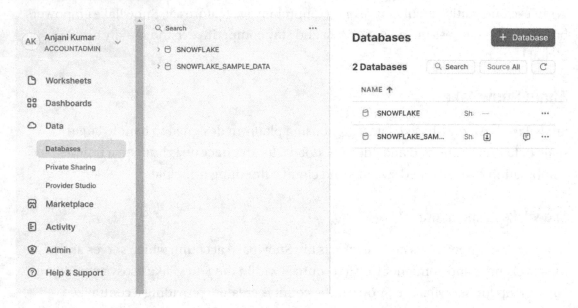

Figure 5-11. *Databases in Snowflake*

To organize data within a Snowflake account, you can utilize databases and schemas (Figure 5-11). Databases serve as logical containers, separating different sets of data, while schemas further help organize and manage data objects, like tables, views, and functions, within databases.

Tables in Snowflake store structured data and can be organized into database schemas. Snowflake supports various table types, including regular tables, external tables (which reference data in external storage), and temporary tables, providing flexibility for different data use cases.

Storage and Query Processing

Snowflake excels in contemporary data analytics, offering scalable solutions. Its standout features include multi-language query support (SQL, Python, JavaScript), facilitating versatile usage. The organization of queries into worksheets enhances practicality, especially in complex projects. Additionally, versioning worksheets in a code repository supports collaborative, controlled development, ensuring effective tracking and history maintenance for teams.

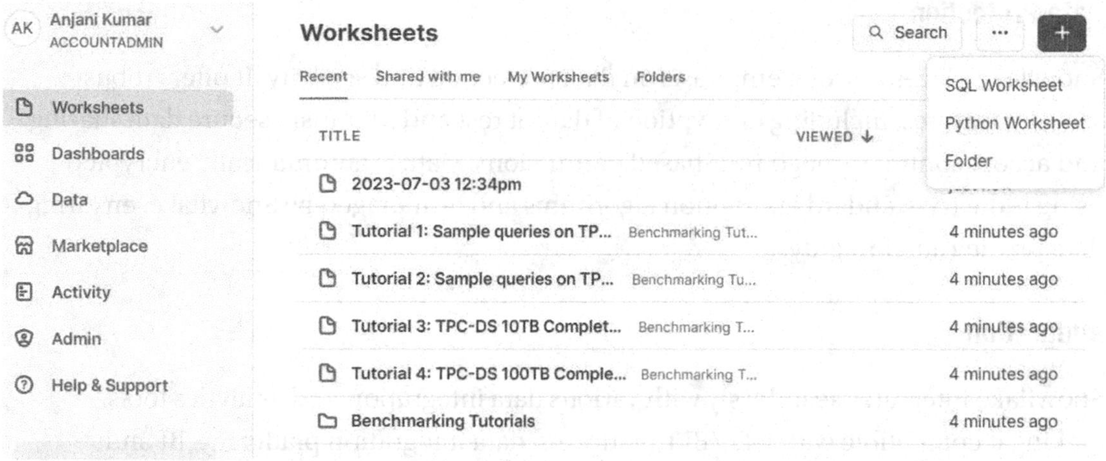

Figure 5-12. *Worksheets can be used to write queries in Snowflake*

Snowflake decouples storage from compute, providing scalable and elastic storage capacity. Data in Snowflake is stored in a columnar format, which offers efficient compression and query performance (Figure 5-12). It manages the storage, replication, and durability of data across multiple storage layers, ensuring data availability and reliability. Based on a shared-disk model, Snowflake's architecture allows multiple compute clusters to access data stored in a centralized storage layer. This multi-cluster, shared-disk architecture enables concurrent access to data and provides the flexibility to scale compute resources independent of storage.

Snowflake's architecture comprises three main services. The query processing service handles the execution of SQL queries, query optimization, and parallel processing. The metadata management service manages metadata associated with databases, tables, schemas, and other objects. The transaction management service ensures data consistency and manages transactions within Snowflake.

Snowflake's query processing engine optimizes SQL queries by employing traditional and advanced optimization techniques. It utilizes a cost-based optimizer that generates optimized query execution plans based on statistics and metadata, resulting in efficient query performance.

Data Protection

Snowflake places a strong emphasis on data protection and security. It offers robust security features, including encryption of data at rest and in transit, secure data sharing, and access control through role-based permissions. Data is automatically encrypted using industry-standard encryption algorithms and is managed by Snowflake, ensuring data privacy and integrity.

Integration

Snowflake integrates seamlessly with various data integration and analytics tools, making it compatible with ETL/ELT platforms, data integration platforms, BI and visualization tools, and programming languages like Python and R. This integration ecosystem allows organizations to leverage their existing tools and technologies while benefiting from Snowflake's scalability and performance.

In summary, Snowflake's architecture provides scalability, performance, and flexibility, making it an ideal choice for handling large volumes of data and performing advanced analytics. With its separation of storage and compute, elastic scaling capabilities, robust security features, and seamless integration with other tools, Snowflake offers a comprehensive platform for building efficient and effective ETL workflows.

Snowflake Support for ETL

- **Data Loading:** Snowflake provides several methods for loading data into the platform. Organizations can bulk load data from files stored in cloud storage platforms like Amazon S3, Azure Blob storage, or Google cloud storage directly into Snowflake tables. Snowflake also supports direct data ingestion from various data sources, including databases, streaming platforms, and third-party services.

- **Snowflake Stages:** Snowflake stages act as landing zones for data during the ETL process. Stages can be used to ingest data from external sources, validate and transform the data, and load it into Snowflake tables. Staging data in Snowflake provides a seamless integration point for ETL workflows and allows for efficient data processing.

- **Transformation Capabilities:** Snowflake offers powerful SQL-based transformation capabilities, allowing users to perform various data transformations within the platform. SQL functions, expressions, and operators can be used to cleanse, filter, aggregate, join, and manipulate data during the transformation phase of the ETL process. Snowflake's support for both row-based and set-based transformations enables organizations to handle complex data transformation scenarios.

- **Stored Procedures:** Snowflake allows the creation of stored procedures, which are reusable SQL scripts that can encapsulate complex ETL logic. Stored procedures can be used to automate repetitive ETL tasks, apply business rules, perform data validation, and orchestrate the overall ETL workflow within Snowflake.

- **External Functions:** Snowflake supports the execution of external functions, which allows organizations to leverage the power of external libraries and services within their ETL processes. External functions enable integration with custom code, machine learning libraries, or specialized data processing frameworks, expanding the capabilities of ETL workflows on Snowflake.

- **Task Scheduler:** Snowflake's built-in task scheduler enables the automation of ETL workflows. Tasks can be scheduled to run at specific intervals or be triggered by specific events, ensuring that data integration and transformation processes occur at the desired frequency or in response to real-time data changes.

Considerations for Building ETL Workflows on Snowflake

- **Schema Design:** Proper schema design is crucial for efficient ETL processes on Snowflake. Leveraging Snowflake's ability to separate compute and storage and organizing data into appropriate schemas and tables can optimize query performance and facilitate easier data transformation and analysis.

- **Incremental Loading:** Snowflake supports efficient incremental loading, allowing organizations to process only the changed or new data during subsequent ETL runs. Utilizing Snowflake's time travel and data versioning features, organizations can easily identify and extract the delta changes, minimizing processing time and reducing the amount of data transferred.

- **Error Handling and Retry Mechanisms:** Incorporating error handling and retry mechanisms within ETL workflows is essential to ensure data integrity and reliability. Snowflake's transactional capabilities enable organizations to handle exceptions, rollbacks, and retries during data loading and transformation, ensuring the consistency and accuracy of the ETL process.

- **Monitoring and Logging:** Snowflake provides comprehensive monitoring and logging capabilities, allowing organizations to track the progress, performance, and issues encountered during ETL workflows leveraging Snowflake's query history, execution statistics, and integration.

Snowflake is a fully managed data platform that goes beyond traditional databases, offering a wide range of features for data storage, processing, and analytics. While it supports SQL queries and stored procedures, its capabilities extend far beyond that. When it comes to data loading, Snowflake provides seamless integration with popular integration and ETL tools like Glue, ADF (Azure Data Factory), and Databricks, among others. These tools enable efficient data ingestion from various sources into Snowflake, allowing for transformations and processing as required. Moreover, you can also utilize standalone code, such as Python, integrated with cloud workflows or integration tools, to load data into Snowflake. By leveraging Snowflake's integration capabilities, organizations can seamlessly incorporate their existing workflows, ETL processes, and integration tools with Snowflake's robust data warehousing features. This integration streamlines data loading and processing, empowering organizations to take advantage of Snowflake's scalability, performance, and flexibility for their data integration and analytics requirements.

Let's look at some of the important features that enable Snowflake for optimized and high-volume data processing as one of the most preferred toolsets for their data engineering and analytics needs.

Continuous Data Loading in Snowflake

Continuous data loading in Snowflake involves ingesting and processing data in real-time or near real-time, ensuring that the target tables are continuously updated with the latest data. Snowflake offers several options to achieve continuous data loading, depending on the data source and the desired level of latency. Here are some approaches to consider:

- **Streaming Data Ingestion:** Snowflake supports streaming data ingestion through its integration with various messaging and streaming platforms, such as Apache Kafka, Amazon Kinesis, and Google Cloud Pub/Sub. By leveraging Snowflake's Snowpipe service or using external tools like Apache NiFi, organizations can stream data directly into Snowflake tables in real-time. Snowpipe provides automated ingestion and processing of data as soon as it arrives, ensuring continuous loading of streaming data.

- **Change Data Capture (CDC):** CDC is a technique that captures and tracks changes made to the source data. Snowflake can integrate with CDC tools, such as Apache Kafka Connect, Debezium, or proprietary CDC solutions, to capture changes from transactional databases. These tools capture inserts, updates, and deletes and deliver them to Snowflake, allowing for continuous loading of the changed data into target tables.

- **Scheduled Batch Loads:** If real-time data ingestion is not required, organizations can schedule batch loads at regular intervals using Snowflake's data loading capabilities. Batch jobs can be triggered by a scheduler (e.g., Snowflake's task scheduler or external schedulers like cron) to load data from various sources, such as files in cloud storage or databases, into Snowflake tables. By setting the desired scheduling frequency, organizations can achieve near-real-time or frequent data updates.

- **External Data Sources:** Snowflake allows direct querying of external data sources, including cloud storage platforms like Amazon S3, Azure Blob storage, or Google cloud storage. Organizations can set up

243

continuous data loading by ensuring that the external data sources are regularly updated, and Snowflake queries are executed to access the latest data from these sources.

- **Snowflake Data Sharing:** Snowflake's data sharing feature enables continuous data loading from external organizations or partners. With data sharing, organizations can securely share datasets, including real-time or near real-time data, between Snowflake accounts. This allows continuous updates of shared data as the source data changes, ensuring synchronized access to the most recent data.

Snowpipe

Snowpipe is a feature in Snowflake that facilitates real-time data ingestion and processing. It provides an automated and scalable mechanism for continuously loading data from various sources into Snowflake tables in near real-time. Snowpipe simplifies the process of ingesting streaming data or rapidly changing data by eliminating the need for manual data loading operations.

By leveraging Snowpipe, organizations can automate the process of ingesting and processing streaming or rapidly changing data, enabling near real-time analytics and decision-making. Snowpipe simplifies the data loading workflow, reduces manual intervention, and ensures efficient and scalable data ingestion in Snowflake.

Key features and characteristics of Snowpipe include the following:

- **Event-based Data Loading:** Snowpipe is designed to handle event-based data loading scenarios, where new data becomes available in the source system. It is typically used for streaming data sources or situations where data updates are frequent and need to be processed in near real-time.

- **Serverless and Automated:** Snowpipe operates in a serverless fashion, meaning it automatically scales and processes data without the need for manual intervention or resource allocation. It automatically detects new files or events in the designated staging area and initiates data loading and processing in Snowflake.

- **Integration with Cloud Storage:** Snowpipe integrates seamlessly with cloud storage platforms, such as Amazon S3, Azure Blob storage, or Google cloud storage. It monitors a specified location in the cloud storage for new files or events, ensuring continuous data ingestion and processing.

- **Snowflake Staging Area:** Snowpipe uses a dedicated staging area within Snowflake to process incoming data. The staging area acts as a buffer zone where the data is initially loaded before being efficiently ingested into Snowflake tables. This approach ensures optimal performance and scalability while separating the data loading process from other activities in Snowflake.

- **Efficient and Parallel Data Loading:** Snowpipe leverages Snowflake's parallel processing capabilities to load data into target tables efficiently. It automatically optimizes the loading process by distributing the workload across multiple compute resources, allowing for high-speed data ingestion.

- **Notification and Event-Driven Execution:** Snowpipe relies on event notifications or polling mechanisms to detect new data and trigger the data loading process. When a new file or event is detected in the designated cloud storage location, Snowpipe is notified to start processing the data. This event-driven approach minimizes latency and ensures near real-time data ingestion.

- **Integration with Snowflake SQL:** Snowpipe seamlessly integrates with Snowflake's SQL capabilities, enabling organizations to apply transformations and perform additional data processing using SQL statements. Once the data is loaded into Snowflake tables via Snowpipe, it can be queried, transformed, and analyzed using the full power of Snowflake's SQL-based analytics engine.

Snowflake Connector for Kafka

The Snowflake Connector for Kafka is a software component that enables seamless integration between Snowflake, a cloud data platform, and Apache Kafka, a popular distributed streaming platform. It allows organizations to efficiently ingest streaming data from Kafka topics into Snowflake for further analysis, processing, and storage.

Key features and benefits of the Snowflake Connector for Kafka include the following:

- **Real-Time Data Ingestion:** The connector enables real-time or near-real-time data ingestion from Kafka topics into Snowflake, ensuring that data is continuously updated and available for analysis as it arrives in Kafka.

- **High-Throughput Data Loading:** The connector leverages Snowflake's scalable architecture and parallel processing capabilities to achieve high throughput data loading from Kafka to Snowflake. It efficiently handles large volumes of streaming data, enabling organizations to process and analyze data in real time.

- **Exactly-Once Data Delivery:** The connector ensures exactly-once data delivery semantics by integrating with Kafka's transactional messaging capabilities. It guarantees that data is loaded into Snowflake without duplication or loss, maintaining data integrity throughout the ingestion process.

- **Schema Evolution Support:** The connector supports schema evolution, allowing for changes in the data schema over time. As the schema evolves in Kafka, the connector can dynamically adapt and synchronize the changes with the target Snowflake tables, ensuring seamless data integration.

- **Flexible Data Transformation:** The connector allows for data transformation and enrichment during the ingestion process. Organizations can apply filters, map fields, perform data type conversions, and apply custom transformations to the data flowing from Kafka to Snowflake, enabling data cleansing and preparation.

- **Integration with Snowflake Snowpipe:** The connector seamlessly integrates with Snowpipe, Snowflake's serverless and automated data ingestion service. Snowpipe detects new data in Kafka topics through the connector and automatically triggers the data-loading process into Snowflake, simplifying the setup and management of the data pipeline.

- **Scalability and Resilience:** The connector is designed to be highly scalable and resilient. It supports parallel data loading from multiple Kafka partitions, allowing for efficient utilization of Snowflake's compute resources. The connector also handles failures gracefully, ensuring data integrity and recoverability in case of any disruptions.

By using the Snowflake connector for Kafka, organizations can unlock the power of real-time data analytics and enable seamless integration of streaming data from Kafka into Snowflake's cloud data platform. It facilitates the processing, analysis, and storage of streaming data alongside traditional batch data, providing a unified view of data for comprehensive insights and decision-making.

Example and Use Case

Delta lakes have gained popularity as a reliable solution for processing delta files in data lakes. Regardless of the technology used, the steps for processing delta tables remain consistent as long as the technology supports delta table processing.

In this particular use case, Azure Data Factory (ADF) is utilized to process delta tables. ADF is chosen as the preferred option due to the scenario where new clients, particularly those with C-suite executives not involved, may be hesitant to adopt technologies like Databricks or Spark. These clients might prefer Microsoft-agnostic solutions, and in such cases Azure Data Factory serves as the best and easiest way to gradually introduce them to the benefits of using delta tables.

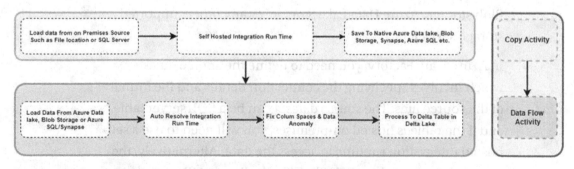

Figure 5-13. *Flow for delta table creation using Azure Data Factory*

To process files in delta tables using Azure Data Factory, you can follow these steps:

Set Up Azure Data Factory

- Create an Azure Data Factory instance in the Azure portal (Figure 5-14).

- Select the appropriate subscription, resource group, and region for your data factory.

Figure 5-14. *Azure Data Factory instance screenshot*

Define Source and Sink

- Identify the source where your files are located. It could be Azure Blob storage, Azure Data Lake Storage, or any other supported storage service.

- In Azure Data Factory, you need to define the source dataset, which involves specifying the connection details and file format of the source files. The source dataset can be a SQL server table, and if the table is hosted on-premises, you will need to use a self-hosted integration runtime to access the data. Alternatively, the source dataset can be a CSV file, TSV file, Parquet file, or other supported format.

Create a Pipeline

- Within Azure Data Factory, go to the Authoring section and select "Pipelines."

- Create a new pipeline and provide a name for it.

- Add a copy activity to the pipeline that represents the file-processing task.

- Configure the activity to use the appropriate source and sink datasets.

- In case the data is being copied from an on-premises data source such as a file or on-premises database, you need to copy data first to a Native Azure source, such as Azure Delta Lake Storage, Azure SQl, Azure Synapse, using a copy activity.

- Load the data as CSV, Azure SQL/Synapse table, or Parquet in the Native Azure data source.

The Figure below, labeled 5-15, illustrates a typical example of loading a Delta table via data flow in Data Factory along with other dataprocessing activities.

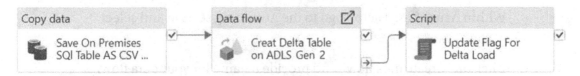

Figure 5-15. *Azure Data Factory high-level activity for delta table load*

Identify the target delta table where you want to load the processed data.

- Define the sink dataset in Azure Data Factory, specifying the connection details and format of the delta table.

Some Constraints and Options

Writing data in delta format is only supported through data flow in Azure Data Factory. Therefore, if the data is located on-premises, you will need to migrate it to Azure native Blob storage, ADLS Gen2, Azure SQL, or Synapse to proceed with delta format utilization.

To work with delta format in Azure Data Factory, you can utilize the self-hosted integration runtime by employing the copy activity. This allows you to save the data in Parquet or CSV format, which can then be further processed in delta format using Data Flow.

Alternatively, you have the option to use Python in Spark or Databricks notebook for data processing. These notebooks can be executed using the Azure Data Factory option to execute notebooks, enabling you to work with delta format seamlessly.

By considering these approaches, you can effectively work with delta format in Azure Data Factory. If the data is on-premises, ensure its migration to compatible storage, employ the self-hosted integration runtime for saving in compatible formats, or leverage Python and Spark capabilities via Databricks notebook execution in Azure Data Factory.

Add Data Flow

Figure 5-16 illustrates a Dataflow activity, an advanced feature in Data Factory that facilitates both data transformation and advanced capabilities, including Delta table loading.

Figure 5-16. *Azure Data Factory data flow activity*

- Within Azure Data Factory, go to the Authoring section and select "Data Flows."

- Click on "Create data flow" and provide a name for your data flow.

- Select the source dataset that contains the data you want to load into the delta lake.

- Configure the source dataset by selecting the appropriate file format and defining the schema.

The figure below, labeled 5-17, outlines the interface for configuring settings related to a datasource within a Dataflow.

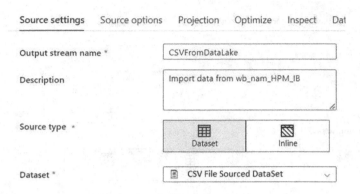

Figure 5-17. *Azure Data Factory data flow source settings*

- Specify the connection details for the data source, such as Azure Blob storage, Azure Data Lake Storage, or any other supported storage service.

- Within the data flow designer, add transformations to manipulate and shape the data.

- Use transformations such as Select, Filter, Aggregate, Join, and Derived Column to transform the data as needed.

- Apply any additional data cleansing or enrichment operations required for your use case.

- Add a sink transformation to define the destination of the data flow.

- Select the Delta Lake format as the sink type.

The figure labeled 5-18 delineates the interface for configuring settings associated with a data destination "sink" within a Dataflow. When loading data from the source into a Delta table, please ensure that the Inline dataset type is set to Delta.

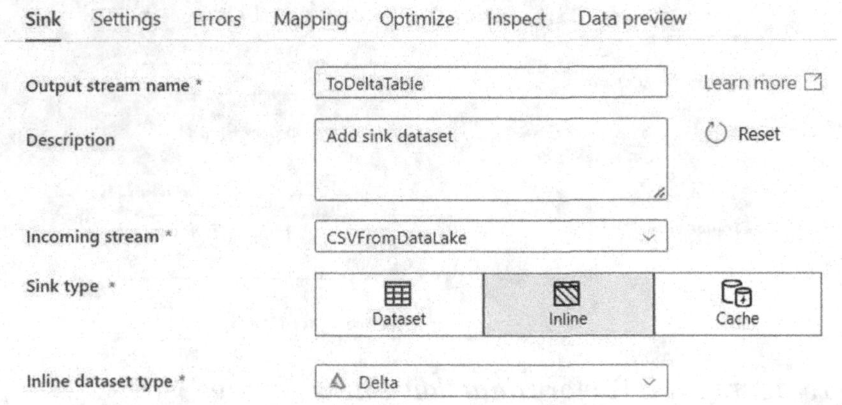

Figure 5-18. *Azure Data Factory data flow sink settings, note the delta format in inline dataset type*

- Specify the output folder or container where the Delta Lake files will be stored.

- Configure the sink dataset, including the connection details for the storage service.

- Choose delta table format as an option, remember to remove extra spaces from columns with tools like regex for all input columns; e.g., [regexReplace($$,' ','_')]

The diagram marked as 5-19 illustrates a standard column cleaning procedure necessary when a column contains spaces that need to be replaced with underscores. The Delta table processor, as of the current version during the writing of this book, does not support spaces in column names for Delta protocol versions below 2.5.

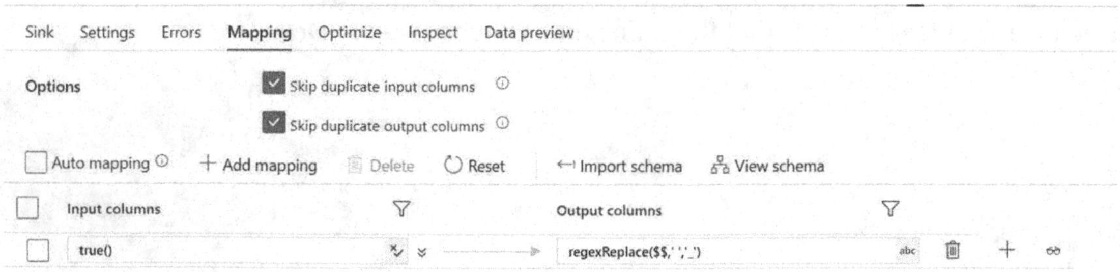

Figure 5-19. *Azure Data Factory mapping setting for cleaning spaces in all the input column at once*

- Once the data flow is designed, publish it to save the changes.

- Create a pipeline within Azure Data Factory that incorporates the data flow.

- Configure the pipeline with appropriate scheduling or trigger settings.

- Execute the pipeline to run the data flow and create/update delta lake.

Publish and Execute the Pipeline

- Once the pipeline is designed, publish it to save the changes.

- Configure the pipeline with appropriate scheduling or trigger settings.

- Execute the pipeline to start the file processing and loading of data into the delta table.

Monitor and Validate

- Monitor the execution of the pipeline using Azure Data Factory's monitoring capabilities.

- Validate the results by checking the delta table to ensure the processed data is correctly loaded.

- You can also use Azure Data Factory's logging and error handling features to identify and troubleshoot any issues during file processing.

By following these steps, you can leverage Azure Data Factory to process files and load the data into delta tables. Azure Data Factory provides a scalable and reliable platform for managing file processing tasks and integrating with delta lakes for efficient data storage and processing.

In this chapter we have explained multiple options, like data lake, data lakehouse and data mesh, that can be used to create an enterprise data warehouse. The topic here describes the need to cater to different aspects when building an enterprise data warehouse.

Summary

In conclusion, this chapter has presented a comprehensive overview of data orchestration, covering various concepts, examples, and use cases. We delved into the details of pipelines, integration tools, and ETL, and discussed different tools and their respective use cases, providing valuable insights for individuals involved in defining data engineering solutions. Furthermore, we explored how emerging data storage and processing technologies are revolutionizing the field of data orchestration and integration. The architectural guidance has shifted toward reducing data duplication and centralizing data in a unified location, such as a data lake or delta lake, to efficiently manage the entire data ecosystem, including processing, storage, governance, delivery, and analytics.

The evolution of multiple cloud tools has formed an ecosystem that supports engineering teams throughout the entire data lifecycle, encompassing data discovery, cataloging, processing, unified storage, data governance, and seamless analytics, employing both traditional and machine learning methods. Today, orchestration focuses on minimizing data movement and storage while maximizing speed and delivery, accommodating diverse scenarios such as real-time processing and traditional batch processing with strong governance and data democratization.

CHAPTER 6

Data Democratization, Governance, and Security

Modern data democratization, governance, and security in the modern data warehouse environment is not conceptual anymore—it is essential. Data needs are growing in volume, velocity, veracity, and complexity, so governance and security are becoming more and more challenging. Data democratization and security are at opposite ends of the spectrum, but governance is essential to balance both. There are a plethora of tools and techniques available for the same, but concepts, activities, and possible pitfalls are found in the same services available in the cloud.

   In this chapter, we will explore the following:

   Introduction to Data Democratization

- Self-Service

- Data Catalog and Data Sharing

- People

- Tools and Technology

   Introduction to Data Governance

- Data Stewardship

- Models of Data Stewardship

   Introduction to Data Security

- Security Layers

- Data Security Approach

- Types of Controls

© Anjani Kumar, Abhishek Mishra, and Sanjeev Kumar 2024
A. Kumar et al., *Architecting a Modern Data Warehouse for Large Enterprises*,
https://doi.org/10.1007/979-8-8688-0029-0_6

- Data Security in Outsourcing Mode

- Popular Information Security Frameworks

- Major Privacy and Security Regulations

- Major Modern Security Management Concepts

Practical Use Cases for Data Governance and Data Democratization

- Problem Statement

- High-Level Proposed Solution

Objectives

After studying this chapter, you should be able to

- understand the fundamentals of data democratization, governance, and data security; and

- identify scenarios and requirements where you can use data democratization, security, and data security.

Introduction to Data Democratization

Data democratization is defined as the willingness and ability to make information accessible to required business and technical users of information systems without having a gatekeeper or outside help to access the data. Democratizing data helps users gain unfettered access to important data without creating a bottleneck that impedes productivity.

Factors Driving Data Democratization

Several factors drive data democratization, including the following:

- Business managers get frustrated with the lower-than-expected quality, mismatched requirements, and delayed timeliness of IT deliverables. This has led business to demand autonomy for their own initiatives.

- The level of technical skill and competence found in business teams has increased.

- The rise of as-a-service delivery, cloud infrastructure, and low-code/no-code environments has made designing and delivering new services and solutions less expensive and easier for businesses. It is just a technical change to simplify development and integration.

- The shift in trend from IT-led to business-led data leadership makes data a shared responsibility.

- The shift in trend from working in silos to effective coordination between interrelated business and IT teams

- The shift from top-down to co-created, adaptive governance to empower cross-departmental teams

- The shift from monolithic to reusable technology to provide cross-departmental teams with reusable technology components to build digital capabilities quickly, securely, and efficiently

- The need to provide cross-departmental teams with data, tools, and infrastructure to build digital capabilities

Responsibility for delivery has been shifting from the IT department to the business one, driven by the business area's desire for more control and ownership. The business teams responsible for digital delivery often have little or no link to the IT department. While this is a positive trend, there is a risk that organizations will become fragmented and highly inefficient. The correct method would be to formalize the right combination of business stewardship and IT stewardship to maintain efficiency and at the same time provide ownership to the business side. This way, IT would focus as an enabler of business.

Benefits of this strategy include the following:

- Increase focus on the specific and important business goals and outcomes.

- Have better understanding of customers and their needs.

- Increase ability to change quickly and easily.

- Increase innovation and collaboration across the organization.

- Develop optimal solutions and remove duplicated efforts, resources, and solutions.

- Integrate local "black box" solutions, best working practices, and best methods to integrate into an enterprise-wide architecture.

Layers of Democratization Architecture

To get the best from a democratized organizational model, and to avoid many of its problems, we need to architect the organization across three interrelated layers.

Platform Architecture — Technology Component

The platform architecture consists of the technical platform and core services consumed by the business and technical teams. The platform provides a core set of reusable and shared platform services, a minimum viable architecture to meet local domain and department needs, and a shared strategic architecture that enables collaboration among stakeholders. For example, key business applications such as ERP (enterprise resource planning), CRM (customer relationship management), POS (point of sale), and so on, along with other services, such as security, infrastructure, and data management. The platform is architected, with reusability as a core tenet, using a modular API and service-oriented architecture (SOA).

Team Architecture — People Component

Turn the enterprise architecture (EA) practice group into a team of subject matter experts that offers a set of expertise services to meet the needs of stakeholders in each layer. Create multidisciplinary teams in which technology and business experts work together and share accountability for business and technology outcomes.

This defines the architecture that supports and enables the teams. To be effective in doing their work, teams use a minimum viable architecture that is common to them all. This contains a simple framework, design patterns, principles, and policies that will be helpful to those teams in fulfilling local needs. We should see localization as a tenet here, creating agility and flexibility for individual teams to meet their local needs.

Shared Architecture — Processes Component

Use the enterprise architecture to enable collaboration across each layer previously mentioned, bringing key teams and expertise together at the right place and time. This sets the shared governance direction for the organization. It defines the strategy, goals and objectives, governance model, and strategic roadmap. This ensures that those involved understand the direction and objectives and can make their local decisions within that context.

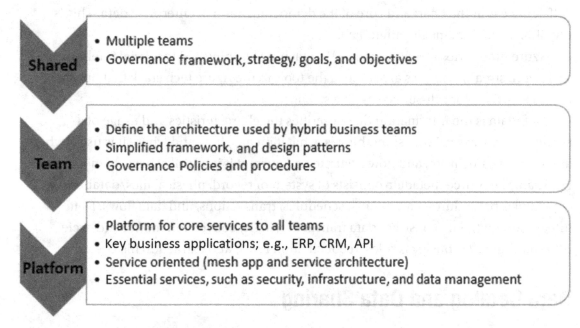

Shared
- Multiple teams
- Governance framework, strategy, goals, and objectives

Team
- Define the architecture used by hybrid business teams
- Simplified framework, and design patterns
- Governance Policies and procedures

Platform
- Platform for core services to all teams
- Key business applications; e.g., ERP, CRM, API
- Service oriented (mesh app and service architecture)
- Essential services, such as security, infrastructure, and data management

Figure 6-1. *Layers of architecture for democratization*

Enhancing the capability of data discovery is essential for democratizing data. An enterprise gets the most value when information is presented in a standardized way. Cataloging business rules, data dictionaries, and business definitions makes sure that users understand the data in the same way without confusion. Users also want to know where this data is coming from, along with the meaning of data elements. Information— like flow of data through multiple systems, or lineage of data sources at a granular level[mdash]need to be analyzed by analysts to make sure that meaning and understanding of data is the same as intended.

For example, the Azure platform, Azure DevOps is an example of sharing codes. Data definitions or business glossary are managed through Azure data catalog at the enterprise level. Sharing data outside the organization can be done through the Azure data share tool from the Azure technical stack. As a part of data democratization, the preceding tools are used for sharing the data for the purpose of increasing innovation.

Self-Service

Self-service is at the heart and core of the democratization of enterprise data. This is possible through managing metadata.

Azure time series insights, Azure ML (machine learning), AI (artificial intelligence), and Azure stream analytics are some of the tools in the Azure tech stack that business users can utilize for self-service in data science.

Metadata is the information that describes the characteristics and usage of a particular data asset. What something is, what it means, how and where it is used, where and when it came from, and how accurate and current it is are all aspects of metadata. For example, source metadata consists of system of record, physical files/databases, copybooks, procedures, parameters, schedules, transactions, and data flows. Data integration metadata consist of data transaction logic, conversion matrix and cycle, reformatting rules, business rules, reconciliation rules, and extraction history.

Data Catalog and Data Sharing

Data catalog is defined as the inventory of organized presentation of metadata that consists of glossaries, dictionaries, data models, lineage, data quality metrics, and data usage. The purpose of a data catalog in the context of data sharing is to provide a standardized understanding of data definitions and business definitions in a single place so as to interpret the data in a standardized way. The owners of the data catalog can add, delete, or change registered data assets. A clear ownership framework is a prerequisite for success. The data catalog can be shared and integrated with other systems through REST APIs.

Data dictionary is the system catalog of databases for IT or data engineering teams to understand physical data assets. It holds technical metadata, such as names, attributes, keys, indexes, formats (length, type, etc.), valid values in columns, default values in columns, and relationship of fields within table as well as with other tables.

The purpose of a *business glossary* is to create clear, consistent, and standard meanings of business terms, key indicators (KPIs), and formulas of these KPIs across the enterprise, as well as to help everyone arrive at the same understanding. The business glossary contains a collection of business terms in the language familiar to business users, with definitions, contexts, examples, and variations across business domains.

Figure 6-2 demonstrates that a data catalog consists of two categories: data dictionary (technical metadata) and business definitions (business metadata).

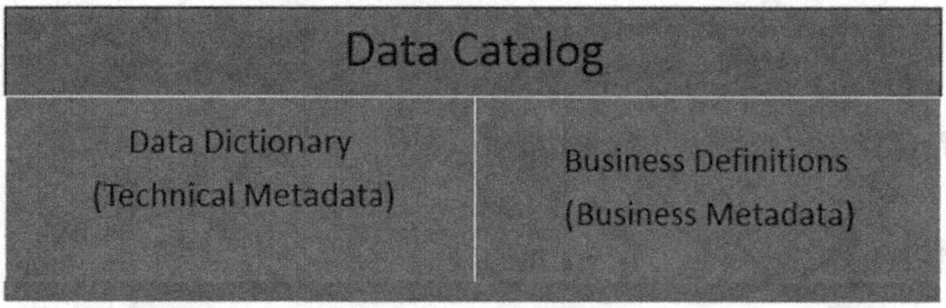

Figure 6-2. Data catalog

For the democratization of data, a data catalog makes it easy to discover data sources and eases the understanding of data. This resolves the challenges related to maintenance and discovery of information assets. Data catalogs add value by making it easy for users to find patterns, meaning, and a sense of the data.

There are multiple tools available in the market by cloud vendors or for on-premises servers. Some examples of tools found within the Azure cloud platform technical stack are as follows:

- **Azure Data Catalog:** Enables data catalog inside an enterprise

- **Azure Data Share:** Enables management and sharing of data outside the enterprise. It also allows everyone within or outside the business to contribute their insights.

Figure 6-3 demonstrates the relationship between types of metadata and the class of the metadata in an organization that includes metadata of source, data integration, data warehouse, metrics and reporting, and reference data.

Metadata

Types	Business Metadata				Business Development and Planners, Corporate Pollicy and Standards, Corporate Strategists, Corporate librarians, Regional Management		
				Business SME's , Business Data Stewards, Data Stewards, Business Analysts, Data Mining Analysts			
		Project Managers, System Managers, Operations, Developers & Testers, Integrators, Production support					
	Technical Metadata	ETL developer, data modelers DQ stewards,DBA, Data and Process architects, BI Developers					
Class		Source Metadata	Data integration Metadata	Data warehouse Metadata	Metrics and reporting metadata	Reference Metadata	
		System of record	Data transformation logic	Reference subject area	List of Data marts, objects, classes	Asset Catalog	
		Physical files/Data bases	Conversion matrix and cycle	logical entities	List of Dimension and fact tables	Document reference Libraries	
		Copybooks	reformating rules	domains & classes	List of reports	Data mining metadata	
		Procedures, parameters and schedules	business rules	process models	Meaning of Data	Corporate policy and procedure library	
		Transaction flows	reconciliation rules	Business definitions	List of Data stewards	Standards and Best practices	
			extraction History	external data	Data quality metrics		
				Data warehouse and Data marts			

Both Business and Technical Metadata
Technical Metadata
Business Definitions

Figure 6-3. *Types and classes of metadata*

Types of Metadata

Metadata is classified by the type of user that is going to use it; e.g., business metadata and technical metadata.

The other method is to classify the metadata by its usage, as follows:

- Intrinsic metadata is the information that is extracted directly from the data itself; for example, name of the document, size of the document, and content of the document.

- Administrative metadata is the information that is used to manage the data; for example, who created the document, date created, and date revised.

- Descriptive metadata is the information that describes the data; e.g., title of the document, subject of the document, who the audience is, etc.

- Semantic metadata describes the data's ability to extract content within the metadata; intelligent metadata.

Business metadata is defined as data about the business data, which includes asset catalogs, document reference libraries, data mining metadata, corporate policy and procedure library, and standards and best practices. This is used by business SMEs, business analysts, IT data stewards, business data stewards, business analysts, and data mining analysts.

Technical metadata is data about technology and is used by technical teams. Business metadata is data about the business and is used majorly by business teams.

There is another category/type of metadata that is used by both technical and business teams.

Classes of Metadata

There are five classes of metadata, as follows.:

1. Source metadata

2. Data integration metadata

3. Data warehouse metadata

4. Metrics and reporting metadata

5. Reference metadata

Source metadata is data about various sources in physical files, databases, copybooks, procedures, parameters and schedules, and transaction flows. This metadata is used by project managers, system managers, operations, developers, testers, integrators, and production support.

Data integration metadata is data about data transformation logic, conversion matrix, business rules and reformatting rules, extraction history, and reconciliation rules, to name a few examples.

Data warehouse metadata is data about reference subject area, logical entities, domains and classes, process models, business definitions, external data, data warehouses, and data marts, for example.

Metrics and reporting metadata is data about lists of data marts, objects, classes, lists of dimensions and fact tables, list of reports, meaning of data, list of data stewards, and data quality metrics, to name a few.

Reference metadata is data about asset catalog, document reference libraries, data mining metadata, corporate policies and procedures library, and standards and best practices, for example.

People

As part of self-analytics, business stewards and IT data steward teams are the core units of work within a democratized framework, and IT data stewards' teams are the core teams that support a wide range of internal and customer-facing data challenges and work within a democratized delivery model. They share accountability for technology and business outcomes. Technology becomes important and essential to achieving growth and gaining competitive advantages.

Hybrid teams manage business capabilities in multiple domains, such as order management, supply chain, and so on, which includes ERP, payroll, or an internal employee portal. This hybrid team also manages and acts as doorman for access points, tools, and processes to digital services, such as campaign management.

Hybrid teams working in the product area manage commercial products that either augment existing ones or are new revenue streams; e.g., customer prediction models, product engagement applications, etc. To succeed in the long run and to be confident in its end-to-end capabilities, it needs to offer excellent services. To sustain delivery and content, it needs to fit with the business case to gain wide acceptance across organizations. Only by adoption and getting wide acceptance can data governance be sustained for the long term.

Tools and Technology: Self-Service Tools

There are different layers at which self-service is provided, as follows:

- **Access to data:** All tools for self-service. There are different tools and technologies that can be used for providing self-service capabilities to business users.

- **BI layer:** This is the layer that is used frequently by power users. *Self-service capability* means enabling users to provide access to data within tools so that users can create ad-hoc reports. All BI tools have a semantic layer of data for summarization purposes and the data model associated with it. Power BI, Tableau, and Cognos are few tools but not all of them.

- **Semantic layer:** Providing read access to the semantic layer enables users to do ad-hoc data reporting. This solution works for end users who are business decision-makers and want to get more granular data for further analysis.

- **Data server layer:** This layer of data is present in the data server. Again, this is providing access to the data server layer itself, which could be bronze, silver, or gold, or a combination of these. Because there are raw data, structured or unstructured data associations are required by data scientists and advanced users or IT business analysts.

- **Source layers layer:** Access to this layer is provided to highly skilled users and developers through logical layers to explore the source level of data. This approach is used when data is not centralized when collected. Logical layer/data fabric layer is connected through multiple sources or through one-by-one sources painfully.

From a security perspective, row-level security can be built into data platforms and BI platforms.

The different layers require different data governance tools.

Data Governance Tools

Data governance tools are required to sustain over the long term and increase the capabilities of a business.

Data Discovery and Management

Organizations actively use both structured (products, human resource management, finance, etc.) and unstructured (legal documents and requirement analysis from regulators) data. There are many Data discovery and Classification tools available in the market. These tools are capable of indexing, searching, and analyzing both structured and unstructured data sources. The following are a few benefits:

- Data discovery and Classification tool solutions are in compliance with EU (European Union) and GDPR (general data protection regulation). It enables security operations, compliance, and access to automation features. These tools have the capability to monitor access based on categorization and classification.

- Part of DDMS (data discovery and management software) extracts and provides detailed metadata, content, and contextual information for reference; guidance to improve regulatory compliance; for risk management, and storage management and data analytic capabilities. Formerly known as file analytics, the renamed and improved (document management software) DDMS has added data sources and capabilities. This helps in enforcement and update of policies, procedures, and remediation actions.

- DDC (Data Discovery and Classification) tools solutions enable an organization to manage repositories, search documents, and find metadata of unstructured/structured data in cloud, hybrid, or on-premises. This increases the searchability of disparate and unorganized sources of information.

- DDMS solutions allow security and compliance teams to improve insights about policy adherence, including personal information (PI) data; increases visibility of data sources; data ownership; and creates data visualization maps to better identify the value and risk of the data.

- DDMS solutions reduce business risk by safeguarding sensitive data and identifying access permission issues. Some of the actions, like data breach, data exfiltration, and personal data (PD) and intellectual property (IP) exposure, can lead to auditing and regulatory fines. Identification of sensitive data and implementation of effective data management initiatives will lower business risk and increase efficiency and effectiveness of storage utilization.

- Identifying and removing redundant and outdated files increases storage efficiency. The tool is capable of identifying sensitive data and implementing effective data management initiatives. The DDMS solution enables data tracing, including where it resides and who has access to it, and has ability to explore data for driving business decisions.

Tools: Spirion; Congruity360

D&A (Data and Analytics) Platform Governance

A data and analytics platform governance covers the set of integrated data and analytics technology capabilities of the platform. This platform enables governance and stewardship for a range of policies and procedures spanning security, quality, access, retention, and privacy. This includes execution and enforcement of policies for all stakeholders (e.g., business and data stewards, business analysts, internal/external business users, and governance board members).

Analytics teams require the following:

- Ability to find critical data and linkages among data relationships; e.g., workflow of data, identification of data sources, association of business terms to technical artifacts

- A platform for fast processing and storage space irrespective of the size of data

- Easy access and interoperability to multiple sources within organization or external data

- Availability of high-quality data as source of truth. Auto-generation and execution of DQ (data quality) rules by implementing DQ rule engine

- Effective support in governance and enforcement of policies, such as privacy, security and data quality. Also data definition and automated classification of sensitive data

- Transparency in creation, consumption, and control of data

- Easy access to capable reporting and dynamic visualization tools

An organization needs to have federated but distributed, integrated, automated, synchronized, and cost-effective governance solutions. All of these requirements can be provided by a single platform. There are multiple technology platforms and vendors available in the market that can satisfy these requirements. Single platform does not necessarily mean single tool; it can minimize the number of tools and solutions if it has all the mentioned capabilities.

Tools: Collibra, IBM, Informatica. SAS

Analytics Platform Governance

As organizations are adopting advanced analytics including AI, the platform for analytics is marked with wide data, Big Data, and lake houses. All the major cloud platforms has the capability of self-service, advance analytics, predictive models, and artificial intelligence. The platform is capable of MLOps and rapid prototyping of analytics outputs by users closer to the point of build decisions.

An analytics platform governance charter is validated with policy setting and enforced through stewardship and policy execution through management, along with your analytic tools. This will reduce redundancy, save money, and lead to improved outcomes.

The tool can be enabled by lineage, but tracking data lineage is not data governance. That is nice, but not sufficient. Organizations need to prioritize and select the most important domain in the organization's data and analytics that drives its most important business outcomes.

Analytics governance tools can utilize data and analytics platform tools. Data lineage and third-party and regulatory compliance with data privacy, security, access, and quality can be covered by tools available in the market.

Suggested Tools: Collibra

Capabilities Covered by Tools

Data discovery is a process of automating the identifying, classifying, and tagging of sensitive data in both the source and the target. For large volumes and varieties of data moving in and out of multiple systems, it becomes costly to identify and manage sensitive data. Data discovery enables organizations to accelerate the data life cycle and scale the enforcement of data privacy rules consistently.

The data catalog consists of the data dictionary and business definitions.

Data Integrators and connectors with ability to access hybrid or multi-cloud environment systems (e.g. connection among clouds, connections from cloud to on-premise.

Lineage is the ability to track the linkage of data systems from source to target. If there is a change in a column in a source, one should be able to see the flow within tables and its impact on integrity.

Auditing is the ability to gather real-time data usage/adoption to ensure compliance. Auditing and reporting capabilities help you keep track of who is accessing what when and how.

Visualizing capabilities are the ability to visualize tables' metadata, linkages, classifications, high-level data model and reporting for the benefit of easy representations and understanding of stakeholders.

Data governance tools provide the ability to establish and enforce processes, policies, standards, and tools for defining and managing data. They also provide the ability to collaborate with business users to accept or decline data change requests through a data workflow approval system, along with version control.

It is also good to have a built-in SQL editor for data analysis without switching applications.

Introduction to Data Governance

Data governance is defined as the orchestration of people, processes, and technology to manage the company's data assets by using roles, responsibilities, standards, policies, and procedures to ensure the data is accurate, consistent, secure, and aligned with overall company goals and objectives.

Today, effective data governance is a key challenge in the data and analytics space. Enhancing data quality, reliability, and access is a top priority. This provides data and analytics practitioners with a framework for effective data governance and quality in the era of Big Data. Effective governance provide guidance on establishing data governance's scope and objectives, defining and implementing data stewardship programs, meeting data standardization and quality goals, and tracking ongoing improvements.

One of the core reasons for the formal introduction of data governance is to get the support of senior executives. Pressure to meet business deadlines on key IT programs can lead to more focus on immediate priorities and better handling of tactical business objectives. Many organizations have no budget for strategic data quality initiatives and ignore the risk of putting in place centralized teams for data administration.

Even though all organizations have different reasons for governance, effectiveness, efficiency, and government regulations are some of the common ones. Here are some of the challenges faced by organizations, which could be the reason to implement data governance at the enterprise level:

1. **Inability to persuade business partners that data is a business concern, not an IT concern.** Even though most business domains agree on the importance of high and consistent data quality, most of them push back on having ownership of data, perceiving that managing data is an IT department responsibility alone. Continued IT ownership puts a middleman between the ultimate beneficiaries of quality data and the strategic decisions involving that data and hinders progress toward accuracy and insight of reporting and analytics.

2. **Difficulty to adopt consistent data governance processes and policies.** Without a formal governing body with both business and IT representation and a targeted scope, governance processes will fail to be adopted and benefit will be diluted.

3. **Failure to come to consensus on common enterprise business definitions.** Every business unit in an organization tends to view their business definitions as unique rather than consistent with other areas of the enterprise. They are ingrained in the particular uses and nomenclatures in their silo with nominal concern for enterprise standards, leading to a continuation of sub-optimal reporting capabilities and an inability to get a holistic view of basic customer, employee, and vendor data, for example.

4. **Inconsistent approach to data across projects.** An inconsistent approach across the enterprise risks project solutions' being at odds with one another and fails to achieve scalability, slowing down projects as tasks and documentation are reinvented for each project.

5. **Difficult to define and sustain a path toward a target state of data competency.** Achieving data quality, accuracy, and consistency is a vast and amorphous objective. Organizations struggle to identify a realistic target state of data competency and the interim milestones to reach in the near- and mid-term. Without a maturity path that delivers tangible value along the way, data initiatives risk being deferred due to time and resource intensity coupled with distant payoff.

Despite any reason, the goal of data governance is to manage the data of an organization as an asset. This is done by providing oversight and creating policies, procedures, and processes. Other deliverables are also achieved by creating a framework or metrics. To achieve these goals, data governance should be incorporated into the organization's culture and development methodologies. These goals and impacts should be measured and improved upon consistently and continuously.

Ten Key Factors that Ensure Successful Data Governance

Organization in modern times need a data governance that encompasses a wide spectrum of use cases, from business intelligence (BI) to artificial intelligence (AI). With basic principles of accountability, transparency, compliance, and quality, Here are the following factors to consider for the successful data governance program.

1. **Clarity:** *Clarity* means having a clear scope of the data governance mandate and objectives. Preplanning and clarity of purpose will help focus the efforts and value of the money spent in terms of scarce resources that are most important for governance activities.

   Creating and implementing clear policies and procedures to guide interaction among governance bodies is vital; e.g., What, when, why, where, how and with whom to exchange information with consistency to improve data quality.

2. **Type of Data:** The application of varied degrees of governance and types of governance depend on the type of data. All data are not the same. Depending on the highest business value, volume, and usage, rigor should be applied accordingly, and priorities are decided accordingly. Start with the most valued data.

3. **Sponsorship of leadership:** Having continuous sponsorship of leadership from the conceptualization and initiation to the maturity of the governance program is essential for the success of the program—and more so at the time of conceptualization and initiation.

4. **Measuring success:** Providing continuous metrics to measure the success factors. Depth or width of key parameters can be different depending on the life cycle, maturity of program, industry, and the organization itself. Define milestones and overall progress across data domains.

5. **Partnership with business:** For sustenance of governance programs, it is important to collaborate with business at all times. Identify business stewardships, making sure that business is part of council and committees and is involved in decisions about data.

6. **Stewardship and ownership:** Stewardship and ownership is another factor. The information technology department is custodian of data. Clear ownership of business entities and data would put back ownership of data back to business. Without the consent of owners, IT should not change or modify the data, as an owner business would know all issues and plans, and progress of fixes by IT around the Entities owned by the business. Start with organization Chart and Data entities mapping to define the ownership and stewardship.

7. **Standardization:** Take all opportunities to standardize processes, data, integration, and technology requirements. The business glossary, data dictionary, and definitions are the first steps of standardization. Tracking lineage, metadata, master data management, and version control enterprise solutions are a few such items.

8. **Data quality:** Data quality is at the core of a successful data governance program. Concrete steps should be taken to improve the data quality. Quality is looked at from multiple perspectives, from users and multiple contexts. The confidence of business users in the quality of data is essential for any data governance program.

Data Stewardship

Data stewardship is a way to describe the accountabilities and responsibilities of data and related processes to ensure effective and efficient control of the use of data assets.

The main focus of data stewardship is as follows:

- **Creating and managing core metadata:** The metadata includes business terminology, data about data, business glossary, etc.

- **Standards:** Business rules and standards are applied across different domains consistently at the enterprise level. Stewards help surface these business rules and standards to ensure that there is consensus about them within the organization.

- **Managing data issues:** Stewards are responsible for the identification and resolution of data-related issues. Data issues are identified, raised, and resolved though governance committees and prioritized through data programs in the governance council.

- **Operations:** Day-to-day operations of data governance activities ensure policies, procedures, and initiatives are adhered to. They enable data ownership decisions to ensure data is managed to support goals of the organization.

Models of Data Stewardship

All organizations have different kinds of data needs. As the organization evolves, different systems, technologies, skills, and processes also evolve.

There are different models of data stewardship. Which models to apply in an organization depends on multiple factors, like organization structure, organization culture, and industry. Regulations are some of the factors in deciding the governance framework.

Model 1: Data Steward by Subject Area

As per this model of stewardship, data owners own the data and data stewards manage a specific data subject area of their expertise. The customer data steward is different from the product data steward. Depending on the organization, the product of data is owned by product stewards.

In an organization, risk management is a part of corporate governance. A data governance council can drive data governance policies and should be responsible for decisions regarding strategy and program delivery. This means that IT security governance can affect the ownership of system and application security policies. It can also impact data access and protection policy implementation.

Figure 6-4 shows the data governance framework by subject area and demonstrates how each data steward is aligned with expertise of the subject area.

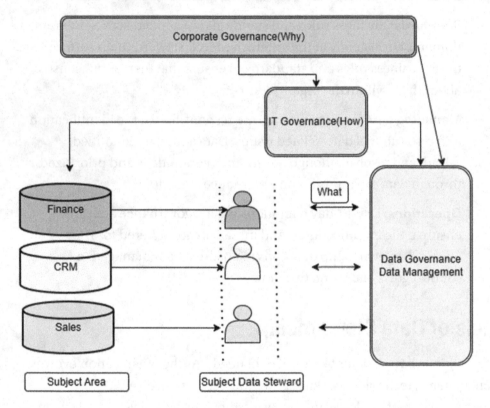

Figure 6-4. *Data governance by subject area*

Because the business department knows about the respective content and meaning of data more than anyone else, the data governance council involves data stewards from business. As the business domains can be further divided into subdomains (for example, the finance domain can be divided into collections, vendors, supplier domains, etc.), it is natural for individuals to gain expertise in their respective domains. One of the data stewards may be aligned into one of multiple domains.

The effectiveness of this stewardship model depends on the complexity of the data, subject areas, industry, and size of the organization. Generally, this stewardship model works best for medium- and large-sized companies where multiple departments share the same data.

Some of the benefits of the stewardship model by subject area are as follows:

- Stewards from business and IT are clear about their respective responsibilities.

- It is easy to implement and pitch stewardship and ownership responsibilities in this framework.

- Knowledge about the systems and business rules about the respective subject areas increases incrementally.

The following are the challenges of stewardship by subject area:

- Data stewardship efforts take manual effort in all business areas. One measures data stewardship improvements in terms of business benefits and quantifies these benefits in monetary terms. Quantifying data quality improvements is one of the ways to measure success, but linking business benefits—e.g., customer retention—with data quality improvement is another challenge.

- The effectiveness of this model of stewardship is tied to business initiative. Tried and tested long-term relationship building with each department's subject area experts is the key to success.

- Depending on the systems, data domain, culture, and other factors in an organization, data stewardship can become a political landmine, as people can become resistant to change and hold off the knowledge in fear of ceding control.

Model 2: Data Stewardship by Function

As the name suggests, managing data stewardship by function, a.k.a. organizational data stewardship, focuses on managing data by lines of business or organization departments.

As there are multiple departments organized by function—e.g., marketing department, finance department, etc.—this data stewardship model focuses on the functional area. In our example, the marketing department in the retail industry can consist of data related to campaigns, customer details, promotions, purchasing history, and product details, as well as external data related to demography, customer credit scores, etc. The following are the benefits of this model:

- It is easy to establish a business glossary and data definitions by business function as they understand the context of the data. It becomes easy to assign and align data stewards by business function. There is good possibility of finding knowledgeable business data stewards.

- There is a good likelihood to get the sponsorship and the commitment of time from departments regarding aligned stewards.

Data stewardship by function has the following risks:

- Putting a boundary of responsibility of data entities where there are multiple departments that may take ownership results in duplication of efforts and can become political. This may result in contradicting policies, procedures, and definitions of the same data. Getting a clear ownership matrix by entities will help in this scenario.

- In some cases, data stewards may feel reluctant to coordinate across department boundaries. Sponsorship from leadership may help regarding conflict resolution.

- This stewardship model does not work in companies that are looking for initiatives with a singular, consolidated, and standard view of data across the organization. For example, with a global organization, trying to create a singular financial data model for all countries—which have different tax structures, rules, and regulations—would be challenging to tie together within the same department. Strong data governance with a conflict-resolution process would be helpful in this scenario.

Model 3: Data Steward by Business Process

Data stewardship by business process means data stewardship is assigned to an individual business process. This stewardship model is very effective for companies that already have a high level of mature processes and understanding about data at the enterprise level.

Data stewardship responsibility is assigned by specific business processes. A single business process consists of multiple data domains, applications, and systems. One or several data stewards may be assigned to each business process based on the complexity, scope, and size of the domain area. For instance, tech companies with corporate software products e.g., sales process (from quote to cash business process) can have one business data steward assigned to this process and multiple IT data stewards assigned. There would be primary and secondary stewards assigned to subject matter experts (SMEs).

Benefits of stewardship by business process include the following:

- It is easy to manage the predefined business processes as a natural extension of process definitions.

- Measurement of business benefit, data quality, and data availability in terms of business process is straightforward and reliable.

- It is easy to justify the cost to expand the stewards for processes. This is an efficient and effective way to extend stewardship across organizations.

The risks of stewardship by business process include the following:

- A data ownership model becomes difficult to assign to multiple process stewards as they use the same tables, elements, and domains. Implementation of an enterprise-wide data governance program is important to manage this situation.

- As the business grows, the size and complexity of data and processes increases. The several data stewards assigned to the same process could cause confusion.

Model 4: Data Steward by System

This approach focuses on taking ownership and stewardship by system. At most companies, systems are defined. As the organization grows, a lack of understanding grows about the data found within systems. The duplicated, redundant data appears in multiple systems. This combines with a lack of master data and source of truth to create challenges. Organizations can propagate data quality of systems in a sustainable way by addressing data issues in the upstream systems at the point of origin. The system-oriented stewardship model is an effective way for an organization to introduce the concept of data stewardship.

Figure 6-5 shows the data governance framework by system, demonstrating that each data steward is aligned with the expertise of the subject area.

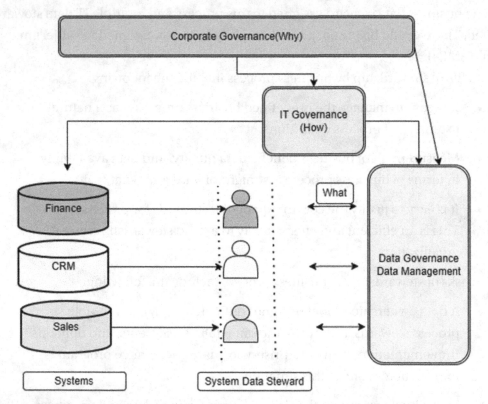

Figure 6-5. *Data stewardship by system*

All systems are identified with storage, processing, and visualization of data.

There could be more than one physical or virtual system with different domains. As a business puts all its focus on growth, physical system ownership is taken by the IT department themselves. Any change in the system, including data, is owned by IT. This model is the default model in many organizations.

The benefits of system-oriented data stewardship include the following:

- The IT department takes ownership of data improvements when business teams are reluctant to claim ownership or involvement in stewardship because of one or multiple reasons, like bandwidth issues, organization structure, lack of education, or benefits related to data governance and stewardship.

- Data stewardship by system can grow in an organic way or bottom up. This allows IT to start stewardship by involving business through regular education about standards, rules, policies, and procedures as the system grows to meet the needs of the business and to make the data valuable to the business.

- Each system having at least one data steward is an established practice in this model.

The challenges of system-oriented data stewardship include the following:

- IT's taking a leadership role may create confusion in the business department as to the role of IT as data owners instead of data custodians. This makes any issues related to data IT issues, and business avoids involvement in issue resolution. By default, businesses may not bother about policies and procedures related to data.

- System stewardship by system can lose the big picture as they maintain the integrity of the data only on their system, which comes under the preview of their responsibility.

- System-level data stewardship constrains involvement and communication between business and IT.

Model 5: Data Steward by Project

A data stewardship approach by project may be the fastest way to introduce the data stewardship concept to organizations. Generally, consultancy companies prefer this approach by introducing stewardship on high-profile, data-intensive strategic initiatives. Some examples are data integration– and business intelligence–related projects.

Responsibilities related to provisioning and data quality are given to experienced team members. This approach is applied where the project implementation team is strong. As team members are starting, expertise in the data domain grows with time.

Figure 6-6 demonstrates data stewardship by project. Data governance under corporate governance umbrella of corporate governance and IT governance through project management office.

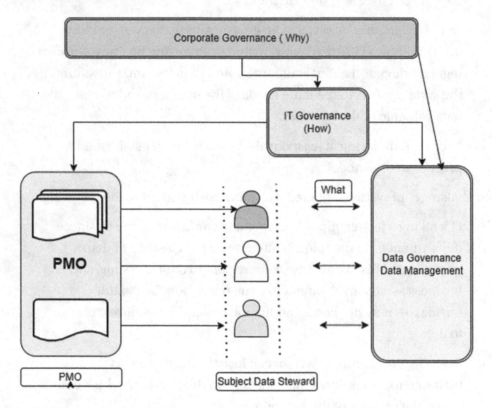

Figure 6-6. *Project stewardship*

As part of organization hierarchy, corporate governance includes management of IT governance. The IT governance team manages the project management office (PMO), along with data governance. This model is a temporary measure until the project ends. The PMO manages data stewards to interdependent projects ensuring synergy with primary and secondary domain expertise assigned. This gives an opportunity to formalize and extend data management standards, policies, and procedures, and to introduce data steward roles to other projects.

The benefits of data stewardship by projects are as follows:

- Increase speed of execution by introducing stewardship quickly

- Flexibility to customize data stewardship processes as per organization culture and desired outcomes

- Ability to Ability to realize initial and quick benefits and then subsequently extended and refined for broader deployment

The challenges of project-oriented stewardship are as follows:

- As projects are of finite time and effort, once a project finishes, the team may get dispersed or allocated to different projects, which means that data stewardship can lose its momentum.

- Finding incumbent skills can be challenging for small companies or companies that use project-oriented or consultancy approaches. It is difficult to find skillful resources in data management, governance implementation, and execution.

As data stewardship is extended to different projects, adoption of the idea of data stewardship increases, and the role and model can evolve. Either the model will shift to another model or is modified or combined with another model to make it a hybrid; e.g., using both functional and system experts. The framework described is good for the introduction of data stewardship to an organization to prove value and without any significant disruption.

There are multiple levers through which data governance is implemented. As mentioned earlier, data governance includes designing and implementing the operating model, assigning stewardship by establishing role, responsibilities, and tasks, and enabling tools. This helps organizations better understand and protect data privacy and security, and fulfill compliance obligations.

Data governance framework comprise of following three capabilities.

> **Process:** Understanding and setting up legal requirements, operating model policies, enacting procedures as per strategic objectives to consolidate business requirements, metrics, and rules associated with these objectives. Processes are set up around people and technologies.

People: Setting up teams consisting of individuals from within the organization with clearly defined roles, responsibilities, and tasks, and providing resources to them to perform duties, and also providing guidance. Increasing and including new skills about processes and technologies.

Technology: Using technologies including tools to aid people and processes in identifying and analyzing dataflows and reducing risk.

Data Security Management

Data security management is defined as the planning, development, and execution of security policies and procedures to provide proper authentication, authorization, access, and auditing of data and information assets as per an organization's risk strategy.

Even though IT security management is a wide area, data security is a subset of it. The following are the purposes of data security management:

- Prevent unauthorized or inappropriate access to data assets.

- Ensure that the privacy and confidential needs of all stakeholders including government regulations are met.

- Ensure confidence in the capability of the organization, including users, by creating systems, processes, policies, and procedures to provide the required and expected level of protection against data breaches or loss of data resulting from any reason at any point in time.

This is achieved by focusing on the CIA (confidentiality, integrity, and availability) rule. *Confidentiality* means to protect against unauthorized or inappropriate access of data. *Integrity* means to ensure right data is available at the right time to the right person. *Privacy* means personal information is used only for the specific purpose for which it was collected. Some of the techniques to achieve the security principals are database audit and protection (DAP) techniques, data loss prevention (DLP) services, privacy-enforced techniques, and data life cycle management techniques.

Some deliverables to manage data security are policies, procedures, privacy and confidentiality standards, user profile management, passwords and memberships management, data security permissions, data security controls, data, access view permissions, document classifications, authentication, access history, and data security audits.

Key considerations and identification of potential business risks for not being conservative in data security are as follows:

- Data breaches and ransomware

- Project disruption

- Loss of customer retention

- Loss of reputation

- Financial penalties or fines

- Data manipulation and data loss

- Insider threats

- Industry, economic, or environmental events

Figure 6-7 demonstrates the major data security implications and respective impact on business outcomes.

Data Security Implication	Impact on Business Outcomes
Slowing access to data	Reduced employee performance; indirect monetary impact
Removing staff access to data	Prevents analytics can lead to slow Performance to reduced quality of Business decisions in absence of right data
Lack of or bad privacy management	Reduced customer loyalty and Brand image
Data breaches and ransomware	Impact can vary from Disruption, Financial penalties and reduced customer loyalty.

Figure 6-7. *Direct Business Impacts*

Security Layers

The security of data is paramount, and data is money. There are seven layers of security, with data at the core. The innermost layer has more value than the outer layer. Accessibility decreases as you travel to the innermost layer.

Figure 6-8 demonstrates the seven layers of security: (1) human layer, (2) physical parameter layer, (3) access point/end point, (4) network layer, (5) infrastructure layer, (6) application layer, and (7) data layer.

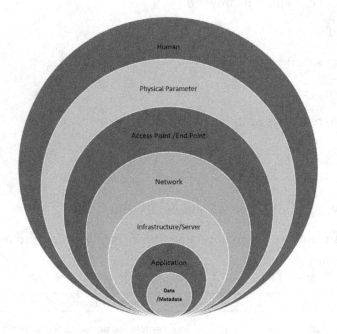

Figure 6-8. *Seven layers of security*

"Data is money." Data is the center of all security, and the purpose of security is to save data.

Understanding the different layers helps in safeguarding your company's reputation in terms of managing customer data. This knowledge says that client-facing portals should be reliable, compliant to regulations, and safe to use. It is essential to safeguard the company's reputation by saving the data.

Human Layer

Once a device is compromised, cybercriminal hackers may gain access to your partial or entire network. People can be the weakest link in the organization's information security program.

Out of the seven layers, the human layer is the first line of defense. Employees, contractors, external partners, and business vendors make up this layer. The human layer is the outermost layer of security in terms of having the most vulnerability in security. Thirty-two percent of breaches are caused by phishing attacks, and malware delivered through emails is one of the major reported incidents. Hackers use social engineering frequently to manipulate the users or stakeholders to obtain access to information about a system.

The human layer is more vulnerable than the non-human layer in IT security. This vulnerability can be reduced substantially by increasing proactiveness. The goal of actions is to increase the degree of proactiveness in IT security at this layer. Some of the ways to reduce vulnerability are as follows:

- Regular and mandatory awareness training of all stakeholders. Making sure that all stakeholders understand their role and actions in case of attack

- Creating tools and technology components as part of an IT security program

- Increasing the technical skills of non-technical employees, contractors, and vendors; e.g., training to prevent non-technical staff from clicking on suspicious emails and links. Increasing awareness through training and education to spot phishing attacks

- Creating policies, procedures, and awareness—and subsequently implementation of training.

Physical Perimeter Point/Layer

This is the second outermost layer out of seven layers. This is the first layer of physical infrastructure or perimeter/computers. This layer consists of physical infrastructure that is the interaction point for humans. This layer consists of computers, laptops, mobile phones, and printers. In the case of IOT (Internet of Things), systems that interact with

285

external environments are also considered to be within this layer. As data can flow inter-layer or intra-layer, we should know what devices/systems are involved and the criticality of the data moving through these systems.

Physical devices need to be protected as these are the physical entry points through the perimeter/devices, irrespective of their location (office, home, cloud farm, or call center.

The example of securing all these devices with perimeter points includes firewalls, encryption systems, anti-virus, device management, etc.

Network Layer

As the devices in the organization are connected to each other or to the application or data server, once one physical point is breached, there is a risk for all the devices within the network. Security in this layer is focused on the security activities within the network.

The internal network layer stops most attackers. For example, this layer is responsible for stopping the spam using automatic scanning tools. The perimeter layer is the most effective layer from the standpoint of stopping attacks, but this layer is often the worst configured, such that a single mistake can allow anything in.

A limited-access approach to the network is one way to achieve the desired security level. Providing access based on the principle of least privilege access applies to all layers, including network layer. This may not stop hackers fully, but at least it will slow down if not fully stop them from achieving their objective of reaching target data.

Secure design is about ensuring that users are traveling through the network in a limited and secure way, and can include secure design and topology, VLAN (virtual local area network), and multi-layer firewalls or switches. Browser-based applications of SAAS (software as a service) use sandboxes to prevent unauthorized users from entering the network. This way, damage is limited to the specific part of the network accessed by external threats. Some examples of how secure networks are enforced include wi-fi security, regular vulnerability scanning, SOC (SECURITY OPERATIONS CENTER)/SIEM (security incident and event management), regular patching, and content filtering.

Endpoint Layer/Protection

An endpoint layer consists of any device connected to your network. Smart devices connected to the network can be a desktop computer, laptop, phone, or server. For endpoint security, antivirus software is prevalent in the market; however, it comes to the market with heuristic, behavior-based, or signature-based flavors. Some of the examples are Antivirus software, firewalls, breach-detection agents, desktop firewall, content filtering, patch management, etc. Even though it is helpful and will stop most attackers, to make it robust, mobile device management (MDM) is a critical part of endpoint security. End-to-end encryption of all endpoint devices is key for robust security by restricting access to specified devices and managing devices remotely.

There are many devices connected to the network. Smart devices need high-bandwidth or high-speed internet to work. As these devices can be used anywhere and anytime, this increases the attack surface as well as vulnerability. Robust measures need to be put in place to ensure devices in the network are secure.

Operating systems must use an automated security patching and compliance reporting tool. Operating consoles should be used if available. Use the Security Remediation and Patch Management Standard and Infrastructure Security Standards for applicable server configuration standards.

Application Layer

The application layers deal with the software and applications you use in the organization for different purposes; e.g., Microsoft Office, Zoom, Google Meet, emails, Slack, and other applications necessary to carry out daily tasks. Application security entails software applications that provide protection from data exposure resulting from transaction compromise or failure.

These applications must be secured. The easiest way to ensure security is to update all the apps to the latest versions. Vulnerabilities found in regular reports should be handled by tools to ensure patching and updates are done in a timely and comprehensive manner. There are additional security measures that should be taken to protect the integrated application. Sandboxes are used in browser-based applications to prevent any unauthorized users from entering the network.

Data Layer

Data and metadata of a business is the heart and aim of any security breach. This layer requires the most attention. Payments, customer information, Social Security numbers, and intellectual property (IP) are the high-value and high-risk data and are the most regulated. They are highly vulnerable to penalties and could be reason for eroding the reputation and wealth of an organization.

Extending the example, once hackers/thieves get hold of an account, a.k.a. deposit box, they find a treasure map in this box. However, they are not able to read or make sense out of it. In another example, if a laptop gets stolen and hackers get hold of the hard drive, if this hard drive is encrypted it cannot be opened. It is useless. Even in situations where hackers got hold of email but email is encrypted, they cannot open the email, hard drive, dataset, or column within dataset. In the absence of a decryption algorithm, even if someone is able to have data open, it is of no use. When data is in motion or in procession it still needs to be protected.

Governance and implementation of data management policies along with security features like encryption, authentication, regular data backups, are some of the ways to secure data layer.

Mission-Critical Assets

Mission-critical assets are those assets of organization that are critical for the survival of the organization. It could be software, hardware, electronic systems, patents, financial records/data, and much more. Analysis is done to identify which assets are considered core and necessary for business and mission critical for the implementation and working of six layers of security. These assets are mandatory to follow industry, state, country, and international laws.

Data Security Approach

A model was created by John McCumber to provide a representation of the architectural approach used in computer and information security. It is a 3 x 3 x 3 cube with all 27 cells representing an area that must be properly addressed to secure modern information systems.

The McCumber model is used within the combination of structured and unstructured techniques to make a threat elicitation methodology within the model-driven architecture framework: price model, information assurance model, asset protection model, CNSS (Committee on National Security Systems) model, etc.

Figure 6-9 shows the McCumber Cube, demonstrating the relationship between dimensions (critical information characteristics, information states, and security measures).

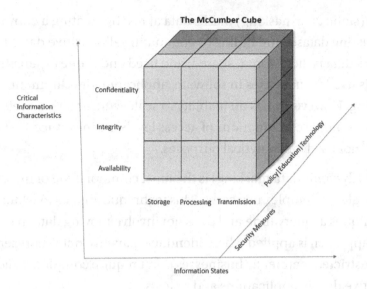

Figure 6-9. *The McCumber Cube*

As per the framework, there are three dimensions, which are security measures, critical information characteristics, and information states. Confidentiality, integrity, and availability are handled at the storage, processing, and transmission states by creating policies, providing education to people, and providing appropriate technologies.

At the cross-section of technology, transmission, and confidentiality lie authorization and authentications. The data is either moving from one end to another or at rest. Hence, data is also safeguarded, whether at rest or in motion.

Data must be encrypted as per data management encryption standards and data classification and protection standards. Cryptographic keys and digital certificates must be created, distributed, maintained, stored, and disposed of securely. This is done by Hardware based encryption (HBA)-based encryption, array-based encryption, and drive encryption.

Data masking, also known as obfuscation, makes sensitive data unidentifiable but available for storage and analytics. SDM (static data masking) and DDM (dynamic data masking) are two ways of masking, each with its own strengths and weaknesses and usage scenarios and fit for use cases:

- SDM (static data masking) masks data at rest by creating a copy of an existing dataset and hiding or eliminating all sensitive data. This copied data is then stored, shared, and used and is free of sensitivity. This is used for use cases in software, application development, and training. However, it has an inability to scale with larger datasets where multiple combinations of access levels are introduced. Also, this is not used for analytical purposes.

- DDM (dynamic data masking) is the most common type of masking and scales to complex use cases. This technique applies masking techniques at query time and does not involve moving data in or out. This approach is applied where identified sensitive data is presented in a restricted manner as businesses don't require complete access to sensitive data in applications and reports.

Meeting the regulatory compliance rules in non-production environments is also essential. Data loss prevention and Digital rights are also required to be managed and secured.

Types of Controls

There are two types of controls: active and proactive responses. The proactive security control purpose is to spot threats before they materialize.

Once data security breaches or incidents happen, you need to know how to respond to a range of incidents, from innocent breaches to targeted hacking disasters. As we know that the availability of data is one of the factors to consider, if a breach means customers can't access data because of any reason, it doesn't matter if the root cause is a DoS (denial of service) attack or a fire.

The responses of many disaster recovery and data breach controls overlap; e.g., applying software patches that close security holes, backing up data, and using high-availability systems.

Proactive data security controls include monitoring networks and systems and running intrusion-detection systems, as well as encryption of data at rest, in motion, or processing.

Technical controls are how the software and hardware tools put data security in place.

Operational controls are defined to keep systems and applications secure. The principle of least privilege is one of the common policies organizations should have. ACL (access control list) is one of the ways to install policies. These policies ensure that you stay in compliance with regulations like GDPR (general data protection regulation).

Architectural data security controls work on how you connect to and between different systems; e.g., systems like VPNs (virtual private networks) and cloud applications use networks. If these systems aren't secure, data is vulnerable. These controls look to improve on vulnerability points and set up policies and procedures to close those gaps, such as penetration testing, vulnerability assessments, and design reviews.

The purpose of monitoring authentication and access behavior is as follows:

- Finding out who is connecting, for what, where, and when, and who is accessing information assets, which is a basic requirement for compliance auditing.

- Alert security administrators to unpredictable, unusual, suspicious, and unforeseen situations, and compensate for oversights in data security planning, design, and implementation.

Major Categories for Security Controls

There are six major categories for security controls, as follows:

- **Operational:** Rules and procedures to protect systems and applications

- **Administrative:** Admin controls in terms of actions, policies, and procedures to enforce standards.

- **Architecture level:** Security control is interconnected between systems.

- **Software level:** Putting security controls at software level

- **Active control:** Putting controls to respond to incidents when they happen

- **Proactive control:** Controls to spot active threats

Data Security in Outsourcing Mode

In modern times, outsourcing is common for development, maintenance, and even security administration. Outsourcing led to additional data security challenges and responsibilities across the world. Keep in mind that companies share responsibilities; control mechanisms are transferred, but not responsibilities and liabilities. These tighter risks are managed by the following:

- **Clauses in outsourcing contract:** Limited liability mechanism provisions; service-level agreements; right to audit; and clear, precise, and pre-defined consequences for breaching these provisions.

- **Monitoring and controls:** Frequent and detailed data security auditing and lineage; monitoring of vendors' system activities; tracking the lineage, chain of custody, and flow of data across systems; constant communication with the service vendor and having data security reports from the vendor; controlling unauthorized access to your organization's data; and clarity in RACI matrix (Responsibility, accountability, consulted and informed) for all roles vendors and geographies to make sure what action would be taken by whom in case of realization of an event.

Guiding Principles

The following are some of the guiding principles for security management at the data layer:

- **Collaboration:** Data security is managed by the IT security team, along with IT stewards. It is governed by, collaborated with, and directed by multiple stakeholders, from the data governance council and committee members, to business stewards, internal and external audit teams, and legal department. Data security policies should be reviewed collaboratively and approved by the data governance council.

- **Enterprise-level approach:** Standards, policies, and procedures must be designed and applied consistently across the entire organization.

- **Clear accountabilities:** There should be clarity in roles, ownerships, and responsibilities across enterprises, including customers, suppliers, and business partners.

- **Metadata-driven:** Data security is driven by metadata. Having classification for data elements is an essential part of data definitions and business definitions. Security of the data layer can be achieved by putting in multiple controls, like version control, access control, identity roles management, groups management, password management, data and group membership management, etc.

- **Proactive management:** Being a step ahead in data security management is critical. Additionally, regular engagement with stakeholders, managing organization, and cultural change is essential. Regularly monitoring the servers and systems for the flow of information is helpful.

- **Reduce exposure:** Minimize sensitive/confidential data in all layers of security.

Popular Information Security Frameworks

Technical aspects of managing information security risks fall to the IT function. It is necessary to have familiarity with the following common frameworks IT uses to manage security risks:

1. ISO/IEC 27001 and 27002

2. NIST Cyber Security Framework (CSF)

3. Cybersecurity Capability Maturity Model (C2M2)

4. HITRUST Cyber Security Framework (CSF)

5. IASME Governance Framework

   ISO/IEC 27001 and 27002: With a joint effort from the International Organization for Standardization (ISO) and International Electrotechnical Commission (IEC), frameworks were published in 2005. The frameworks are the most widely recognized and are meant to be widely applicable across industry and company size.

NIST Cyber Security Framework (CSF): The National Institute of Standards and Technology created a cybersecurity framework that can be applied across industries irrespective of size or type of organization. This framework focuses on the following five core functions related to security incidents:

1. Identify

2. Protect

3. Detect

4. Respond

5. Recover

The framework provides an organization-based context and view on cybersecurity risks. This helps to manage the cybersecurity risk through putting processes in place.

Current risk management methods try to mitigate the threat environment within legal and regulatory requirements and business objectives and constraints. Risks are mitigated through tier selection, which meets organization goals, identifies critical assets, and reduces cybersecurity risk to acceptable levels.

The organization identifies three tiers of risks: Tier 1 (Partial), Tier 2 (risk informed), and Tier 3 (repeatable). These tiers are based on the risk management process, as well as having an integrated risk management program and external participation. These are not maturity levels. The three-tier model encourages movement to a higher level of risk to reduce risk and be cost effective.

Cybersecurity Capability Maturity Model (C2M2): Though created by the U.S. Department of Energy, this model can apply to organizations of all sectors, sizes, and types. It includes a supplemental toolkit to be used in conjunction with the model itself to evaluate the organization's information security program maturity.

HITRUST Cyber Security Framework (CSF): The (HITRUST) Health Information Trust Alliance is based on the ISO/IEC 27001/27002 frameworks. It incorporates requirements from healthcare-related federal legislation and is intended for organizations handling personal health information (PHI). HITRUST received NIST CSF certification in 2018, providing a means to assure compliance with NIST framework's objectives.

IASME Governance Framework: The IASME (Information Assurance for Small and Medium Enterprises Consortium) governance framework is designed to improve small and medium enterprise (SMEs) cybersecurity services. This framework is similar to ISO 27001 but with high-end security tools at reduced cost for SMEs. This IASME certification allows organizations to get free cybersecurity insurance in the United Kingdom.

Major Privacy and Security Regulations

All of the privacy and security regulations should be taken into consideration while defining policies and procedures for an organization.

The purpose of regulations like HIPAA, GDPR, data security standards, and many other regulations is to actively prevent unauthorized access and to safeguard data through all means. These regulations make sure that organizations create comprehensive data management strategies, including data security, privacy, and data protection to safeguard customers and consumers at large.

There are multiple major privacy and security regulations affecting data security standards in countries across the world. Some examples of region- and country-specific rules/regulations and laws are seen here:

European Union: Data Protection Directive of 1998

Italy: Data Protection Code of 2003 Italy: Processing of Personal Data Act, Jan. 1997

Australia: Privacy Act of 1988

Brazil: Privacy currently governed by Article 5 of the 1988 Constitution

Canada: The Privacy Act - July 1983, Personal Information Protection and Electronic Data Act (PIPEDA) of 2000 (Bill C-6)

Chile: Act on the Protection of Personal Data, August 1998

India: Information Technology Act of 2000

United States: Some examples of the regulation of the United States are Federal Information Security Management Act (FISMA), Privacy Protection Act of 1980 (PPA), Video Privacy Protection Act of 1988, etc.

There are industry-specific (financial, telecommunication, health care, infrastructure, and energy, etc.) protection and security laws within the country. There could be state laws along with country-specific security laws; e.g., California Senate Bill 1386 (SB 1386).

GDPR (general data protection regulation) is a set of data privacy laws enacted by the European Union to ensure consumer privacy. These laws have become an international standard across industries. The purpose of the law is to ensure the privacy and safety of data that can be exploited. The personal identification data is defined as data by which a person can be identified; e.g., name, SSN, address, etc. Such data privacy standards should be put in place to ensure a comprehensive data strategy is in place for data security. This data security strategy includes successful identification and classification of personal identifiable) PI data. As part of GDPR, organizations have to disclose policies and procedures that are implemented and governed across organizations. This law gives the right to consumers to determine how their data can be used. In the absence of implementation of these policies and procedures, or in the case of data breaches, heavy penalties are imposed upon those organizations.

Major Modern Security Management Concepts

Along with fundamental concepts of information security (confidentiality, integrity, availability, authenticity, and non-repudiation) cross all five pillars of information security (Physical, people, data and infrastructure security, and crisis management).

Following are few major long term modern security management concepts:

Centralized Enterprise Key Management

Encryption is used to enforce data-access policies across different structured and unstructured storage platforms, including on-premises and public cloud services. This provides a symmetric, centralized software or hardware appliance for multiple encryption solutions by enabling secure key distribution, storage, and administration, and maintaining key life cycle management.

Implementing encryption or tokenization is a critical component of a data security strategy. These mitigate growing data residency and privacy requirements to prevent data breaches due to hacking or malicious or accidental incidents. Enterprise key management provides consistent key life cycle management to help mitigate these risks and reduce the risk of accidental shredding of data in case keys are lost.

Enterprise key management enables cryptography to protect the data/files in storage or to protect data fields stored within files accessed from SQL and NoSQL platforms.

Enterprise-wide key management is expected to support enterprise-wide data security governance (DSG) policies that complement a broader set of product controls, such as database activity monitoring (DAM), data access governance (DAG), data loss prevention (DLP), and data access privileges in on-premises or multi-cloud environments.

Data access governance helps across connections with multiple systems. This includes interoperability of unstructured and semi-structured data. Governance includes assessment, management, and real-time monitoring of systems. These controls include system-level, row-level access, and table- or schema-level access control, along with other security controls at the storage and processing levels. Data classification identifies which class of data needs to have more access controls, audit trails, and permission activities.

Data access governance products help organizations solve data security and privacy regulation issues, specifically where data access tracking is critical, including financial services, banking, health care, federal and pharmaceutical, legal, insurance, and retail. This helps in the protection of data related to intellectual property in multiple industries.

Data Protection Cloud Gateways

Deploy a combination of forward/reverse proxy and API adapters to public cloud SaaS providers. They can apply encryption or tokenization to structured or unstructured data as it flows to the SaaS provider to mitigate inappropriate access that could lead to a breach. This helps meet data residency requirements for data protection and privacy. Functionality-wise, this ability is also provided by some security service edge (SSE) products.

Increasing volumes of sensitive data are stored across multiple public SaaS (software as a service) based tools, which increases the need to control data residency and access to data to mitigate security and privacy risks. CDPG (cloud data protection gateway) software is important to help reduce these risks by restricting access to data to specific staff, as well as potentially blocking access by the CSP (content security policy).

Secure Instant Communications

Typical regulations are the Health Insurance Portability and Accountability Act (HIPAA) and the regulations issued by the Financial Industry Regulatory Authority (FINRA).

Data Classification

Data classification is a process to classify the risk for data within all systems across organization, using factors like the value, security, access, usage, privacy, storage, ethics, quality, and retention requirements of the data. The higher the risk rating, the more precautions is required to securely manage the data. First step is needed to classify the sensitivity of the data so as to process and enable management and prioritization of data.

Classification and organization of information assets uses a process of categorization and finding relationships between business domains and subject areas. Because data classification is the process of organizing, it includes the application of tagging and labeling to a data object to facilitate its use and governance. This is done through the application of controls during its life cycle, or the activation of metadata using data fabric.

Data classification has an impact on a wide range of areas in data management, from identification, control and mitigation of risk in an application, and data security and compliance, to metadata management, master data management, content and records management, data stewardship, and multiple DataOps, among others.

Identifying and tagging all the organization's data is the first step for maturity of data security and risk management. Increasing data classification capabilities in an organization also increases security and risk management capabilities. There are multiple automation and AI tools available for cloud and on-premises data-based applications.

TLS Encryption and Decryption

The Transport Layer Security (TLS) encryption/decryption platform is a dedicated appliance (in-line or out-of-band) used to decrypt and pass TLS traffic to the other end of the destination to multiple stand-alone security inspection solutions, then encrypts the traffic before it proceeds to its final destination for data processing.

The TLS decryption platform can be used to decrypt inbound and outbound traffic. This is important because as an ever-greater percentage of inbound and outbound network traffic is encrypted, security and risk management leaders must consider how to gain visibility into potentially malicious activity.

This technology can solve visibility issues in organizations outside of highly regulated nations. In nations with data privacy and data sovereignty laws, decisions to decrypt must be coordinated with legal and human resources. Enterprises tolerant of additional appliances can use a dedicated TLS decryption platform for the greater visibility necessary to protect their data and let other security tools inspect traffic. Midsize enterprises are likely to leverage existing solutions to solve visibility problems.

Data Security as a Service

Data security as a service (DSaaS) provides data security and protection capabilities as a service. Enterprises and organizations hand over their data to the service provider. The provider stores, protects, transforms, and shares it back to them or with third parties while achieving the required compliance and secrecy goals.

DSaaS makes complex or expensive data security controls accessible to mainstream organizations. It enables clients to shorten the deployment times of data security from many months to several days, bringing them into a position to match the speed of cloud and DevOps initiatives. It achieves this by consistently meeting the customers' and regulators' control objectives without the need for the customer to care for the implementation.

Data can be secured while at rest and in motion. It can flow securely among individuals and organizations. However, an increased number of data-related regulations and associated legal, security, and privacy risks are blocking this data sharing. DSaaS will be instrumental in solving this challenge.

Data security controls and data security architectures are frequently complex, and the customer is loaded with both hardware and software—putting thorough, scalable, and agile data security out of reach of most organizations. At the same time, most organizations must step up their data security controls to address constantly evolving privacy regulations, prepare for open data initiatives and artificial intelligence/machine learning use cases, or enable monetization of data with ever-changing ecosystem partners. This tension will lead to accelerated adoption of DSaaS.

Ideal Scenarios

For unstructured data, the use of AI/ML supports semantic analysis and data discovery. For example, depending on the context, a date can be a date of birth, a purchase date, or delivery date in the purchasing life cycle. Each data type will need an appropriate level of protection.

In summary, for data security there is no one single panacea solution. There are evolving gaps, which are driving the need for tools that orchestrate and integrate controls across data security, identity access management (IAM), and privacy and application management tools and platforms. In the meantime, it is important as new technologies are added to address emerging data security use cases, to use a digital security guard (DSG), a data recovery agent (DRA), and a privacy impact assessment (DPIA/PIA) to create data security policies that address these product shortcomings or gaps. The emergence of new technologies such as DSP (digital security program) and DSPM (data security management) is expected to help bridge these gaps in a more orchestrated, scalable way. Continued innovation in data protection techniques has seen the emergence and growth of confidential computing, differential privacy, homomorphic encryption, zero-knowledge proofs, SMPC (secure multiparty computation), and KMaaS (key management as a security). Technologies that can monitor user activity with data are evolving, such as cloud-native DLP (data loss prevention), multi-cloud DAM (database activity monitoring), DSaaS, and DSP.

Practical Use Case for Data Governance and Data Democratization

Following is a business use case that provides a real-world example of how combining data governance and data democratization helped an organization.

An assessment was done to find out how to improve the efficiency and effectiveness of the data and education analytics landscape of AI Fabric School.

AI Fabric School (pseudonym) was under pressure to improve outcomes and efficiencies in all aspects of its operations, with severe shortages in faculty and staff adding to this pressure. The effective use of data and analytics offers a means to do so. Increased and better use of data will be a key differentiator among organization going forward.

After talking to analysts from all departments, it is found that there are multiple pain points and multiple things to do to improve the data and analytics maturity of AI Fabric School. The organization is facing multiple issues that lead to wastage of resources, time, and money.

Problem Statement

Here are a couple of observations and pain points of different departments after talking to analysts working on the ground:

- Analysts of all departments are working on data, analytics, and reporting in silos.

- A lot of time is taken and effort exerted to create, store, and process BI reports. Senior management is asked about the number of analysts by each department as analysts' bandwidths are fully occupied.

- If reporting frequency is inconsistent, there are long delays.

- IT department is unable to persuade business stakeholders that data is owned by business, not by IT.

- Lack of standardization on data, processes, and BI reporting technologies.

- Lack of automation and interoperability within existing and internal sources.

After further deep analysis, the core problem was identified, even though there are multiple core suggestions provided to AI Fabric School. These can be further classified into two parts: (1) technology and (2) process improvements.

Motivation

Motivation is to collect data, analyze current state of data maturity and find pain points, suggest actionable insights to improve the state of data maturity in organization with a purpose of aligning with business goals and objectives.

Business Drivers

Business drivers are (1) optimizing business processes through automation and artificial intelligence; and (2) leveraging data to inform decision making.

Technology: Analytics Platform

In the presence of information from both internal and external disparate data sources, information must be managed to ease and reduce the time taken to retrieve it. This can be achieved by providing self-service capability. For uniform, standardized, and quality information, we need a platform where analysts of all departments can store, process, and clean data and automate reporting. AI Fabric School must get ready for the future by enabling machine learning and AI. There is a need to upgrade staff and analysts for future-ready skills.

Efforts/Processes Improvement

Data Strategy: Even though all resources are working hard, there is a clear lack of data strategy, management, and standardization across AI Fabric school in all data domains. This includes business intelligence, data integration, storage, data quality, reference data, data modeling, data security, document and content management, and metadata management for tools and processes. The execution style must shift from reactionary to strategic.

Data Governance: There must be collaboration across departments for digitalization and data-related projects and BI reports. The conflicting priorities of each department regarding projects need to be managed as part of the governance council and governance steering committee. The governance council and committee need to work with the IT department to prioritize issues related to IT inventory of work.

Stewardship and ownership of systems must be properly identified, assigned, communicated, and accepted, along with the responsibility of training, problem resolution, and communication with the user. Second, the workload must be visible, primarily through communicated priorities, project plans, and cross-departmental resource loading.

Data governance also includes creating data and business dictionaries so that the whole organization has uniform definitions of functional terms used across all departments.

High-Level Proposed Solution

The first part of the proposed comprehensive solution includes setting up data strategy, data governance, and skills and process improvements; these steps are essential to improve the state of data and analytics of AI Fabric School.

The second part of the solution is the essential technology component. An education analytics platform needs to be implemented that can (1) connect to all systems that contain data from domains like finance, student, academics, and others; (2) clean, process, and standardize data from those systems; (3) analyze and manipulate data themselves, providing self-service capability to analysts; (4) analysts can create and automate reports and share those reports in a secure and automated way; and (5) able to create predictive and AI models in the future. This solution can be given different names, like data warehousing, data lakes, data lakehouse, etc., with some technical design and capability differences.

When the education analytics platform is combined with setting up the governance framework as mentioned in the previous section, and the data dictionary and business definitions and dictionary are created and used, the number of benefits is huge. These benefits are mentioned in the next section.

Tools

Even though there are many vendors and solutions provided in the market, after initial and high-level analysis and considering multiple factors like robustness, flexibility to work in multiple languages, ability to provide resources, interoperability with other systems, and so forth, we came up with the data lakehouse from Databricks, Inc. as a possible technical platform solution. This will provide self-analytics solutions for analysts, teachers, and leadership across the organization; provide current and cleaned version of source of truth across all departments; and get the organization future ready for the next decade in view of AI, automation, and predictive modeling capability.

Cost

At a high level, the estimate of implementation of these tools, and including skilled resources, is around $450,000 to $500,000. This central cost component is a one-time technology and tools implementation cost; hiring skilled staff, and governance implementation.

Proposed Tools: Data lakehouse/data warehouse from Databricks

Financial Benefit: High

Medium: Benefits* mentioned next

Long-term benefits: Cost optimization through business processes, accelerated time to development through automation and artificial intelligence, customer responsiveness, risk and compliance effectiveness, trust and governance effectiveness, and increased trust in data and governance.

Short-term benefits: Will recover the cost by removing inefficiencies and redundancies, removing dual licenses, and time saving of resources.

The major benefit would come through cost saving. There are many indirect benefits, like leveraging data for better decision-making through analysis regarding students, creating future-ready curriculum, and more.

Example of Business Case 1: Currently the finance reporting is all manual and takes five months for closure. Having an automated weekly/monthly balance sheet and expense report from platform will provide better control and transparency of costs and expenses for all line items, help close data gaps, and plan and provision finance and budget in a better way. This will reduce the time taken to close the end of financial year from five months to one month.

Example of Business Case 2: Running predictive analytics to see which intervention and recommendation to make to students based on individual needs, life cycle, and performance over time; e.g., educational games, vocabulary lessons, extracurricular activities, etc.

Summary

In conclusion, we learned the basics of modern data democratization, governance, and data security.

We started with an introduction and factors that are driving democratization. Then we explained the benefits of democratization. We moved on to the three layers of architectures from the perspective of governance framework, team, and platform, which is a prerequisite for self-service enablement and successful democratization of data.

We then moved to explain self-service, the concept of metadata sharing, and modern ways to use tools, people, and technology levers.

Then we introduced data governance, reasons why organizations need to adopt governance, and key factors that ensure successful data governance programs. We explained stewardship and five different models of data stewardship; e.g., by subject area, by function, by process, by systems, and by projects. We can have a hybrid of these models, which are combinations of two or more of these models.

We explained seven different layers of security and that data is at the center of it. Then we moved on to explain the approaches used for data security and six types of control to put in place. Each of these types is a critical part of data security activities. Understanding each one and how they fit together is important. We must grasp the popular information security frameworks and the major privacy and security regulations in place to protect data. Last but not the least, we explained major modern data security management concepts like data security as a service.

At the end, we discussed an example of a real implementation use case for data governance and data democratization (name of client has been changed). We started with a problem statement, motivation, and business drivers, then moved to the high-level proposed solution with processes and technology. We talked a little bit more about modern technology and tools to be implemented that are ready for at least the next ten years and flexible enough to upgrade after the ten-year time frame.

CHAPTER 7

Business Intelligence

Business intelligence (BI) is an area of information technology that interacts with business domains on the front end of user interactions and is important in terms of its impact on business. Business intelligence in a modern data warehouse environment is not only conceptual, but also essential. In the last chapter, we discussed self-service. It would not be possible without enabling business intelligence tools.

Structure

In this chapter, we will explore the following topics:

- Introduction to Business Intelligence
- Business Intelligence Tools
- Trends in Business Intelligence
- Data Strategy
- Summary

Objectives

After studying this chapter, you should be able to

- understand the fundamentals of business intelligence; and
- identify scenarios and requirements where you can use business intelligence.

© Anjani Kumar, Abhishek Mishra, and Sanjeev Kumar 2024
A. Kumar et al., *Architecting a Modern Data Warehouse for Large Enterprises*,
https://doi.org/10.1007/979-8-8688-0029-0_7

Introduction to Business Intelligence

Business intelligence (BI) is an activity aimed at understanding both organizational activities and opportunities for the organization. As the word itself means the intelligence of business, its purpose is to enable the organization to ask the right questions using data from all or any business operations, customers, and competitors within or outside the industry, and to find new opportunities to grow—or survive. Business intelligence also refers to the set of technologies that bolster decision support tools, which enable users with a wide range of capabilities, from simple querying, advance analytics, and statistical analysis, to predictive and scenario modeling, and to visualize results using reports or dashboards.

There are multiple definitions that have evolved over time, however. *Business intelligence* was first defined in 1958 by Hans Peter Luhn in the *IBM Journal* article titled "A Business Intelligence System." This defines *business intelligence* as an ability of systems to present and understand the facts and relationships between these facts in such a way to guide action toward desired objectives and goals. Decision support systems (DSS), query, reporting, OLAP (online analytical processing), statistical analysis, forecasting, and data mining are some of the examples under the domain of BI technologies and applications. As noted, the definition of *business intelligence* in the beginning included activities like data gathering, storing, providing access, and analyzing data.

Another way *business intelligence* is defined as a set of methodologies, processes, architectures, and technologies that transform raw data into meaningful and useful information that can be used to enable more effective strategic, tactical, and operational insights or decision-making.

As per DMBoK (Data Management Body of Knowledge), *business intelligence management* is defined as the planning, implementation, and control processes that provide decision support data and support knowledge workers engaged in reporting, query, and analysis. This definition is one of the most consistent and standard definitions of *business intelligence*.

At a broad level, there are three types of BI report. Figure 7-1 demonstrates these.

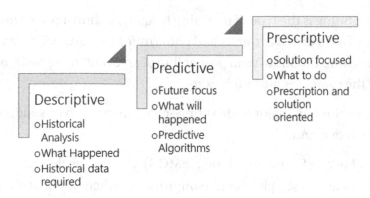

Figure 7-1. *Types of BI report*

Descriptive Reports

Descriptive reports are the reports that represent what happened in the past using graphs and key parameters indicators (KPIs). They explain or describe why the event happened by performing a root cause analysis.

Operational reporting is a good example of descriptive reporting. It is used to analyze the performance of ongoing business operations and related short-term business trends and patterns from historical data. These reports are the main bread and butter of BI reporting for lower and mid-management levels. There is no department or domain where operational reporting cannot be used. These reports are the most common type of reports used to describe or measure the existing state.

A simple example of assessing metrics is the expense report of a utility bill that shows energy consumption by day, month, or year. This report is based on the services and electricity already consumed by the consumer. These include multi-dimensional analysis (OLAP) and OLTP (online transactional processing)/web.

Predictive Reports

The second set of reports are those that use historical data but additionally use a statistics and predictive algorithm to provide a prediction for the near future. Predictive models/algorithms may or may not be available for the subject area as per the pre-defined required confidence interval required.

Predictive reporting is the type of reporting to analyze short-term or long-term business trends so as to discover trends and patterns for the future. This type of reporting uses algorithms to find the short-term probability of an event in the near- or long-term future. Some of the examples are as follows:

- Navigate through major trade supply-chain disruption or sudden spikes in demand.

- In Fast Moving Consumer Goods (FMCG), Predict the flow of materials across supply-chain to improve the efficiency of inventory and operations.

- In FMCG, predict demand of FMCG final product. In traditional clinical processes, use trial simulation without recruiting patients.

- In health care, predict a patient's length of stay and help hospitals save money per patient every year. Some additional areas of benefit are disease identification and diagnosis, medical imaging, and drug discovering and manufacturing.

Some of the algorithms are neural networks, logistic regressions, linear regressions, naïve Bayer classifiers, k-near neighbors' algorithms, random forest, k-means clustering, regression analysis, decision tree learning, gradient-boosted models, boosting, and more. Even though there are multiple algorithms, the application of these algorithms changes use case to use case.

Prescriptive Reports

As a requirement of the third step of the ladder, once we have historical data, prescriptive reports use algorithm models to do prescription for the respective situation to solve the problem or advice with a sufficient higher degree of confidence interval.

The fitness of these models depends on multiple factors. These factors and parameters that are input into these models may be fed into another model. These factors can be fine-tuned, and there can be interdependence among these factors.

Understanding and knowledge of influence factors, and how these factors will change and their impact on the outcome, and converting these factors into simple and interpretable business language in business terminology. One can provide a "prescription" to business by suggesting changes in these factors (increasing, decreasing) in business language.

Business Intelligence Tools

To capture the descriptive, predictive, and prescriptive reports, there are multiple business intelligence software and user interface tools available on the market. However, it is not rare for companies to develop their own tools.

The many kinds of BI tools are made for different purposes and have different capabilities to handle the information width and depth required by different stakeholders in an organization.

IT developers creating statistical reports need to produce complex statistical coding. Analysts and information workers use business queries for development for their work. Executive and managers use dashboards, OLAP, interactive reports, and scorecards for management. For management, reports are more summarized than what analysts and developers require, but cover information spread across multiple domains. Front-line workers, such as sales persons in retail or assembly line workers, are users of embedded reports and published reports. They require reports of very summarized information; e.g., sales amount, sales quantity at end of day, etc. These reporting tools use operation system reporting and query tools like Unix, Linux, or Windows. The production reporting tools require to fetch data from production environments instead of lower environments. Regulatory reports are some of the consumers of production reports. This information requires a wide variety of information across all departments but in summarized form.

Figure 7-2 demonstrates the classification of different kinds of tools, like published reports, scorecards, interactive reports, OLAP, spreadsheets, dashboards, embedded BI, system reporting, and statistical reports on factors like information width, depth, and complexity of use.

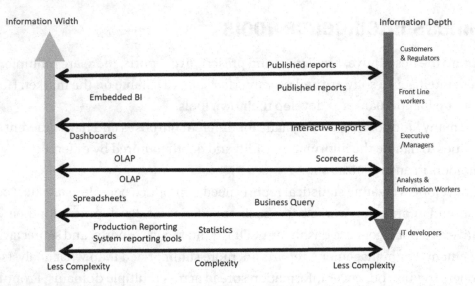

Figure 7-2. *Reporting tools on information width, depth, complexity, and ease of use*

There are multiple BI tools, such as query and reporting tools, OLAP tools, analytical applications, dashboards, production reporting, statistical tools, spreadsheets, embedded BI, published reports, and interactive reports.

Such reports can be grouped by complexity and information depth. Complexity in development means skills required to develop these reports. This complexity can be in terms of skills and training required to operate or develop or code reports. Information depth means granularity of information and types and sources of information.

Some of the factors to consider when deciding which business intelligence tools to use are as follows:

- Ability to meet diverse and changing requirements of users

- Wide variety of functions as per the requirements

- User interface (UI) ease of use

- Flexibility to use UI for both drag-drop and code

- Ability to create standard and ad-hoc reports

- Scalable to number of users and high processing requirements.

- High performance while processing and accessing; e.g., <5ms to access the reports

- Low cost of ownership, including acquisition, execution, implementation, and Maintenance

- Ability to use DevOps, and CI/CD tools for fast deployment.

- Ability to integrate with existing tools of organization and cloud tech stack

- Support for different output types

- Ability to integrate and connect with multiple databases, including legacy, on-premises, and cloud

- Distribution and scheduling options like refreshing at ad-hoc and scheduled time and upon an event

- Compatibility with existing setup

- Width, variety, and ease of doing administrative activities

- Secure access and security

- Vendor reputation and support of tools

- Others

Note   All these factors cannot be fulfilled; they need to be prioritized and optimized as per the requirements and technical, time, and monetary factors.

Query and Reporting Tools

There is a spectrum of BI tools. OLAP tools use dynamic drill up/drill down functionality. Power users require static charts, data maps, tables, formatting capabilities, and ad-hoc query and reporting functionality. These reports became standard at some point in time.

Depending on the user group's needs, BI tools consist of two kinds: query and reporting.

Those who develop reports are called developers, and very much interact with query tools, even though UI tools are also used for development. Power users generally interact with data through visual tools, whether static or dynamic. However, there is a common layer in which end users are skilled in and/or want ad-hoc query analysis for finding new patterns or reports; e.g., users may require query tools to query data sources and create a report, such as an invoice. These data sources could be internal or external.

Business operations reporting requires different capabilities. Users can also use these tools for management reporting. The tools related to management reporting generally do not come with query tools. Business users require a user interface with good pixel quality and good color combinations for dashboards. There is a semantic layer in reporting tools that is used for aggregation, normalization and create a business logic.

While developers create any kind of reports, they need the capability to access data warehouses, data marts, or external data. They also require query tools or UI tools. However, users of management reports need to connect to existing databases, including legacy databases.

All major vendors provide tools capable of both query and management reporting. These delivery mechanisms include web, email, and applications. Figure 7-3 demonstrates the relationship of information width and depth with the management hierarchy.

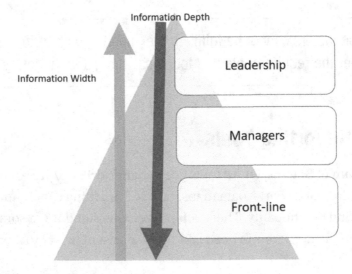

Figure 7-3. *Information hierarchy*

As the responsibility in the management ladder increases, the width of information required across departments and domains increases. The number of summarized key performance indicators (KPIs) needed across domains increases, while the number of KPIs needed per department decreases. However, as you go lower in the hierarchy of the organization, the number of KPIs increases, and they are in much more detail and of finer granularity.

Online Analytical Processing (OLAP) Tools

Online analytical processing (OLAP) tools enable the arrangement of data into multiple dimensions so it can be represented as or called cubes. This is useful for fast analysis and looking at data from multiple dimensions. OLAP tools generally have two component architectures; the first one is a server-side component and the second one is a client-facing component. This client-facing component can be on the web or on the desktop. The architecture, like that of ROLAP, MOLAP, and OLAP tools, can offer multi-dimensional capabilities to provide interactive analysis with drill-down/drill-up functionality with different levels of granularity and detail.

Figure 7-4 demonstrates an example of an OLAP multi-dimensionality cube with dimensions like products, time, and geography.

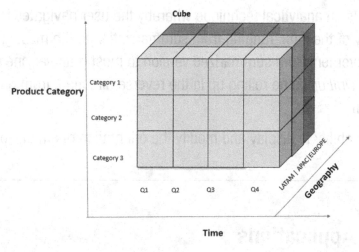

Figure 7-4. OLAP cube

Within categories of BI tools, OLAP cubes generally use a star schema data model. The OLAP cubes are capable of showing 360-degree views of data using a combination of measures within facts and non-measures in dimensional tables. These cubes can be on-demand or batch jobs.

A benefit of using OLAP tools is the availability of a 360-degree view of data. This leads to a reduction of the chance of misinterpretation. Analysts have a mental model that requires a specific or a combination of multiple permutations and combinations of multiple facts and dimensions to navigate. The availability of OLAP tools helps in aligning with an analyst's mental model, which enables the analyst to navigate the full or subset of data through continuous interaction. Common OLAP operations include slicing and dicing, drill up/down, roll up/down, and pivot.

Note   Slicing/dicing (refer to light-blue color shown in Figure 7-4): in a simple analogy, if the cube is a cake, slice is the subset of this cake with a single array of multidimensional cubes consisting of combination of horizontal or vertical member of dimension.

Dicing is the slicing of more than two dimensions of a data cube; these dimensions could be consecutive dimensions.

Drill *down/up* is an analytical technique whereby the user navigates through the granularity of the data, ranging from summarization to the most granular detail. The movement from summarized version to most granular one is called drilling down. *Drill up* is the rolling up in the reverse direction, from granularity to summarization.

Pivoting is the ability to display and modify the orientation of dimensions of the report.

Analytical Applications

Analytical applications include applications that process data extracted from source systems, varying from legacy systems to modern applications, from static data models to flexible ones. Applications provide custom or pre-built reports, cubes, and dashboards to multiple business functional areas across the breadth and width of industries.

In build-versus-buy decisions regarding the analytics scenario, the buy decision adds value by offering a quick start that can lead to shortened time to market and delivery.

There is a plethora of analytical applications available. However, there are multiple factors to examine to decide the right fit. The first question to ask is about the business goal. What are we trying to achieve? What would be the impact from the technological, infrastructural, and process prospectives? The results would come out of comparative calculations on direct and indirect costs, with the value coming out of the Implementation of Analytical applications.

While deciding the inhouse vs buy decision, compare cost and value of making fewer modification vs buy from vendor. following are the factors while making these decisions However, in absence of implementing right-fit features or missed ones all advantages to save time and money can get lost. Examine the following factors:

- Business requirements: focus on the problem

- Comparing the build-versus-buy analytical application

- Converting into specific features required to buy analytical application

- Comparing multiple features; which features are required?

- Considering skills and long-term total cost of ownership

How many source systems do we need to integrate? Fewer sources means a better fit. How much work is required to customize this? How many dashboards and reports and KPIs match? How much of the existing infrastructure matches, and what extra infrastructure is required?

Performance Management Tools

Performance management tools are considered business performance management tools and include tools for budgeting, financial consolidation, and planning. Planning includes financial metrics, workforce, capital, and so on. These were originally considered operational reporting tools. but still part of business intelligence. The popular tools from vendors are the same. However, the details of reports are granular, as their purpose is operational. Modern tools are capable of detailed reporting.

Three purposes of performance management tools are as follows:

- Monitor information: To monitor performance of department and organization at high level

- Analyze information: To summarize and analyze detail information

- Transactional information: Most granular information at transaction level

Three types of dashboards or reports are as follows:

- Dashboards or scorecards summarize key strategic information for executives.

- Operational dashboard/reports monitor operational or ongoing activities by managers and front-line workers.

- Tactical dashboards capture tactical KPIs for cross-department management or activities that can be created on an ad-hoc basis, or KPIs, which are used for less than one year and can be changed frequently.

Dashboards are a visual and dynamic representation of key performance indicators and can include charts, graphs, or other visuals. Dashboards are primarily used by the range of management staff for monitoring operational activities efficiently and in a standard way.

A scorecard-like dashboard is similar in terms of functionality except it is focused on strategic goals and used at the management and leadership levels. Dashboards provide a holistic view of management's performance, and a scorecard provides a holistic view of an organization's performance.

Scorecards focus on metrics related to key performance indicators and compare them to a target or a previous year. Key performance indicators reflect a simple status by color (red, yellow, or green) as per business rules.

Dashboard and scorecard creation is supported by most of the tools presently on the market.

Predictive Analytics and Data Mining Tools

Predictive mining tools are a specific kind of tool that mines historical data for the purpose of predictive or statistical analysis to find the probability of a future event, patterns, and direction of trends. Another use case for data mining tools is for fraud detection, root cause analysis, anti-money laundering (AML), segmentation, scoring, and market basket (MBA) analytics.

Traditionally, statisticians have extracted sample data through files. Processes, models, and required analyses were run in a data warehouse. However, in modern times, the existence of multiple data warehouses and data marts presents a lack of interoperability and integration among different systems and departments. Hence, DB vendors and BI vendors are providing tight coupling with analytical processing. Available standard models utilize user interfaces and produce statistical reports and charts. Modern BI tools integrate analytical processing and storage.

There is a process to create predictive models and machine learnings. ML-Ops (machine learning operations) enabled tools are used to build Machine learning algorithms and operationalize these tools. Then these are run for periodic file extraction or to provide access to data for self-service analytics.

Advanced Visualization and Discovery Tools

Business users are required to perform analysis through two means: either through visualization tools or through direct access to a database.

Modern visualization tools utilize in-memory architecture to interact with large amounts of data in a visual way. It is hard to find patterns in a row and column–style dataset. A pattern can be picked up visually in a better way either by querying the data or by using graphs, charts, etc. for quick analysis without manual coding.

The best practices and standards for visualization include directly interacting and analyzing through visualization as compared to a tabular data display. The high degree of sophisticated analysis and visualization are some of the reasons to adopt advanced visualization and discovery tools.

Figure 7-5 demonstrates the classification of different kinds of tools, like published reports, scorecards, interactive reports, OLAP, spreadsheets, dashboards, embedded BI, system reporting, and statistics reports on factors like information width, depth, and complexity of use.

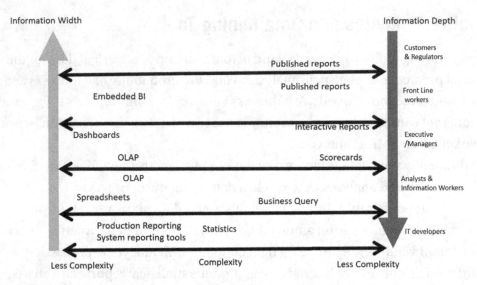

Figure 7-5. *Business intelligence tools classification*

Three classical implementation approaches are as follows:

- ROLAP: Relational online analytical processing

- MOLAP: Multi-dimensional online analytical processing

- HOLAP: Hybrid online analytical processing

Capabilities of modern BI tools are as follows:

- Analytics catalog: Easy to display and search analytic content to make it easy to find and consume

- Automated insights: Ability to use machine learning (ML) techniques to generate automatic insights for end users

- Collaboration: Capability to collaborate with broad spectrum of users, like development and end users, internally or externally

Data science integration includes the following:

- Ability to interconnect with wide variety of data sources—structured, unstructured—irrespective of location of data source, whether on-premises or in the cloud

- This involves creation of and support for highly interactive dashboards and data through manipulation with multiple visualization options, including charts, images, heat and tree maps, and more. Also the ability to combine and narrate data visualization interactively

- Ability to run reports or dashboards on ad-hoc basis or at a user-defined schedule

- Ability to use verbal or written communication using Google-like interface to run natural query (NLQ) though verbal or written communication, which enables users to ask questions about data

- Ability to share and collaborate with developers to co-produce or share final results with business users internal or external to boundary of organization

- Ability to apply machine learning (ML) techniques to generate insights for end users

- Ability to track, audit, control, and manage information (reports, dashboard, data, etc.)

- Ability to prepare data, drag-and-drop, and query through code and user interface to cater to data science and business applications

- Ability to create searchable content from catalog and ability to make recommendations

The following are categories of users, which each have different needs:

- Consumer of BI: The high-quality pixels and color combination for visualization, metrics, ability to do self-analytics are important. Ability to share and collaborate with external users

- Data scientist: Integration with data science capabilities, self-analytics, ability to collaborate with other users. Connection with wide variety of sources

- Business Analyst: Ability to blend disparate data together for visual analysis

- Developer: For developers, connectivity of data sources, ability to have flexibility to develop reports through UI (user interface) or through coding. Ability for developers to have ready-made graphs, codes, or metrics

Trends in Business Intelligence (BI)

There are multiple trends going on in the area of business intelligence. These trends are not mutually exclusive. Their basic motivation is the same: speed, quality, and quantity, at reduced cost. In the center is the data.

Business Decision Intelligence Analysis

A business environment is dynamic, complex, and unpredictable. There is a need to remove the unstructured, ad-hoc decisions that are siloed and not connected with other departments. Local optimization is done at the expense of organization-wide efficiency. The combination of human collaboration and AI techniques such as NLP (natural language processing), ML (machine learning), and so forth helps foster automation and consistency in making decisions, reducing the risk.

Tighter regulations from risk management teams are more prevalent. From privacy and legal guidelines, new laws impact decisions. It is important to track decision-making and provide consistency regarding decision-making across the organization.

Transparent but structured and automated decision-making combined with AI techniques is another trend that is improving and automating the decision-making process. This process is intended to improve decision making by understanding how decisions are made and how outcomes are evaluated, managed, and improved.

Generally, the metrics in BI and reports keep on accumulating with time. There may be KPIs that are not key indicators for business and do not add value. However, on the other end of the spectrum, there may not be indicators that are key in making decisions but are not included in reports/dashboards.

Evaluating how a decision is made reduces technical debt and increases visibility. This improve the impact of business processes and increases the sustainability of organization decision models based on the factors like transparency, auditability, resilience, and relevance.

Proper coordination between business units (BU) and helpful critical decision flows among them bring effectiveness of efforts. Being transparent about the way decisions are made and encouraging collaborative efforts among business units and buy-in from leadership is critical.

Decision modeling across the organization often focuses only on technical skills, but we also need to focus on social, economic, and physiological factors. Creating a Center of Excellence for BI/BA/AI would be helpful for sustainability.

Improve the predictability and alignment of decision makers by simulating their behavior.

Develop staff expertise in traditional and emerging decision automation techniques that include description, diagnostic, prescriptive, and predictive analytics. Also, collaborate with SMEs (subject matter experts) in AI and business processes.

Self-Service

The responsibility for delivery has been shifting from the IT area to the business area. Driven by business' desire for more control and ownership, business teams responsible for digital delivery often have little or no link to the IT department. While this is a positive trend, there is a risk that organizations will become fragmented and highly inefficient. The right method would be to formalize the right combination of business stewardship and IT stewardship to maintain efficiency and at the same time give ownership to the business department. This way, IT could focus on being an enabler of business.

Benefits to this arrangement are as follows:

- Increase focus on the specific and most important business goals and outcomes

- Have better understanding of their customers and their needs

- Increase ability to change quickly and easily

- Increase innovation and collaboration across organization

- Develop optimal solutions and remove duplicate efforts, resources, and solutions

- Integrate Local build black box solution with the enterprise-wide architecture using best working practices, standards, and methods.

- Self-service analytics require advance tools that necessitate building descriptive, predictive, and prescriptive capabilities. However, data management with drop-and-drag capabilities is limited to descriptive capabilities.

- Data science and machine learning platforms require governance of data science models and tools.

Advanced BI Analytics

Text analytics: Derives business insights from structured/unstructured text data. Determines, classifies, and extracts key entities, and summarizes text and identifies the tone or sentiment of texts.

Most organizations have large quantities of unstructured text data in the form of memos, company documents, emails, communications, websites, social media posts, and blogs. Most businesses don't know the value of data, what to extract from where, or where, when, or how to extract value from text data. Some of the use cases for text analytics are text categorization, text clustering, concept extraction of the most relevant text, assessment of opinions and sentiment, and summarization of documents. These use cases may analyze the contents of both internal and external documents, including emails, social media posts, etc.

Sentiment/opinion analytics: Seeks to extract data from text, video, or audio data to understand opinion, attitude, or sentiment of internal or external consumers. The advance polarity sentiment analytics can also go further by classifying the emotional state of person by using facial expression. This type of BI analytics is popular for social media data where people are showing a variety of emotions. Health care, insurance, finance, legal, retail, marketing, law enforcement, and digital publications are some examples of industries, but not all.

Image analytics: Seeks to extract information for images and processes images for the purpose of finding patterns and metadata. After processing, needs to recognize these images or graphics.

Image analytics can be used in facial recognition in the security industry. Another use case is recognizing brand or product in photographs shared on public social media platforms for the retail industry. Casinos use face recognition to identify high rollers and provide special treatment. Image recognition in medical CT scanning is a value addition. Some other use cases can come from security services/forces. An important point here is to identify value through answering strategic questions and delivering on long-term goals.

Voice analytics: Another important case is voice analytics. Gathering, storing, and processing files, and having voice analytics in the customer relations management area, can lead to insights. These insights could help you to spot these potential pitfalls before customers take to social media to complain. Another popular use case is related to the security industry.

Some of the use cases related to voice analytics are as follows:

- Proactively identify upset customers by analyzing the pitch and intonation of conversation.

- Proactively intervene in cases before escalation.

- Help to identify underperforming customer service representatives for additional training or coaching in call center.

- Secure the devices by implementing voice recognition.

- Other cases in security industry

Stream analytics: This is the stream processing of events for the purpose of stream data integration. This is applied to data in motion to enable real-time situational awareness and near-real-time responses to threats and opportunities, and they merge, or it stores data streams for use in applications downstream. This enables faster and more precise decision-making. Sources can include IOT sensors, digital control systems, social computing platforms, news and weather feeds, data brokers, and so on.

Natural language analytics: Business users utilize an interface for the creation/consumption of analytics content. They search for information via a query/search/chat box using business terms, whether by typing or through their voice. These queries are translated into natural language questions using NL processing technologies and/or by using a keyword search. These are supported by supporting the querying of structured data or a semantic search of multiple structured bits of information.

Foundation models like BERT (bidirectional encoder representations from transformers) and generative pre-trained transformer (GPT) techniques, advanced text analytics, deep learning, natural language generation (NLG), and natural language query techniques.

NLQ can interpret geospatial questions and immediately deliver location-based answers and business insights; e.g., relevant food, hospital, and businesses nearby.

Graph analytics: Exploration and discovery of trends and relationships between entities, people, and transactions can determine any connections across data points. This is a multi-context visualization tool that can inform insights and decision-making by using path analysis, network coordination, clustering, outlier detection, Markov chains, and more. Knowledge graph insights can be used for analyzing optimized supply tracing, disease tracking (not forgetting COVID-19), fighting fraud, supply chain tracing, etc., by identifying outliers and unusual patterns in relationship data. This consists of models that connect the dots across data points in the form of visualization for better insights and decision-making. Established AI techniques can increase the power of knowledge graphs.

ModelOps: Model operationalization is primarily focused on the life-cycle management of ML (machine learning), AI (artificial intelligence), and NLP (natural language processing) models. This includes creating policies, procedures, and rules optimizations and dependencies associated with models, such as the following:

- ModelOps helps in enabling standardizing, scaling, AI, and analytics by combining statistical and machine learning models.

- Move models from the lab environment to production environment.

- Operationalize and scale these models.

- Monitor and govern machine learning model.

There is a wide range of risk management concerns across different models, like drifting, bias, integrity, and so on. Comprehensive governance also includes data, application, and infrastructure.

As the number of analytics, AI, and decision models at an organization increase, and as projects become more complex and complicated in needing to manage different type of analytics, AI, and decision models, governance policies and procedures for development, testing, automation, and maintenance are required. Governance ensures collaboration among all business departments regarding development of analytics models and associated KPIs and deployment of these models in production.

Extend the skills of an organization's ML experts to operationalize a wide range of models. Recruit/upskill additional AI to cover graph analytics, optimization, or other required techniques for composite AI. Skills for knowledge engineering should also be available.

DataOps: Data operations is a part of data management focused on improving interoperability, automation, observability, and operations. It involves analyzing and developing dataflows—through process-oriented methodologies—for designing, developing, and delivering analytics in an agile and collaborative way.

DataOps is a response to friction around the consumption and use of data across the organization. Some of the metrics for DataOps are as follows:

1. How much time is taken to deliver data pipelines

2. How many usable datasets are delivered

3. How often codes, tables, etc. move to production

4. How many request tickets related to data are resolved

5. Error rate in production (code errors, data integrity errors)

6. Measuring qualitatively, how the delivery process has become predictable, observable, and repeatable

7. Self-service: what is the adoption rate of self-service users with enabled tools?

8. How many data features are reused or foster reusability and standards

Data Literacy

As self-service analytics is getting traction, it is essential to have the ability to write, read, interpret, and understand data across the enterprise.

Individual knowledge workers should have the ability to understand the analytics regarding business value or outcome. Data and analytics are pervasive in all domains of business. Data literacy is fundamental for self-service analytics and today's data-driven culture. One must be able to identify, access, integrate, and manage both internal and external data and draw insights relevant to business use cases.

Some of the ways to increase data literacy are as follows:

- Create organization-wide standards, terminology, business glossary, data dictionary, and dataflow diagrams. You can use industry-wide data models.

- Increase data visualization skills and increase business curiosity about data by using trainings and certification.

- Regularly measure the overall adoption of BI initiatives.

- Increase the initiative to address cultural and data literacy challenges within strategies and programs.

Edge analytics: Edge analytics is a subpart of analytics where processing is executed in distributed devices, gateways, or servers located in the edge (where data is created and executed).

Figure 7-6 demonstrates the flow of data from source, processing, and output flow for edge analytics.

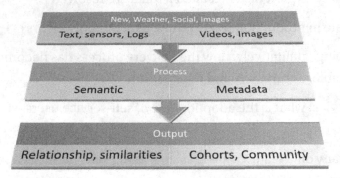

Figure 7-6. *Edge analytics dataflow*

Growth in 5G networks, combined with mobile edge computing and the connectivity and demand for IOT, is increasing the scale, complexity, and number of use cases. Given the demand for real-time event analytics and decision-making, autonomous and fault-tolerant applications will eventually likely increase across industries.

Some edge analytics benefits are faster response time, reduced network bottlenecks, better data filtering, and reliability.

Governance issues related to sensitive or regulated data, and the storage location of that data, which can violate sovereign regulations, combined with mobile edge computing are some of the challenges that can constrain D&A (data management and analytics) teams.

Real-time intelligence: Real-time analytics are integrated in business operations to process current and contextual data and prescriptive actions with which to respond. It provides automation in decision-making and support. This can be achieved by a combination of machine learning, event stream processing, augmented analytics, data quality, and the business rules engine.

It is important to have the capability to trigger an automated response by sending messages to other systems that can trigger business processes.

The first level of D&A capabilities is descriptive analytics, and the second level is predictive modeling. The third level is prescriptive analytics. This means using analytics for supplying prescriptive information about the best available action in the current context.

The growing complexity—and the desired scalability, speed, and automation of decision-making—fuel the adoption of decision intelligence. Constant monitoring of systems looks for threats and opportunities, and offers suggested or automated responses to those events.

Advanced intelligent systems require the following:

> Full integration of real-time analytics with cross-functional business processes

> New, modern skills like enterprise architect, advanced data engineering, and data scientist, along with cross-functional advance knowledge of business required to implement such a system

Here are some of the examples of real-time BI use cases:

> Providing real-time observations, using sensors, about drivers' behavior, creating a safety score insurance companies can use to recommend products; find the purchasing behavior of insurance products; and sale and marketing decisions for insurance companies.

> Another example is providing GPS/positional data tracking of vessels to dry bulk operators, which can collect operational and engine data that can impact business decisions regarding reduction of fuel consumption and operational cost. Being transparent and proactive in sharing such data and supply-chain metrics with customers can improve the business and save consumption and operation costs. These benefits can traverse all domain areas, functions, and layers of a business.

> Shorter latency of data means proactive decisions can be made by identifying additional business capabilities and use cases from active and passive metadata. While the first step is to collect data to monitor operations for the purpose of observation, there are a few actions/decisions that can be taken instantly, and there are other decisions that need due diligence. Decisions that require due diligence need shared data kept in data store for later.

Analytics Governance

We explained and discussed data governance in Chapter 6, "Data Democratization, Governance & Security," in detail.

However, as we discussed about data governance, people sometimes get confused that it deals more with enterprise data management governance: policy and procedures for analytics pipelines governance. As it is similar to data stewardship, analytical stewardship need to be clearly specified. Policies and procedures for data practice are related to the data analytics/BI life cycle.

Data Analytics Life Cycle

There are six phases of data analytics that must be followed in data science projects. The framework for data science projects is simple and cyclical in nature, both backward and forward, but has to be one step after another. The steps are as follows:

1. **Data discovery and formation**: It starts with defining a goal, objective, and benefits the organization wants to achieve. Next, it evaluates and assesses required data and comes up with high level goal with objectives. The next step is to create an evaluation and assessment of the data. Create a basic hypothesis related to the objective.
   This stage consists of mapping out the potential use and requirements of data: what data is required, where to find the required data, and how to get this data.
   Mandatory activity in this phase is structuring the business problem in the form of an analytics goal and formulating the initial hypothesis to test and start learning from the data.

2. **Data preparation and processing**: This stage consists of anything related to storing and processing the data.
   Data is ingested from external sources/internal systems and sources. After ingestion, data is prepared and transformed. Sample data is prepared to using business logic. This phase takes the longest time in the life cycle to make sure that data requirements match with business requirements.

3. **Designing a model**: After mapping out the business goals, collect structured, semi-structured, or unstructured data.

   These steps include the team to determine the best methods, techniques, and workflow to build the model in the subsequent phase. Model building initiates with identifying the relationship between data points to select the key variables and eventually find a suitable mode.

   Datasets are developed by the team to test, train, and produce the data. In later phases, the team builds and executes the models that were created in the model planning stage.

4. **Model building**: In this step, after designing a model, we develop, test, and train a dataset. Experts build the model that was built in step three. Experts use different modeling techniques using coding or user interface tools. Some of the examples of algorithms are linear regression analysis, logistics regression, neural networks, etc., as per requirements for building and executing the model. This step may have multiple iterations within and makes sure that a model is tested, fit for purpose, finalized, and ready for production.

5. **Communicating and publishing**: After model is ready for production, communication and collaboration are started regarding the success or failure as per predefined criteria. Business value is re-evaluated.

6. **Measuring effectiveness**: The data is moved to a live environment from the sandbox and monitored to observe if the results match the expected business goal defined in previous stage. If outcome deviates from the goal set out in first phase, you can move backward in the data analytics lifecycle.

BI and Data Science Together

The implementation of data warehousing (DW) and business intelligence (BI) has eleven guiding principles, as follows:

1. Executive commitment, sponsorship, and support is paramount.

2. Secure business SME (subject matter expert) support in understanding, correcting, and user acceptance testing UAT) of data, and validation of KPIs.

3. Priorities to be driven by business.

4. Maintaining high-data quality is mandatory and critical to ongoing business intelligence and data science program success.

5. Build and show incremental value.

6. Customize according to business domain requirement. One size does not fit all.

7. Provide transparency and self-service along with context to provide value and satisfaction to business.

8. Design and architect with global standards, but build with local business rules in mind.

9. Collaborate and integrate with other data initiatives across business for synergy—and avoid duplication.

10. Start with a clear objective and goals in mind.

11. Summarize and optimize in the end. Build on the granular data and add aggregates of summaries needed for performance.

Companies regularly interact with customers; develop and design products; and create strategic plans and make decisions according to market forces. Modern data warehouses have modern expectations, like being well governed, consistent, and fast in delivery of quality data. Value can be brought to organizations through a well-governed strategy for getting required data from customer, supplier, partner, application, and systems.

Data Strategy

A data strategy is defined as a set of choices and decisions that will guide and enable a high-level course of action to achieve high-level business goals.

Data strategy has the following purposes:

- Alignment with business and providing guiding principles

- Data strategy defines the vision, mission, and goals of the data management program. The execution of a data strategy is about making strategic decisions about the individual areas of data management, like Big Data, data quality (DQ), document and content management, data warehousing (DW), data integration (DI), reference and master data, storage and operations, modeling and design, and data security, through tools, technologies, and processes.

- Create a communication strategy for sponsors and stakeholders, and define success factors for the data strategy program.

- The main goals of a data strategy program are to either focus on running operations or focus on growing the business.

   Focusing on the growth of business aspects tends to increase focus on analysis, which allows one to see ways to increase business growth through innovation by data exploration and seeking of patterns, and intent the ability to predict results and generate new insights and innovations.

   Focusing on running operations requires standard and production reports using reports, dashboards, automation, and workflow to optimize business processes and increase performance.

- Reconcile contradictory points of view.

Figure 7-7 demonstrates the data as a bullseye of business-driven, self-service, data governance, and data infrastructure and service programs to either grow revenue or reducing costs.

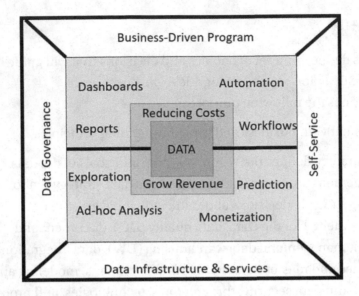

Figure 7-7. *Data as bullseye value*

The main goal of data strategy is to balance and reconcile two contradictory points of view. This helps provide direction to efforts. However, balancing this depends on many factors, like industry, organization culture, business strategy, and so forth. The following are examples:

How much to focus on regular operations versus how much to focus on innovation

Where and how much to centralize versus how much to decentralize. Note how many and how much process to centralize.

How much to focus on speed versus how much to focus on standards. Note that the absence of standards would increase the speed of implementation temporarily. Increasing the standards provides consistency long term.

How much to focus on self-service versus how much to focus on governance. Note that too much governance across processes leads to increased dependence on IT processes.

How much and agility versus architecture. For example, in the absence of standard architecture, users have the flexibility to create schemas as required by user. However, the presence of architecture standardizes the way data is arranged in systems, which increases predictability and sustenance.

In both cases, it needs to sync up with business strategy. The Amsterdam model— also called a nine-cell model—is used to synchronize business with information and subsequently with information technology (IT). This model has three columns representing business, information, and technology. The three rows introduce an intermediary level between strategic and operations.

Figure 7-8 demonstrates the business, information, and technology alignment with strategy, tactical, and operations.

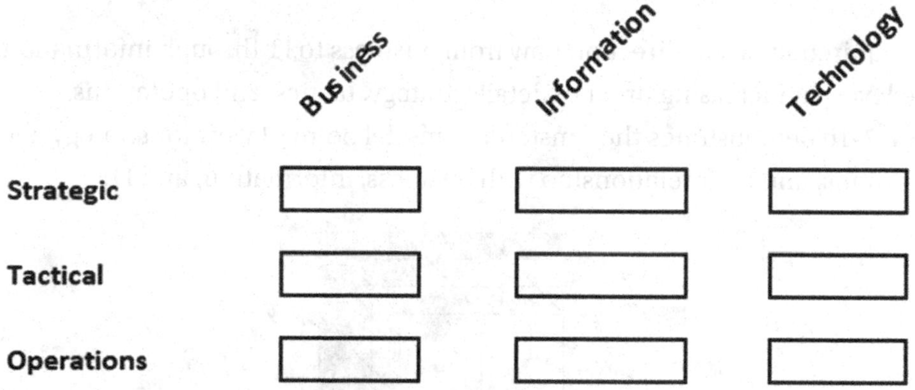

Figure 7-8. *Strategic alignment matrix*

The term *strategic alignment* references tactics deployed and how operational level should be aligned with business strategy.

IT strategy and governance should be aligned with information strategy and governance, and both should be aligned with business strategy and governance. IT architecture and planning should be aligned with information architecture and planning, and both should be aligned with organization processes. Similarly, IT services and execution should be aligned with information management and use, and subsequently it should be aligned with business execution at the tactical level.

Figure 7-9 demonstrates the Amsterdam model point of view for the alignment of strategy, tactics, and operations, and the flow of alignment from business to information and to IT.

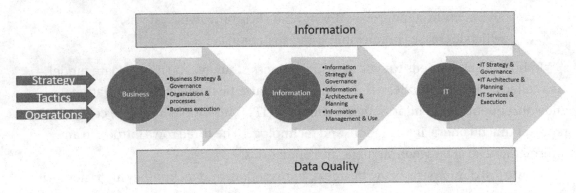

Figure 7-9. *Amsterdam model point of view 1*

The requirements and direction flow from business to IT through information. There are three levels in increasing order of detail: strategy, tactics, and operations.

Figure 7-10 demonstrates the Amsterdam model point of view for strategy, tactics, and operations, and their relationship with business, information, and IT.

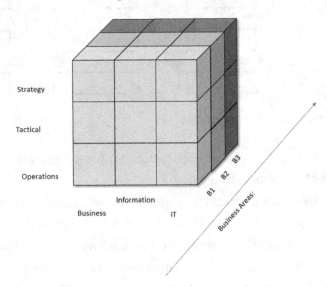

Figure 7-10. *Amsterdam model point of view 2*

Typically, data strategy comes under data management program and is involved in data management program strategy and in planning for maintaining and improving data quality, integrity, security, and access.

Business plans use information to competitive advantage and to support enterprise goals. Data strategy inherently derives data needs/requirements that should meet business goals and sync up with business strategy.

Guidelines for data strategy are as follows:

- Create the vision for data management program and initiatives.

- Create a business case to demonstrate the qualitative and quantitative value for business and business sponsorship.

- Create guiding principles from management perspective.

- Create the mission and long-term directional goals of data management.

- Create measures to quantify success for data management. These measures should be SMART (specific, measurable, actionable, realistic, and time-bound) for both the short and long term.

- Create descriptions of data management roles, responsibilities, and decisions to be made by individuals.

- Create scope and high-level data management implementation roadmap for next three to five years (projects and action items).

- Describe all the technical and non-technical decision-tracking issues impacting strategy.

Data and Analytics Approach and Strategy

The strategy of an organization flows from business strategy to information strategy, which includes application and data strategy. It is essential that information strategy matches with business strategy. Information strategy consists of application strategy, data strategy, business intelligence strategy, and analytics strategy; all of these must align with the business strategy.

Generally, there are three areas of strategic focus for data and analytics strategy. Even though the definitions of *utility*, *enablement*, and *driver* change as the availability and capabilities of tools and technologies increase in the market, moving from utility to enabler to driver increases the organization's capabilities. See the following:

- **Data and analytics as a utility**: Providing utility services means providing analytics capability to all individuals across business domains and departments. This is about the basic functionalities provided to complete the intended business purpose. One of the examples is providing Excel and Access database capabilities.

- **Data and analytics as an enabler**: Being an enabler means to resolve the pain points of business by providing modern tools and technology and creating processes to enable fulfillment of all current needs or to meet specific business goals. An example is providing advanced data warehousing, architecture, and metadata capabilities, as well as self-service capabilities, to business users.

- **Data and analytics as a driver**: Being a driver is one step further than being an enabler. It generally means enhanced capability and future readiness, or a means to achieve new business goals. New tools can uncover new insights, and new data types can lead to new business questions; both drive new business ideas and revenue sources.

Core Strategy of Business

At a high level, there are four business focus areas, as follows:

1. **Operational excellence**: By focusing on operations, a business tries to bring value by reducing costs in business or IT operations to gain a competitive advantage; e.g., by focusing on new or modified business processes to make it robust, efficient, and effective.

2. **Innovation**: By focusing on innovation, businesses create value through designing and creating new products and services to grow or capture new markets.

3. **Customer understanding**: By focusing on the customers and their behavior, a business can focus on product and services that are fit to customers' needs. Also, if a business does not have the best products, they are a good fit for a targeted segment of customers.

4. **Risk management**: By focusing on the Risk management, Business create value by reducing and managing the risk for customers and business.

Mappings

The purpose of this matrix is to align the focus of business strategy with data analytics strategy. Like all the programs, questions to be answered include, What is the value or value proposition for our customers in terms of providing data insights? What business process and response changes give these new insights?

Figure 7-11 shows an example of a matrix that maps the strategic focus of a business with a data and analytics approach.

Strategy Focus	D&A (Data and Analytics) Approach		
	Utility	Enabler	Driver
Innovation	Exampke: Self-service: Use D&A as a tool to support and enable customer service to self-service and organization to focus on innovation through descriptive reporting.	Example: Data and Analytics products: Use D&A to enable new products to drive results through predictive models. Success is defined and measured.	Example: Feedback- Use D&A to enable new predictive methods such as prescriptive models to predict the markets and actions required.
Customer Understanding	Example: D&A as a service: Provide data, reports, and tools to stakeholders	Example: Provide 360 degree : view of data about the individual customer within segments to create a solid understanding of customer.	Examople: Personal analytics Combine 360 degree of data with personal data and reference data of customers to focus on individul customers or by
Risk and Compliance	Example: Compliance Use data for mandatory compliance reporting.	Example: Risk mitigation Uses data to mitigate risks and new venues, opportunities, performance, and security.	Example: Risk leadership: uses data to more accurately assess risk versus compliance and enable to open new venues for performance
Operational Excellence	Set of capabilities that does not required specific set of capabilities	Centers around business cost, time and quality optimization	Completely integrates information value chain with data and analytics used throught the data delivery chain

Figure 7-11. Reference business to data strategic alignment

All organizations use multiple approaches and multiple business strategies.

There are four areas in an organization that are focused on simultaneously. It might be more focused on one area than others, depending on the industry or market forces or time of the year.

The approach varies based on the organization's data and analytics capabilities. When maturity is low, data and analytics are used as a utility only. As maturity increases, data and analytics act as an enabler for achieving business goals, and in the case of highest maturity, data and analytics drive the business goal. The four areas of focus are as follows:

1. **Innovation**: When self-service for analysts is missing. Providing data availability would be the most value addition across enterprise domains. This is the first step to achieve innovation across organization; for example, using data and analytics tool for business users for self-service and enabling the organization to focus on innovative products and services.

2. **Customer Understanding**: As a core strategy, a business must collect data internally, as it is core and central to all analyses. Even though a department may try to analyze data from different points of view and try to connect all data manually, there is a lack of a platform where analysts can have a 360-degree view of data. Having one analytics platform will enable the business to have a better understanding of all domains quickly and with minimal effort. Second, an organization may already be creating new products. However, having an analytics platform will take a driver's seat and actively partake in personal analytics.

3. **Risk and Compliance**: As per current assessment, organizations create compliance reporting. But these reports are used primarily for compliance. Having a data and analytics platform can be enabled for risk mitigation.

4. **Operation Analytics**: This data and analytics enablement centers around cost, time, and quality optimization. However, having a data and analytics platform will not only enable operations analytics but evolve to completely integrate the information-value chain with data and analytics used thought the data-delivery chain of the organization. This generally centers around business cost, time, and quality optimization.

Data strategy is generally owned and maintained by a governance council with the guidance of a chief information officer or chief data officer and other management executives. These executives may retain ownership and control of data strategy. Data strategy has three major separate execution deliverables, as follows:

1. **Data management program charter**: Like any program charter, it consists of overall vision, goals, objectives, guiding principles, business case, measures of success, critical success factors, identified risks, and risk mitigation plans.

2. **Data management scope statement**: Scope of the programming consists of which projects or programs will bring exact business benefits within the planning horizon of usually three to five years and the roles, organization, and individual leaders accountable for achieving these objectives.

3. **Data management benefit realization plan**: Program work breakdown structure consists of the following:

   - Combination of multiple and specific related projects making up the program

   - High-level planning horizon in a range of three to five years

   - Related major milestones of each project

   - Deliverables, program plans and procedure, standards and processes, and public communications

Step to Create Data Strategy

There is a ten-step process to create a data strategy document, as follows:

1. **Build awareness**: This is a first step that creates awareness of the issue and acknowledges the need to create an enterprise strategy and enterprise program. To do so, create awareness about the pain areas related to data and the need to establish a data strategy program at the enterprise level. These pain areas could be different for different companies and may vary across any area in data management; e.g., data integration, data security, interoperability, etc. This step gets executive buy-in by making

them aware of the value of the data program and how companies in and across industries are using data to gain a competitive advantage.

2. **Assemble a team**: After getting partial or full buy-in from the leadership team, the next step is to create a hybrid team from the business and IT departments.

    These motivated individuals have an interest in increasing the maturity of the data and analytics capability across the organization. It is suggested to have an incremental implementation approach in mind.

    This team of senior managers should understand data and any challenges and opportunities. This step makes sure to get commitments from the stakeholders and their supervisors about their bandwidth and participation. Expectations from the team are to commit time and ability to create a data strategy and oversee execution of that data strategy.

3. **Educate the team**: The next step after assembling a team is to create an understanding among the team members about common data issues across the enterprise, different approaches, data trends across industries, and specific trends within the business' industry. As the team is from different domains with different perspectives, it is important to be on the same page about the common vocabulary, best practices, and standards. Internal and external experts with experience in execution and implementation can help to educate the team about the possible opportunities, challenges, and data solutions.

4. **Assess Current State**: The next step is to evaluate and assess the current state of maturity of data practice. Self-analysis is required to find the commonalities, patterns, and core reasons behind these pain points. It is important to align business strategy with information strategy. The purpose of finding the current state is to perform a gap analysis to align with and achieve the objectives of

the business strategy. A prerequisite is to understand the business strategy. Activities include maturity assessment, gap analysis, and SWOT (strength, weakness, opportunity, and threat).

5. **Develop a vision and goals**: The next step is to create a vision and mission for the team. This step completes gap analysis with regard to the business strategy. It motivates the team and provides them with ongoing and high-level direction. This can be done by brainstorming the ideal future state and communicating with stakeholders about vision and how it would be aligned with corporate strategy. Discuss how it will be implemented both operationally and strategically.

6. **Develop Recommendations**: After developing vision and goals, the next steps are to provide recommendations based on the current state, and on the vision and goals for the future. The comprehensive solution and recommendations can be from people, process, and technology prospectives.

Figure 7-12 demonstrates technical levers to govern data management, like data architecture, metadata, data storage and operation, data quality, document and content management, data integration and interoperability, data modeling, and data security.

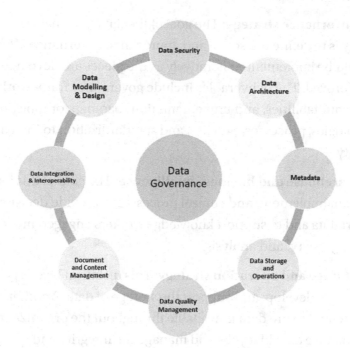

Figure 7-12. *Technical levers*

Reference and Master Data: This requires enabling of sharing information assets across multiple domains across the organization. Master data is defined as being reconciled, verified, quality, and source of truth. Implement standards through data models and data integration (DI) patterns.

Document and Content Management: As the organization grows, systems are complicated and documents grow in number. Managing content and documents is one of the goals. However, one of the many challenges is to only comply with existing country and international legal obligations. Goals are to ensure that systems and data are compliant. A second goal is to ensure storage, processing, and usage are safe; third, to have interoperability capability between unstructured content of documents with structured content.

Data governance strategy: The goal of the data governance strategy is to define the scope and approach to governance efforts. It should be implemented iteratively as the pieces are developed and approved. The deliverables include governance framework and accountabilities, and implementation roadmap for tools, technologies, processes, policies, and standardization to increase maturity.

Data warehouse and business intelligence: The goal of this lever is to plan, implement, and control processes to provide decision support data and to support knowledge workers engaged in reporting, query, and analysis.

Data storage and operation strategy: This technical lever's goal is to design, develop, and support the storage of data. Another goal is to make sure data is available throughout the organization 24x7, manage data lifecycle, and manage the integrity and performance of data assets.

Data modeling and design: The goal of the data modeling management strategy is to design, document, and communicate an understanding of different perspectives, which leads to data management that more closely aligns with current and future business strategy, and create value through forming a data structure of data designed for integrity, capture, and retrieval of datasets.

Data architecture: The goal of data architecture is to identify data storage and processing needs of the enterprise. This is done by designing data structures and plans to meet the current and long-term data strategy of the enterprise. Data architecture strategy needs to align with business strategy. One of the goals of the organization is to prepare to quickly evolve their products, services, and data to take business advantages.

Data security: The goal of data security is to make sure that the right user has access to the right and secure data from the right system at the right point in time. It protects data to comply with all policies, procedures, privacy, and regulations to protect confidentiality, integrity, and privacy of all stakeholders.

Metadata: Metadata is the data about data. Metadata is prevalent in all applications. Usage of metadata in organizations requires standardization of the business terminology, access, and measure of the usage of applications across all domains. The usage of metadata is widespread for multiple use cases that ensures security and quality of data.

Data integration and interoperability: The goal is to make sure that data can flow through the systems connected with each other. Data can be pulled directly from another system or pushed to systems directly; e.g., sharing of metadata through trigger alerts, events, and actions.

7. **Develop a roadmap**: Create a roadmap based on any recommendations. This roadmap could range from three to five years. For example, you were advised to start and increase the maturity of analytics. This is done in two major steps. The first step is to enable access to historical data, tools, and skills for individuals or groups of users, creating governance, policies, and procedures around the data. Once the quality of historical data is provided, advanced skills to create mathematical algorithms and statistics are achieved to advance to the next maturity levels. For example, historical data is required to find what happened, when, where, how, at what frequency. Next is to find the root cause of the problem. Finding out what action is required can also be done with the help of historical data and advanced analytics. Data science is one step ahead, using historical data to find what can happen next with reasonable confidence. Figure 7-13 is an example of a high-level roadmap.

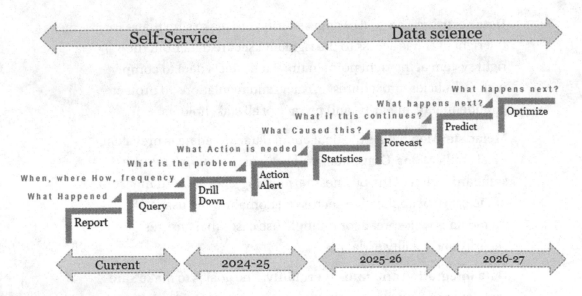

Figure 7-13. *High-level roadmap*

Figure 7-13 demonstrates a framework to increase the data science capabilities and maturity of an organization, from reporting to statistics to forecasting and predictive capabilities.

8. **Develop a business use case**: This step gathers requirements from a business for a specific use case. Gather costs and both qualitative and quantitative benefits to get from these use cases. Find dependencies of these use cases and fine-tune your roadmap based on the bandwidth and the budget allocated. Create specific projects associated with these individual or collection of use cases.

9. **Prepare for change**: This step prepares for a well-informed change management strategy. Create a plan that aligns with all stakeholders' interests, and prioritize use cases. For the implementation of the data strategy, it is important to take all stakeholders on same page. Prepare council and committees and communication plans for all stakeholders and their involvement.

10. **Execute the strategy:** As the data management and business intelligence use cases increase with time, there is a requirement to improve speed in delivering trusted data. Focus on value where there is business impact. Increase the collaboration across data, business, and technical persons. Manage interdependencies across business process. Provide reliable data-delivery service goals and levels.

Operational excellence in data delivery is achieved through predictability in delivery and change management of data.

As tracking of metrics—such as time to deploy changes, degree of automation, developer productivity, code quality, and cost efficiencies in dollar amount—increases, failure rates in production decrease. Direct benefits of DataOps are increased productivity, reduced development timelines, and a robust pipeline to ensure that pipelines don't break frequently and are designed in such a way that change management and fixes can be done easily to ensure lineage, security, and quality.

Self-service analytics required advanced tools that require building descriptive, predictive, and prescriptive capabilities. However, data management with drag-and-drop capabilities are limited to descriptive capabilities.

Data science and machine learning platforms require governance of data science models and tools.

Summary

In conclusion, we learned the basics of modern data democratization, governance, and data security.

We started with the introduction to Business intelligence and the types of BI reports like descriptive, predictive and prescriptive. We then moved to types of BI tools and categorization of these BI tools on the factors like information depth, complexity and users in detail.

In next section there are trends in business intelligence like self-service, Advanced BI analytics, Data literacy, Analytics governance. We then moved to explain the data analytics life cycle. We have also explained the synchronization of Business Intelligence and Data science.

In last we discussed and explain data strategy and explain the way to syncronize data strategy with business strategy. We also explained the steps to create data strategy.

Index

A

Advanced BI analytics
    data literacy, 327–329
    DataOps, 326, 327
    graph analytics, 325
    image analytics, 324
    ModelOps, 326
    natural language analytics, 325
    phases, data analytics, 330–331
    sentiment/opinion analytics, 324
    text analytics, 324
    voice analytics, 324, 325
Advanced intelligent systems, 329
Alation, 37
Amazon Kinesis, 194, 243
Amazon Redshift, 39, 49, 192, 232
Amazon Web Services (AWS), 46, 192, 196, 230
Amsterdam model, 335
Analytics platform, 38, 86, 193, 267, 268, 302, 303
Analytics teams, 267, 328
Analytics tools, 72, 85, 206, 227
Apache Atlas, 37
Apache Axis, 191
Apache Flink, 179, 194, 211
Apache Kafka, 189, 194
    creating Kafka topics, 210
    data analysis, 211
    data consumption, 211
    data ingestion, 210
    data storage, 211

data storage and visualization, 211
data transformations, 210
defining data requirements, 210
identify data sources, 210
installing and configuring, 210
monitoring and management, 211
scaling and performance, 211
Apache NiFi, 14, 194, 198, 243
Apache Spark, 84, 193, 226, 233
Apache Spark and Databricks, 197
Apache Sqoop, 197
Architectural guidance, 254
Artificial intelligence (AI) services, 67, 260
As-is data architecture, 166
Auditing, 100, 269
Automation, 67, 86, 88, 180, 212, 304, 329, 349
AWS Glue, 15, 196
    advantages, 231
    best practices, 234, 235
    data schema management practices, 235, 236
    description, 230
    key components, 232–234
    use cases, 232
AWS Glue ETL scripts, 233
AWS Glue job, 233
Azure Data Factory (ADF)
    cloud-based data integration service, 222
    components, 221
    configuring activities, 223

Printed in the United States
by Baker & Taylor Publisher Services